EFFECTIVE SUPERVISION

Prentice-Hall, Inc., Englewood Cliffs, New Jersey 07632

WILLIAM J. WASMUTH
Cornell University

LEONARD GREENHALGH
Dartmouth College

EFFECTIVE SUPERVISION
Developing Your Skills
through Critical Incidents

Library of Congress Cataloging in Publication Data

Wasmuth, William J.
   Effective supervision.

   Includes index.
   1. Supervision of employees. 2. Personnel
management. I. Greenhalgh, Leonard, joint author.
II. Title.
HF5549.W3475   658.3'02   78-7554
ISBN 0-13-246462-4

Printed in the United States of America

10 9 8 7 6 5 4 3 2 1

Prentice-Hall International, Inc., *London*
Prentice-Hall of Australia Pty. Limited, *Sydney*
Prentice-Hall of Canada, Ltd., *Toronto*
Prentice-Hall of India Private Limited, *New Delhi*
Prentice-Hall of Japan, Inc., *Tokyo*
Prentice-Hall of Southeast Asia Pte. Ltd., *Singapore*
Whitehall Books Limited, *Wellington, New Zealand*

Contents

22

Rights and Responsibilities   *235*

A CRITICAL INCIDENT: The Limits to "Freedom of Speech"
Setting: Foreign Auto Repair, Inc. (small business)   *236*

23

Resistance to Change   *243*

A CRITICAL INCIDENT: An Unwelcome Surprise
Setting: Precision Electronics (production)   *244*

24

Promotion from the Ranks   *251*

A CRITICAL INCIDENT: "Congratulations and Condolences!"
Setting: Foreign Auto Repair, Inc. (small business)   *252*

25

Your Future   *257*

A CRITICAL INCIDENT: What Price Success?
Setting: Globe Housewares Company (production)   *258*

1. WHAT IS A GOOD BOOK ON SUPERVISION?

After much experience in teaching supervisors and future supervisors, we (the authors) knew what we wanted in a book on supervision.

It had to be condensed, first of all. Who wants to read 600 pages if the same knowledge can be conveyed in 300?

Second, it had to give the reader *examples* of supervisors living through real situations. We have found that people don't learn much from being given a set of dry, abstract, "principles of supervision." The learning comes from seeing the principles *applied* in the rich context of a real-life supervisory episode.

At the same time, the language had to be simple. Somebody famous (we've forgotten who it was) once said, "You don't *really* understand something until you can explain it to a small boy." We tend to agree. So the book had to have a minimum number of "high-falutin'" technical terms in it, and a maximum amount of "plain English."

Furthermore, the book couldn't go on endlessly to describe the routine details of what supervisors do. The authors know from experience that when everything is going fine in a department, *anyone* can be an effective supervisor. It's only when the chips are down—when there's a crisis or a dilemma instead of smooth sailing—that top-quality supervision makes a big difference.

Finally, the book had to be designed as a self-contained learning experience. It had to give the reader some feedback as to how he or she was doing. Who wants to wait until the end of a course to find out that he or she didn't understand something?

To make a long story short (and all long stories should be short!), we just couldn't find such a book. So we decided to write it. We were encouraged by Prentice-Hall to do so, since their marketing people knew that most teachers wanted the same things out of a book on supervision that we did.

Preface

2. CONTENT AREAS COVERED

The five subject areas, covering twenty-five major topics in supervision, include virtually everything that will *really make a difference* in the life of the supervisor. The technical aspects of the job have been covered in full detail, but "served" in a way that most readers will find easily digestible.

We have given equal weight to the nontechnical aspects of the job that are important, too. Indeed, they can "make or break" the supervisor! Even though some of these topics are "delicate"—such as "politics" and conflict in the work place, we haven't been shy in writing about them. The supervisor *needs to know* these things!

It should be emphasized that despite the lack of technical jargon, the content of the book is grounded in the very latest theory and research. Although translated into "plain English," the book draws heavily on the various academic fields that have something to offer the student of supervision. It draws on management, organizational behavior, psychology, sociology, anthropology, social psychology, organization theory, political science, and even philosophy.

3. FORMAT OF THE BOOK

The book was designed as a complete, integrated learning experience. The five sections are laid out as independent learning units. Each one starts with a Pretest, so that the reader can test his or her knowledge at the outset. Then the reader can take the test once again (as a Posttest) when the five chapters in that section have been mastered, and then check the answers given at the end of each section to see how much of an improvement has been made.

As a final review, all fifty questions (the ten from each section) appear near the end of the book. The reader is, in effect, offered a final opportunity to measure his or her overall understanding of the book. We hope you'll take advantage of it.

Each chapter starts out by listing the key points (the *learning objectives*) that we want the reader to learn. Then the points are taught by presenting a *critical incident*—a situation in which a supervisor performed particularly well or particularly poorly.

To make sure that the key points were learned, each individual chapter provides test-yourself review questions at the end of each critical incident, followed by answers, in a *programmed-learning* format.

In addition, we encourage the reader to explore in further depth the issues raised in the chapter. We try to guide this exploration by posing three Questions for Further Thought at the end of each chapter. Answers appear immediately after each question.

4. THE SUPERVISORY SETTINGS

The critical incidents take place in four case settings. There's a white-collar office setting, two different types of blue-collar factory settings, and a small business. These provide just about all the *variety* in supervision that the reader is likely to run across.

At the same time, with only four settings, it is possible to get to know the supervisors and their worlds, and to get a feel for the rich *context* in which decisions are made. To aid in this process, we've provided a "preview" visit to each setting in the Introduction to the book. They're worth reading before starting on the chapters and also worth referring back to from time to time.

Furthermore, towards the end of the book, in the Epilogue, we've provided a final look at each organization. This is designed to help the reader recap what has happened over time, and to provide some hints as to what is likely to happen in that organization after we have left it.

5. A WORD OF THANKS

We are indebted to Mrs. Ann VanDeMark, who provided valuable editorial comments as she typed the manuscript and nursed it through the many refinements in its development.

Our thanks also go to Cary Baker, Stephen Cline, and Ann Marie McCarthy of Prentice-Hall, for their constructive support in making this book a reality. In addition, we are grateful to Ronald House and George deLodzia, who helped develop the basic format.

We would also like to thank Bert Morton and Mrs. Norma Wasmuth for their suggestions and support, and Lucy Svagan for her editorial work on the final draft.

Final thanks are also expressed to Don Martinetti who did the illustrations.

William J. Wasmuth
Leonard Greenhalgh

To visit Precision Electronics, you have to drive through the industrial section of a large city. The streets are busy, with a lot of noisy truck traffic.

Finding the plant is not easy. The forty-year-old, three-story brick building looks just like many of the other industrial buildings located near the railroad line. Some of the nearby buildings, however, are unoccupied. Because of the extra costs and delays involved in moving materials and finished goods up and down, from one floor to another, many of these businesses moved to single-story buildings in the suburbs.

Eventually you find Precision Electronics. You have come to visit the President, and you park in the visitor's parking lot (see Exhibit 1). From there, you walk up to the Pine Street entrance, carefully dodging the loading dock traffic.

Just inside the heavy metal door there is a building directory mounted behind glass. You see that the President's office is on the third floor, and that there is a passenger elevator opposite the directory board.

But you're early. So, to kill some time, you decide to wander around the plant. Next to the elevator is the Production Manager's office. He is the only high-level manager not located on the third floor.

Beyond his office door, on your right, is a large area where final product assembly is done. Most of the assemblers are women, and this department has a woman supervisor, Maria. There is a strong smell of solder flux and hot plastic insulation. There's a lot of lively chatter between the assemblers, which doesn't seem to hurt the job. They work very fast.

Diagonally opposite the Assembly Department is the Machining Department. It happens that only men work here, running lathes, drill presses, and milling machines. Vince is the supervisor. There is less talk going on in this department, since the machinists would have to

Introduction
to Precision Electronics
Company

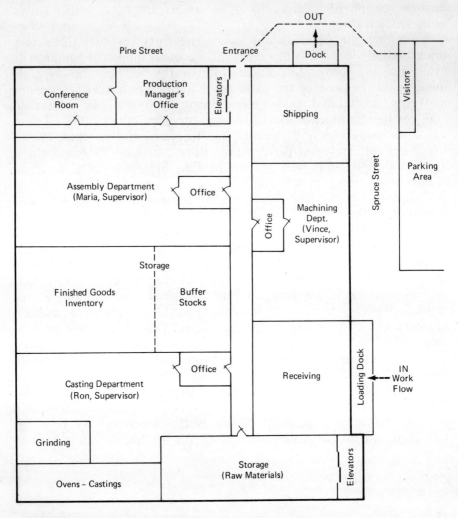

EXHIBIT 1 *First-floor Plan Precision Electronics Company*

raise their voices above the humming of electric motors, the whirring of gears in the machinery, and the constant scraping noise of cutting tools working on metal. There is a strong, kerosene-like smell of cutting oil.

Even farther down the corridor is the Casting Department. Despite the roaring exhaust fans, it is always hot working here. As the castings cool, there is a pleasant crinkling sound of thousands of tiny metallic contractions. But this is almost drowned out by the high-pitched whine of air-powered grinding tools coming from the booths where the castings are deburred.

After a few moments, the heat and the noise get to you, so you wander back up the corridor towards the quieter, cooler end of the first floor, where the elevators are.

On the way back, you are conscious of the storage, shipping, and receiving areas. These may have escaped your attention on the way down, since there is relatively less activity to catch your eye. Nonetheless, you realize that these are vital for running the factory.

You find much less variety on the second floor, despite the fact that there are more people working here. About half of the workers are making and packaging electronic components and spare parts. The other half are working on transistors and integrated circuits.

The second floor is different from the first in other ways, too. Every unit being made here is much smaller, and more intricate. The work is done under bright overhead lights, sometimes with the aid of magnifying glasses. Workers seem to be concentrating more on what they are doing. There is music playing, from a number of portable radios, which drowns out the noises from the first floor.

The third floor is as different again. The large, open office space is quiet. The people working there in Personnel, Sales, Accounting, and Purchasing, are clean and well-dressed. (Few production workers are seen on this floor. They don't feel comfortable here.) The pace of work seems somehow more relaxed than in the production areas.

Next to the elevators is the Quality Control Department—a laboratory where samples of the production output are tested to make sure that quality standards are being maintained.

Next door to Quality Control is the Engineering and Product Development Department. It is sealed off from the rest of the office, and has its own heating and air conditioning system. The company

3

president seems to pamper his engineers. He was once an electrical engineer himself.

On the other side of the elevators are the executive offices. Each spacious, paneled office is "guarded" by a private secretary whose desk is just outside the door. Looking at the size and the expensive furnishings, you would think that you were visiting one of the giant companies in the industry. Actually, Precision Electronics is merely a modest-sized company, employing 400 people, and struggling to keep up with intense competition.

You are shown into the President's office, which is the largest, has a thick rug on the floor, and is the most expensively decorated. It has its own private bathroom. As you sit in a comfortable chair, waiting for him to get out of a meeting, you notice the company's organization chart (see Exhibit 2) hanging on the wall next to you. The secretary brings you some coffee, in a china cup.

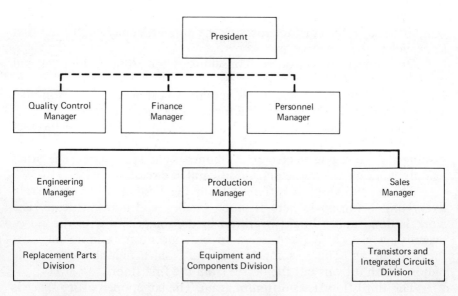

EXHIBIT 2 *Organization Chart Precision Electronics*

You breathe a sigh of relief now that you've finally arrived at the receptionist's desk at Allied Industries.

Finding a parking space was really tough. The employees' parking lot across the street was packed. So it took fifteen minutes of driving through the narrow downtown streets, which were choked up with afternoon traffic, before you were fortunate enough to spot someone just pulling out.

You tell the receptionist you are here to see Marvin Green, Supervisor of the Accounts Receivable Department.

Within minutes, Marvin has come to greet you. You find him quite pleasant and soft-spoken. He offers to give you a quick tour of the building, since this is your first visit.

All of the office work, he explains, is done on the second floor, where you are now standing. Below you on the first floor is the production area. This plant is one of eleven garment factories owned by the same company. The 300 workers "downstairs" are busy cutting, sewing, pressing, packaging, and shipping the men's and women's clothing.

Marvin says he'll be glad to show you around the first floor if you really want to see it, but confesses that he's "not an expert" when it comes to production technology. Assuming that you're more interested in the "white collar" work, he skips the production area and concentrates on a tour of the office.

As the two of you enter the office area, you immediately turn left (see Exhibit 3). The first thing that strikes you is the noise level. It seems lower than it should be for such a large and busy area. You *can* hear phones ringing, typewriters clacking, and people talking, but all these sounds have a muffled tone.

This surprises you, because the office area is quite open. There are only six-foot-high partitions and walls of filing cabinets dividing

Introduction
to Allied Industries

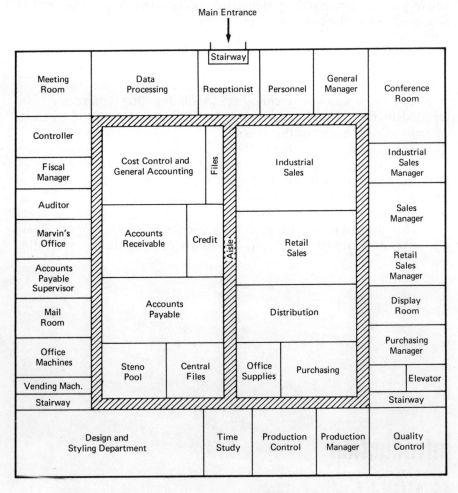

Main Entrance

		Stairway			
Meeting Room	Data Processing	Receptionist	Personnel	General Manager	Conference Room

Controller	Cost Control and General Accounting	Files	Industrial Sales	Industrial Sales Manager
Fiscal Manager				
Auditor				Sales Manager
Marvin's Office	Accounts Receivable	Credit	Retail Sales	
Accounts Payable Supervisor		Aisle		Retail Sales Manager
Mail Room	Accounts Payable		Distribution	Display Room
Office Machines				Purchasing Manager
Vending Mach.	Steno Pool	Central Files	Office Supplies	Purchasing	Elevator
Stairway				Stairway

Design and Styling Department	Time Study	Production Control	Production Manager	Quality Control

EXHIBIT 3 *Allied Industries Layout of Second Floor*

6

the various departments. Even though there is acoustical tiling in the ceiling, the floors are not carpeted: they are covered in plastic tile, just like the passageway you are walking down. The partitions must serve as very effective noise baffles.

Meanwhile, Marvin is explaining the general layout of the office area. This side, he points out, is devoted mainly to sales activities. The other side is mostly accounting and control.

Sales is split into two main divisions, each with its own office staff. The first one you pass is Industrial Sales. This department markets uniforms and work overalls, mostly to institutions. These are manufactured "downstairs." In addition, the Industrial Sales Department sells sheets and pillowcases to hospitals and hotel linen services. These items are not manufactured within the plant, however; they are subcontracted out to local rehabilitation workshops.*

Retail Sales involves several brands of ready-to-wear clothing for men and women. The factory that you are now visiting supplies a four-state area, dealing directly with the clothing stores that carry the brands. Marvin explains that his own Accounts Receivable Department takes over the paperwork once sales are made by either of the two sales departments, and also checks on customers' credit.

You pass the Distribution Department which arranges all the shipments. This can get very involved, Marvin explains, especially when unsold goods are transferred from one store to another, or defective clothing is returned. To further complicate matters, shipments of finished goods are made *directly* from the rehabilitation workshops to "industrial" customers. Marvin knows only too well about these complications; his department has to process *this* paperwork, too. Shipping notices are the evidence that deliveries have, in fact, been made.

You can easily tell that Marvin has a lot of contact with these departments. Everyone who catches his eye smiles or nods at him.

At this point, you begin to notice things about these office workers. All of the men, for instance, seem to be dressed just like Marvin. They all are wearing shirts and ties (but no jackets), and slacks. And they all look neat and clean.

The women are neatly dressed, too. You see skirts and blouses, dresses, and pantsuits, but there are few flashy colors or striking styles. Like the men, the women dress quite conservatively.

You have now walked around as far as the steno pool, and Marvin is telling you that his department has only one secretary. Any typing work that she can't handle is sent down to this group of stenographers.

*Rehabilitation workshops are nonprofit organizations that help handicapped people develop job skills. They do this by performing subcontract work for "regular" business organizations.

You see them typing away, some working from handwritten drafts of letters, others listening to dictating machines. Each work area is neat and tidy, and you suddenly notice that each desk has somehow been "personalized"—usually with photographs of families, but you also see photographs of pets, and even some artwork.

An attractive stenographer gives Marvin a friendly smile, which he returns, blushing slightly. He turns and offers to buy you a cup of coffee, from one of the vending machines.

As the groaning machine dribbles coffee into the plastic cup, you glance through the door of the Design and Styling Department and see a different world. The walls are painted the colors of the rainbow, in contrast to the pale green of the rest of the office area. In the midst of a casual disarray, young designers are dressed anything but conservatively. You figure that these people are tolerated as "creative types," and perhaps are even expected to be a little different. All the same, you notice that their little world seems to be "walled off" from the rest of the office.

As Marvin is explaining about a cafeteria down the stairway that you are passing, it is apparent that the noise level is much higher in this corner of the office, although the sounds still have a muffled tone. The photocopying and mimeographing machines are just on the other side of the vending machines. That also explains a distinct odor in this particular area. It's the wet ink.

When you arrive outside Marvin's office door, he points out the Data Processing Department, which is just ahead of you. Despite the heavy plate glass that isolates that department from the rest of the office, you can still hear the annoying clatter of the high-speed printer.

Marvin tells you that Data Processing is sealed off because of the need for careful climate control for the computer. He also says that the noise drove everyone crazy before the plate glass was installed. But this leaves you wondering how the people inside can stand it. They also look a little different from the rest of the office workers—the majority are men who, with loose ties and collars undone, are casually standing around. The computer must be running smoothly.

Marvin's office is inexpensively furnished. There are few frills in this business. With lots of stiff competition, the General Manager has to keep overhead costs* at a bare minimum. But the office is comfortable, and Marvin has a way of making you feel at ease. He explains the organization chart to you (see Exhibit 4).

*The permanent expenses of running a business that occur every day, regardless of the amount of sales.

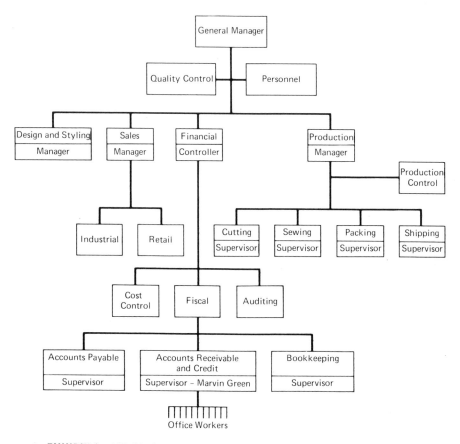

EXHIBIT 4 *Allied Industries Organization Chart*

You've heard all around town that Foreign Auto Repair is the best place to get your car fixed. Their quality is tops and their prices are fair. So you make a phone call, and Alan, the owner, assures you that if you bring the car in that afternoon, he'll take a look at it and tell you how serious the problem is.

When you arrive at the shop, you figure that there must be some mistake. Can *this* be the place everyone's been talking about? Instead of the modern, spotless, automotive "clinic" you had expected, here is a grimy cinderblock building surrounded by junk cars and rusty heaps of discarded car parts.

Well, this *is* just the outside. You figure the inside will be much different. It isn't.

When you walk into the office, you find a mess. The old desk is piled high with parts catalogs and paperwork. Nearby are heaps of new car parts, and there's a soda machine rattling softly in the corner.

This room must also serve as the waiting room. There are several old bucket seats, with stacks of old auto and motorcycle magazines nearby.

After a few minutes, it becomes obvious to you that no one knows you're waiting there. So you wander into the shop, ignoring the sign that says, "Insurance Regulations Prohibit Customers in Work Area." (See Exhibit 5.)

Alan, who is the shop supervisor because he owns the place, is on the other side of the building. He is spray-painting a car. The smell of the acrylic lacquer thinner is almost sickening, even from where you stand. You wonder what the local Fire Marshal would say about the poor ventilation.

You thread your way through the shop, carefully avoiding a multitude of hazards. There are jacked-up cars which seem precariously

Introduction
to Foreign
Auto Repair, Inc.

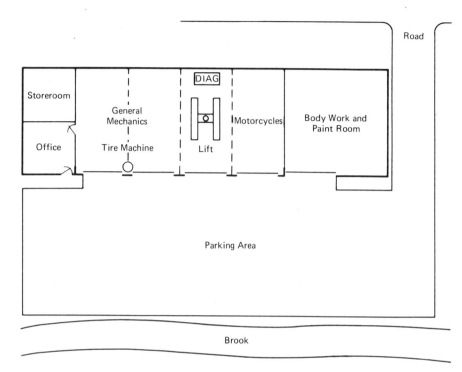

EXHIBIT 5 *Foreign Auto Repair*

balanced; oil puddles, sparsely sprinkled with drying compound, for you to slip on; mechanics' legs sticking out from under cars ready to trip you; a heavy steel chain-hoist, dangling at head-height, threatening to brain you; old engines, lying on their sides, waiting to bruise your shins; and a serpents' nest of extension cords and air lines to ensnarl your feet.

To make matters worse, everything that isn't oily is covered with heavy dust. So you have to be careful not to let your clean clothing brush against anything.

Alan can't be interrupted until the paint-spraying is complete. The paint will clog the spray gun if it is allowed to stand, and it takes almost as long to dismantle and clean the gun as it does to actually do the spraying. Once Alan starts a job, he has to keep going.

Alan thoroughly inspects his work when he's finished. If he's missed any spots, he has to catch them now. Then he hands the spray-gun to Cass, who will clean it. Cass is a big man, twenty-eight years old, who does all the bodywork. He also does all the painting preparation work, and buffs out the paint. The painting itself, however, requires Alan's special skill.

Alan suddenly spots you waiting by the door. He takes off his painting mask and comes over to greet you. Almost automatically, he starts to shake your hand, and then hesitates, looking down at his paint-soaked hand. He shrugs his shoulders and grins.

As Alan is cleaning his hands with more of that foul-smelling lacquer-thinner, you mention to him that in addition to wanting your car fixed, you're also interested in the mechanics he supervises. This amuses him, and since he's an open, frank person, he tells you about each of the mechanics (see Exhibit 6).

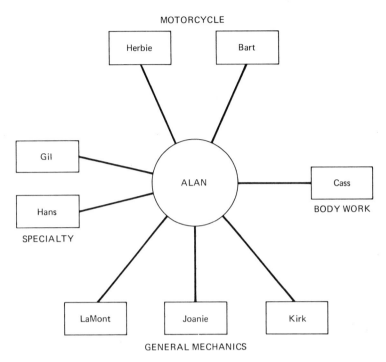

EXHIBIT 6 *Organizational Relationships*

Gil and Hans are the oldest mechanics, and because they are the most highly skilled, they are the easiest to supervise. All Alan has to do is to assign them the work (mostly the high-precision, specialist jobs) and consult with them about how to plan a schedule.

Gil is forty-eight years old, many of those years being spent working in a Mercedes-Benz dealership. In addition to being highly skilled, Gil is highly paid (and always looking for *more* money). He works very fast, very efficiently, and as far as Alan can tell, has never made a mistake.

Hans is forty years old. He was raised and did his apprenticeship in Austria. Though not quite as fast as Gil, Hans seems more adaptable to a variety of jobs, as is Alan himself.

While Gil and Hans are the master mechanics, three younger workers do the jobs that call for lower-level skills, under Alan's more careful guidance. These are Kirk, LaMont, and Joanie.

Kirk was the first mechanic to join Alan, back in the days when Alan was running a gas station and fixing cars as a sideline. Kirk is thirty years old, and has a degree in Industrial Arts. He couldn't get a job in his specialty without moving to another city, and seems to have resigned himself to auto repair work. He likes mechanical things.

LaMont is twenty-four years old, and black. He is a "sports car nut." He is getting to be quite expert at operating the electronic diagnostic machines.

Joanie is a twenty-three-year-old woman. No one seems to know much about her. She does general mechanical work, and does it well. She keeps to herself most of the time.

There are two more specialists among Alan's crew—Bart and Herbie. They run the motorcycle sales and repair operation, which takes up the repair bay next to the paint-room walls.

Bart is in charge of the "bikes." He is twenty-seven years old, and is always careful about his appearance (this is not an easy task in this shop). In addition to doing repair work, Bart is the motorcycle salesman, handling three specialty lines of bikes.

Helping Bart with the bikes, especially during the busy season, is Herbie. If Bart is the best-dressed of the mechanics, Herbie is by far the worst. The other mechanics joke that Herbie must spend hours working on his appearance to get that scruffy look. Yet even at only twenty-three years old, Herbie is a whiz kid at troubleshooting.

Alan confesses he leaves the "bikers" alone, as long as they continue to show a reasonable profit and don't actually run over any customers while doing "wheelies"* in the parking lot (their favorite lunchtime pastime, weather permitting).

You ask Alan about the dirt and the disarray in the shop. He shrugs his shoulders and explains that the mechanics hate doing "clean-up work," and cleanliness is only necessary for certain jobs. Furthermore, after a few bruises, the mechanics learn to be careful around the shop, so that there are few accidents.

Alan listens to your badly running car in the parking lot, opens the hood, and discovers that a wire has fallen off. He reconnects it and tightens the terminal, then sends you on your way without charging you anything.

You'll be back when more serious repairs are necessary.

*Stunts performed with only one wheel on the ground.

Walking through the door from the office area (see Exhibit 7) to the factory can be quite a shock. You are immediately confronted with the Stamping Department, where cold-rolled steel is smashed into shape by huge machines. The noise is a little rough on the nerves at first, but you *can* get used to it.

There are ten press operators working at the stamping presses. They all look busy and cheerful, but they don't seem to be concentrating on what they're doing as much as you'd expect. After all, the presses are obviously powerful enough to amputate anything that gets in the way.

Then you notice that in order for the presses to operate, two separate buttons must be pushed at the same time. That way, *both* the operator's hands must be out of the way before the press will come crashing down. The operator puts his hands in the machine only when he removes the stamped part and throws it into a hand truck.

Sam, the supervisor of this department (see organization chart, Exhibit 8), is talking to one of the press operators, who continues working while they talk. Actually, they are shouting more than talking, since the racket from the presses is almost constant.

Meanwhile, near to where you are standing, an older man from the Maintenance Department is fixing one of the presses. He is wearing a machinist's apron, and has a pencil stuck behind his ear.

You walk further down the corridor, passing a big degreasing machine. Here, you see a man who is taking parts out of a hand-truck and sending them through the machine. Inside the machine, the lubricating oil from the stamping operation is chemically removed. Otherwise, paint will not stick to the metal.

Just the other side of the degreasing machine is the Painting De-

Introduction
to Globe Housewares

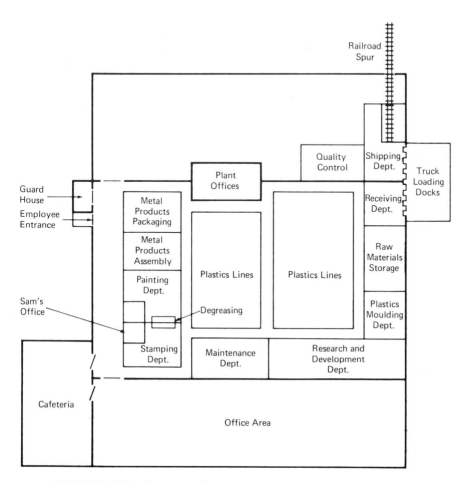

EXHIBIT 7 *Globe Housewares Company*

partment. You notice that there are three subdivisions to this particular department.

First, there is the actual painting area. Here, the clean metal parts are placed in special jigs on a conveyor belt. As they are passed in front of the painters, a powerful electric charge is passed through the parts. This acts like "static electricity" to attract the tiny paint particles towards the parts. It also accounts for the fact that there's very little paint dust floating around in the vicinity of the painting booths. Nonetheless, the painters wear masks, hats, and protective clothing.

Second, the freshly painted parts are sent through large drying ovens, where the paint is baked. When you walk by, you can feel the radiated heat. You notice that the skin of the materials handlers working in this area glistens with heavy perspiration.

17

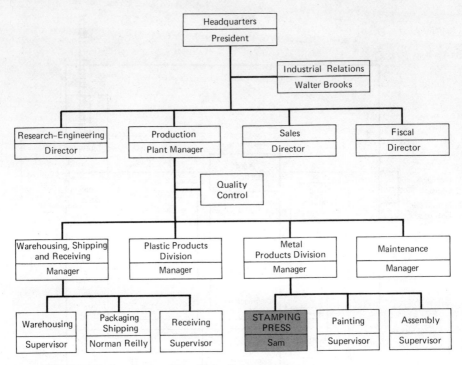

EXHIBIT 8 *Organization Chart Globe Housewares Company*

The third subdivision is the cooling area, where racks of dry parts are left to cool. This area reeks of hot paint.

When the parts are cool, they are taken, a rack at a time, to the Assembly Department, where they are combined with other parts to become complete Globe Housewares products.

When you get this far up the corridor, the constant din from the Stamping Department is only faint, and the heat can no longer be felt. Only the paint smell lingers. The workers here, and in the adjacent packaging area, carry on constant conversation without shouting (or mumbling through paint masks).

Across from the Packaging Department is the guard house. Here, two security guards are stationed to check on people entering and leaving the plant, and going through the heavy metal fire door into the warehouse area. Pilferage is a big problem at Globe Housewares.

The burly guard permits you to enter the warehouse. In contrast to the manufacturing area with its 600 lively workers, the warehouse is somber and cool. The roof is higher here, which permits pallets to be piled to cathedral-like heights. Little fork-lift trucks scurry around the dusty aisles, their electric motors whirring softly.

The Shipping Department, lodged in one corner of the warehouse next to Quality Control, is a stark contrast. Here there is a lot of activity as orders are picked and loaded onto pallets for shipment to customers. The workers here are just as busy as Sam's press operators, except here in Shipping, they look harassed instead of cheerful. This department makes you feel uncomfortable, so you leave.

After once again passing the suspicious eye of the security guard, you leave the warehouse area, turning left. As you look up, you see the large glass windows of the mezzanine-level plant offices. Up there, the Plant Manager can keep watch over plant operations. So does the time-study engineer, who is resented by all of the plant's unionized employees.

Farther down the corridor, you hear the cheerful banter of the Receiving Department workers, as they trade gibes with the truckers making deliveries.

Soon you've passed the raw materials storage area, which seems fairly dull, and you've arrived at the other hot spot on your plant tour, the Plastics Molding Department.

The molding machinery here has to get the plastic hot enough to melt, but also gets the workers hot enough so that they have short tempers. You wonder what it's like to work here on a hot, humid summer day. Just thinking about it makes you feel uncomfortable, so you move on.

There's not much to see of the Research and Development Department. It's walled off from the rest of the plant, and there's a stern notice stenciled on the small metal door advising unauthorized persons not to enter. You figure that you'd better not intrude, even though you have no intention of "stealing" company secrets about new products.

Off to your right, in the open area of the plant, there's a sea of faces. These belong to people working on the several assembly lines for plastic-based housewares. The plastic lines are shorter, less complicated, quieter, and cleaner than the adjacent metal-based housewares assembly lines.

The last department you pass, on your way back to see Sam, is Maintenance. This department services, repairs, and specially modifies the machinery used in the production processes. Thus everyone else is dependent on the skilled craftsmen who work here. They have the most status within the work force, and take home the fattest paychecks. It's a matter of great pride to work in this department.

By this time, Sam is back in his office. He is filling out a production control report. He dislikes this part of his job and is glad you dropped by to interrupt him.

Here are ten questions. Try to answer them before you read the five chapters in Section I. You'll have another chance to try to answer the same ten questions in the Posttest (page 76).

An answer sheet is provided after the Posttest (page 77). You will be able to use this to score your Pretest and Posttest. By comparing the two scores, you will be able to get an idea of how much your knowledge of supervision has improved.

Questions 1 through 6 are to be answered by circling T if the statement is **true**, and F if the statement is **false**.

1. Controlling is a distinctive process that needs to be kept separate from the planning process.　**T**　**F**

2. Supervisors can benefit from giving all of their workers "satisfactory" performance ratings, in order to demonstrate that they have a good work force.
T　**F**

3. The final decision to hire a new worker should be made by the line supervisor.　**T**　**F**

4. Tight controls should be used by a supervisor when there is the first sign of problems in meeting standards.　**T**　**F**

5. A good performance rating plan will focus on "ability to get along with others" and basic personality traits.　**T**　**F**

RUNNING
YOUR DEPARTMENT

6. A supervisor should give preference in hiring to women and minorities even if they don't have perfect job qualifications.   **T**   **F**

For Questions 7–10, choose the letter from the five possible responses listed below which is the *best* answer, and circle the appropriate letter.

7. A supervisor's department is free of bottlenecks when there is:

    a. A source of technical help.
    b. A trained back-up staff.
    c. Smooth work flow.
    d. A preventive maintenance program.
    e. A number of workable standby machines or equipment.

8. A supervisor can help avoid *people bottlenecks* by having:

    a. A source of technical help.
    b. A trained back-up staff.
    c. A surplus of employees.
    d. A preventive maintenance program.
    e. A number of workable standby machines or equipment.

9. The four steps involved in on-the-job training are listed below, but they are not in the proper sequence. Indicate the correct sequence by writing the appropriate number (1, 2, 3, or 4) in the blanks provided.

    supervised work practice: This should be step ____ .
    job breakdown: This should be step ____ .
    follow-up: This should be step ____ .
    explanation and demonstration: This should be step ____ .

10. One of the following statements about on-the-job training is *false*. Which one is it?

    a. Trainees should be watched most closely during training and immediately after it.
    b. A good worker is not necessarily a good trainer.
    c. The *rate* of training should be adjusted to what each individual trainee can handle.
    d. An overqualified trainee can cause as many training problems for a supervisor as one who is underqualified.
    e. Trainees who reach an acceptable level of performance rarely decline from that level.

A PREVIEW

The five chapters in this first section cover the very basics of supervision—the minimum functions that the supervisor must perform if his or her department is to operate at all.

First, the supervisor must try to achieve smooth work flow. A department cannot be efficient if there are sudden disruptions, pileups, or bottlenecks. Thus the supervisor's first responsibility is to **plan** departmental operations in such a way as to avoid such problems. This is the topic of the first chapter.

Once the planning is done, the supervisor can't just *assume* that the plans will automatically be followed. The supervisor's life is not that simple! Rather, in any organization, constant attention must be given to making sure that the work is being done within the limits of acceptable standards. This is the process of **controlling** the department's performance, and is the subject of Chapter 2.

It is actually the work of *people* that is being controlled, and the third chapter focuses on how to **hire** a new staff member without upsetting the teamwork of the other members of the department. This is not an easy task. Apart from having to exercise judgment about how job applicants will fit into the team and how they will be able to contribute to the department's work load, the supervisor must tiptoe through a maze of restrictive company policies, legal pitfalls, and ethical standards of fair treatment. This usually is further complicated by having only limited information to work with.

Once the team members are all "on board," the supervisor needs to find out how well they're doing their jobs, and to let *them* know, too. In a sense, we're back to planning and control: The supervisor plans what workers should do, and then controls their work by **rating** their performance. Chapter 4 explores the benefits of good performance rating systems, and the consequences of bad ones.

The last chapter in this section, Chapter 5, takes the planning-controlling-staffing-rating sequence one step further. It addresses the question, "What if a worker's ratings show that his (or her) performance is 'out of control'—that is, performance is not happening according to *plan*?" The problem here may be one of capability. Workers may *want* to perform well, but may not know how. The solution is on-the-job **training**, or "OJT."

These are the five basic elements necessary to the functioning of any department. The next four sections of the book will deal with special supervisory skills that become important once "the basics" are taken care of.

1. **Identify "the weak links** in the chain"—that is, those operations in your department that affect everything else if they go wrong. These are **operations bottlenecks.** You should plan to give most of your attention to them.

2. Plan ahead to **achieve smooth flow** from one work station to the next. Anticipate **layout bottlenecks** and **materials bottlenecks** before they interrupt the flow.

3. Learn where to get **technical help** to relieve **equipment bottlenecks.** Also, plan to give high priority to **preventive maintenance** programs to minimize **maintenance bottlenecks.**

4. Plan to allow time for training **backup workers** to cover jobs where there is a danger of **people bottlenecks** upsetting the smooth flow.

Planning

A CRITICAL INCIDENT: Starving to Death in the Cafeteria Line

Antonio, supervisor of the Globe Housewares Company cafeteria, called across the counter to Sam, and told him he wanted to "talk shop." Antonio was an old friend from high school days, so Sam agreed to eat his lunch in Antonio's office, a spacious glass-fronted room that overlooked the cafeteria operations.

Antonio really did need help. He had been on the job only a short time and things weren't going well. Customer complaints about slow service were increasing, and Antonio didn't know what to do about it. He had considerable experience in food preparation, but no supervisory training to help on this kind of problem.

Tray in hand, Sam finally arrived in Antonio's office. Antonio immediately came to the point.

"I need some help, Sam," he began. "I remembered you took a course in work flow planning last fall at the Community College. That's what *I* need right now. This cafeteria's a disaster!"

"It isn't *that* bad!" Sam kidded him. "You don't get more than two or three people a week fainting from hunger while waiting in the line. . . ."

"I figure you must have learned *something* in that course," Antonio continued, ignoring Sam's gibe. "Every time I go by your department, it's running like clockwork." Antonio was referring to the Stamping Department, of which Sam was the supervisor.

"Look, Sam, you've eaten in this cafeteria for years. And you know many of the people and the problems better than I do. Really, can you *please* tell me why the line's always so damn slow?"

"Well, I know the line's always slow," Sam began, noticing that Antonio was taking the conversation very seriously, "but it's not always slow for the same reason. For instance, today the line was backed up waiting for the cash register. There are two registers on the line, but only one of them was being used."

"Yes, but that's because there are only two people who can operate them," Antonio explained. "Winnie usually runs the cash register. Vera knows how to run it too, but she's in charge of salads, unless Winnie is out sick."

"But all Vera does in that job is put salads up front," Sam pointed out. "She makes them in the morning. *She* doesn't have to stand there during the rush periods. Anyone can put the bowls out front."

"Yeah, I guess we could have her running the second register. . . ."

Antonio agreed. She'll probably need some more training, though, in order to be as efficient as Winnie."

"You know, I have the same kind of problem in *my* department when we change the stamping dies on the presses," Sam assured him. "There are only two of my press operators who can change the dies properly.

"So, after I screwed up a few times, I learned to plan their vacations so that at least *one* of them is always around, in case a die gets ruined and we have to change it. You really gotta figure out in advance who your critical people are. Then maybe you have to train other workers to pinch-hit for them if they're out sick or something when you need them."

"I don't know how I missed seeing the cashiers as being critical," Antonio said, frowning. "I always figured my *chef* was critical. He's the only person who can make things like casseroles and fancy desserts. So I have to plan the menu so he doesn't have to do *two* special dishes the same day."

"Yeah," Sam said, nodding. "Now you see, you'd really be in trouble if he got sick or something. The chef's another example of a 'people-bottleneck.' That's one of the four kinds of bottlenecks we learned about in class. Another type is 'materials bottlenecks.' These can also slow up the lunch line."

"I'm listening," Antonio said, gesturing for Sam to continue.

"The amount of small change in the cash register is a good example," Sam explained. "When Winnie runs out of quarters or pennies, *everything* stops! This really gets people in line upset. You might just as well put a gate up there to stop traffic! Clean trays and silverware can be just as much of a problem, when you suddenly run out."

"Yeah. Those things happen every once in a while," Antonio agreed. "But I think I know how I should handle *those* problems: It's just a matter of planning ahead to keep more on hand, isn't it?"

"Yeah, that's basically it," Sam assured him. "Only I call it building up an inventory.

"Sure, it costs the company more for me to maintain an extra supply of really important materials," Sam continued. "But it saves money too, since we don't have to shut the presses down because we've run out of something. How much do *you* figure it costs the cafeteria when employees get mad enough to go out to lunch, or bring their own sandwiches?"

"I'd rather not even think about it," Antonio replied. That question really hurt, since he knew he'd been losing business. "Maybe I should order some more silverware and stuff."

"I dunno. Maybe," Sam replied. "Anyway, I was telling you

about the four types of bottlenecks. The third type is maintenance bottlenecks.

"They can be a hell of a problem in the Press Department," Sam pointed out. "When one of the stamping presses is down, I've got a worker getting paid average earnings for doing nothing. Then our efficiency rating takes a dive!

"To try to minimize these maintenance bottlenecks, I've sat down and planned a preventive maintenance schedule with the Supervisor of Maintenance. I've found he has a lot of know-how and is a hell of a nice guy to work with. Finding people like this to help you out on technical problems is a real big help and it doesn't cost your department a cent."

Sam saw Antonio's face brighten. He was listening intently.

"Together we looked over the past records of breakdowns and found out what are the most frequent problems, and how long the presses can usually run before the critical parts get worn out, or at least become risky.

"Then he services the press on a fixed schedule, replacing the parts that are likely to fail. This is done *before* there's a problem. It's too soon to tell yet, but I think I'm going to save a lot of downtime."

"I need to start a program like that with my mixing machines," Antonio said. "When one of those breaks down, we really get fouled up."

"What usually goes wrong?" Sam asked.

"It's usually parts wearing out in the electric motors," Antonio replied. "Obviously, it would make more sense to replace the parts before the machine quits. It's hard to know when this will happen, so I never pay any attention to the mixers unless there's a problem."

"That's how people end up with maintenance bottlenecks," Sam said, grinning.

"Probably what I really ought to do is to fix up the old mixing machine so we'll have some backup capacity," Antonio said. "It's just been sitting out back since the new machine came in. I'll bet it could be made to work fine during an emergency."

"See? You're catching on fast," Sam assured him. "You've got to give the most attention to the weakest point in the system. If it's the mixers that can mess you up the most, then that's the equipment you've got to watch the closest."

As Antonio was nodding in agreement, there was a crash of dishes. Two people had collided in the confused traffic pattern around the condiment table.

Spots of pea soup decorated several pairs of stockings and a pair of white slacks, as people tiptoed through the broken crockery. Two

cafeteria employees rushed over with a broom and a mop, which stopped the traffic completely.

"What do you do about clumsy people?" Antonio asked Sam. "You can't plan for that."

"Come on, man! You're looking at a layout bottleneck, not clumsy people. Here," Sam said, taking a piece of paper and sketching on it, "just take a look at how people have to move around here before they can get to the cashier."

Sam quickly produced a rough diagram of the cafeteria layout, using arrows to show where people criss-crossed and converged (see Exhibit 1-1).

Antonio looked at all the arrows in disbelief. He had always visualized the layout as if people followed a simple line from desserts to salads, then on to either sandwiches or hot dishes before getting something to drink and then paying the cashier.

Without realizing it, Antonio had placed a counter right in the center of traffic, and this had become a "no-man's land"! People came from all directions to this area to put catsup, dressings, or other finishing touches on their lunches. It was never orderly, particularly on a day like today when everyone was hurrying to make up for the delay in the line. So, as Sam pointed out, the bumping and elbowing should be no surprise.

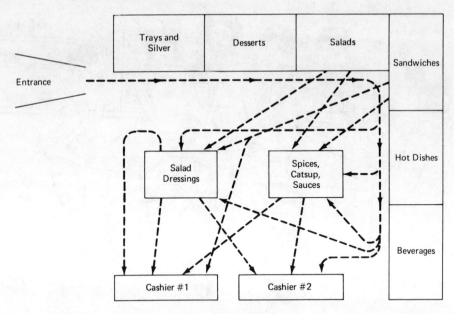

EXHIBIT 1-1 *Sam's Sketch of Flow in Cafeteria*

"OK," Antonio conceded. "I gotta come up with a new layout."

"Don't feel bad," Sam said, reassuringly. "This place still runs a lot more smoothly than the Shipping Department. They're doing so many special orders down there you wouldn't believe the work flow problems! While you've got customers standing around for extra minutes, down there regular orders sit around for days without moving!"

"Why don't you go help them out?" Antonio asked. "You gave *me* a lot of good ideas."

"That's easier said than done," Sam replied. "I doubt if the Shipping Department Supervisor will ever ask for any help. After you've been around here a while longer, you'll know what I mean."

CHECK YOUR PROGRESS

1. What is meant by a "weak link in the chain," and how can the supervisor deal with it?

2. How can a supervisor tell when his (or her) department is free of layout bottlenecks and materials bottlenecks?

3. What are two ways of handling bottlenecks caused by problems with machinery and equipment?

4. What steps can a supervisor take to avoid "people bottlenecks"?

ANSWERS TO PROGRESS QUESTIONS

1. A "weak link," or "operations bottleneck," is an operation in the department that will *disrupt the whole work flow pattern* if it goes wrong. The supervisor should plan to give the weak link *close attention and high priority* in order to spot a potential problem *before* it causes serious trouble.
2. A department is free of layout and materials bottlenecks when there is a *smooth flow* between each of the job stations.
3. The supervisor can get *technical help* or use workable standby machinery to relieve equipment bottlenecks, and plan *preventive maintenance* programs to help avoid maintenance bottlenecks.
4. Good planning involves the *training of backup staff* to take the place of a worker in a critical job operation who is somehow unavailable for work.

Further Thoughts

What is a *plan*?

> The variety of definitions of the term "plan" convey the general sense of what is involved:

1. The setting of goals and priorities to be achieved within a specified time period.
2. A target that allows the supervisor to measure the degree of achievement or deficiency in performance.
3. Establishing who shall do what, where, why, when, and how.
4. Setting objectives so as to help avoid future problems, and achieve future results more effectively.
5. An approach to taking action (and avoiding bottlenecks!) that is less costly than trial-and-error supervision.
6. The specific course of action *within* the department designed to contribute to achieving the overall objectives of the company.

Antonio could have obtained guidance on work flow planning from his boss. Why did he ask *Sam* instead?

> Antonio probably had several reasons for choosing to seek advice from Sam, instead of consulting his boss:
>
> Antonio was probably afraid that by asking his boss's advice, he would be creating the impression that he wasn't competent to handle his job as supervisor of the cafeteria. Since Antonio was fairly new on the job, he probably didn't know his boss well enough to predict how his boss would react, so he "played it safe."
>
> By contrast, Sam was an old and trusted friend, and Antonio could accurately predict that Sam would be supportive. Thus, asking Sam for help was less of a risk.

*Also, since Antonio was fairly new on the job, many of his layout
and bottleneck problems were inherited. Thus Antonio might be faced
with a delicate situation: After all, his boss is ultimately responsible
for the fact that the cafeteria already had these problems when Antonio
came to work there. Antonio will want to avoid making his boss defensive about the inefficiency that had been tolerated in the past.*

*Antonio is probably wiser to get help from Sam, and then go to
his boss and say something very tactful, such as, "I know you've been
busy around here, and haven't been able to give the cafeteria as much
of your know-how as it could have used. I've figured out some changes
that will improve its operations. . . , etc."*

*This approach goes over much better than the risk of criticism
involved in asking the boss's help, where the boss might take Antonio's
request to mean, "Listen, you dummy, you've given me a fouled-up
cafeteria to work with. Now you'd better give me some help in sorting
out this mess!"*

*Antonio can get off on the right foot if he can clean up the cafe-
teria line delay problems, so that his boss gets compliments about the
progress, without any extra effort on the boss's part. In this way, the
boss, at least, will know that Antonio deserves the credit; he will likely
be grateful to Antonio, and will sooner or later give him the reward
that he deserves.*

There are two types of problems that interfere with the smooth running of a department—internal problems and external problems. The supervisor can solve many
of the internal problems by planning a good layout. How can the supervisor handle
interference from *external* sources?

James D. Thompson dealt with this problem in depth in his book,
Organizations in Action *(McGraw-Hill, 1967). Thompson's thesis is that
you design a department's production layout to work efficiently, and
then you figure out ways to prevent "happenings" external to the
department from interfering with that smooth-running system. Thompson calls this "sealing off the technical core from the environment,"
and lists four strategies that the supervisor can follow:*

1. Provide buffers. *Smooth production and high efficiency require
the supervisor to protect his department against downtime and rush
orders. Maintaining inventories can provide the necessary buffers.*

*It should be noted that two types of inventories may be required:
raw materials and finished goods. As long as there is an inventory of
raw materials, there should be no downtime for lack of inputs. (Skilled
labor may also be considered a raw material, in this context, so that
training backup staff is like storing skills in inventory.)*

Sudden demands for output can be very disruptive of departmental efficiency. Thus it is best to be able to accumulate a buffer supply of outputs in a warehouse to supplement the normal (efficient) flow of finished goods out of the department.

Sometimes, however, there will be good reasons why maintaining buffer inventories will be out of the question. Perhaps the cost of maintaining an inventory will be prohibitive. A shipbuilder, for instance, cannot keep a spare oil tanker hanging around his dock in case someone decides he needs one right away.

Sometimes it is the nature of the product that prevents buffering: A cannery, for example, cannot indefinitely keep a supply of fresh fruits and vegetables in a warehouse, so as to buffer the "inputs" to their production operation.

The company that manufactures the cans for the cannery cannot store its production outputs, because empty tin cans take up a vast amount of space: all the can-maker's profits would be lost because of the cost of the huge warehouse that would be necessary.

Thus, although buffering is always "desirable," it isn't always feasible.

2. Smooth out the demand for outputs. When buffering doesn't solve the problem, for one reason or another, and the supervisor is faced with speedups and slowdowns in the demand for his department's finished goods (or outputs), the supervisor should next see if smoothing is feasible.

Smoothing is particularly appropriate for departments where the demand for outputs (either goods or services) is cyclical. Long-distance telephone calls represent one of the most obvious examples of cyclical demand, and the telephone company displays one of the most familiar smoothing strategies: Long-distance calls made during the busy daytime hours are expensive, to discourage "unnecessary" calls. The cheaper night rates encourage customers to call during the phone company's slack time. The greater efficiency increases the phone company's profits.

The cafeteria is a good example of how the supervisor can use smoothing to the advantage of his own department. The bottlenecks in the lunch line occur during the rush hour. Perhaps Antonio should be working out an arrangement with higher management to "stagger" workers' lunch periods. If the various departments were let out at ten-minute intervals between 11:30 AM and 1:30 PM, the line wouldn't be so choked up with people.

3. Try to forecast the disruptions. If buffering and smoothing are not technically feasible, then the supervisor should try to predict when the disturbances will occur.

The automobile body-shop presents a good illustration of this (at least in northern states!). Body shops do two kinds of work—paint and touch-up work, and crash-damage repair.

There is always a sudden increase in crash-damage repair work after the first snowfall. The supervisor running a body shop should forecast this sudden flurry of activity and not have too many touch-up jobs (such as routine repainting) with tight deadlines around this time of year.

4. Ration output to the most needy. *During slack times, the supervisor can meet the needs of everyone who uses the outputs of the department. However, there may be a sudden increase in demand that could not be buffered, smoothed, or forecast. In these circumstances, rationing is the only available alternative.*

Rationing involves establishing priorities to determine who will receive the "scarce" outputs of the department. In a veterinarian's office, for example, a dog that suddenly arrives after being hit by a car will be treated immediately, while another dog waiting for a distemper shot will have to wait. Another example: During peak times, cafeterias prepare ready-made sandwiches or salads, and precook some foods (such as turkey), which are featured as specials so that more people can be served without long delays.

1. Make the most of **control measures** that **pinpoint the acceptable limits** for the use of resources (such as labor hours and materials). When usage drifts beyond these limits, it is **out of control.**

2. **Set tight controls** when there are **large costs** involved in being out of control. Use looser controls when the costs are not so serious.

3. Take **corrective action** as soon as you see that an operation has **drifted out of control.** Don't wait until the problem has become severe.

4. **Keep control standards flexible.** Tailor them to changing conditions and changing control needs.

Controlling

2

A CRITICAL INCIDENT: Where Have All the Profits Gone?

The bookkeeper at Foreign Auto Repair finished up the previous month's profit statement and put it on Alan's desk. Then she left for lunch.

A few minutes later, Alan returned from road-testing a customer's car. He slumped into his chair and began eating a sandwich he'd picked up on the way. When he saw the bottom line of the profit statement, he stopped eating. He'd lost his appetite all of a sudden!

The previous month had been the busiest that Alan could remember since he'd opened his auto repair shop. His eight mechanics had been working "all out," and there had been so many customers looking for service that for the first time in a long while, he'd had to turn business away. Alan had figured he'd make close to $3000 for the month. But the profit turned out to be less than $500.

When the bookkeeper returned from lunch, Alan decided he'd better have a talk with her. He normally avoided getting involved with "that end of the business," as he called it. He hated "numbers and paperwork and red tape." He would much rather spend his time working on foreign cars alongside his mechanics.

Alan had never received any formal training for operating his business. He'd gone from building hot rods and pumping gas, during his high school days, to operating his own service station, which spe-

cialized in foreign car repair. He'd picked up what he needed to know to supervise a crew of mechanics somewhere along the way.

However, it now seemed that there were too many loose ends. Alan suspected that his job had become too complicated for him to "keep the whole thing in his head." He figured he had to do something more than just let the bookkeeper collect the minimum information required by law. It was time to listen more carefully to what she had to say.

So Alan forced himself to sit patiently while the bookkeeper explained where each of the figures on the profit statement came from. She also assured Alan that the low profit figure was accurate. She'd already triple-checked it.

Alan admitted to her that he was really baffled—he didn't know where the profits were going. The bookkeeper quickly made it clear that she didn't know *exactly* why the profit figure had been so low, either, but had some hunches about likely problem areas.

The bookkeeper's job actually put her in a position to have a good, intuitive feel for where the profits might be going. She processed all the invoices for parts coming into the shop, and made up the payroll. She also was the one who totaled up each day's customer bills.

"Well, if *I* managed this shop, I'd start paying attention to the time the mechanics actually *spend* working on jobs. I'd start comparing this with the labor hours that customers actually get *charged* for at flat rate,"* she suggested.

Alan thought to himself that this *could* be a possible cost problem. From time to time, he'd billed jobs at the flat rate when he *knew* that the mechanic had worked on the car for a much longer time.

Alan had not wanted to be bothered with checking the details of each job, however. So he had always figured that on most jobs, he would come out *ahead* of flat rate—by more than enough to offset the occasional problem job. Now he wasn't so sure.

"How much of a problem do you think this is?" he asked her.

"It seems to be more of a problem with *some* mechanics than with others," she replied, telling him something else he already "sort of knew," but preferred not to think about. She was referring to the sometimes erratic work done by Kirk, the mechanic with the most seniority.

"Where else do you figure we're losing money?" Alan asked her, not wishing to pursue her last point.

Her second "hunch" was that customers were not being charged

*A listing of the standard hours, in manuals provided by various auto companies, which customers should be billed for specific service or repair jobs.

for all the cans of oil and antifreeze that were actually used. She remembered processing invoices for many caseloads of each during the past month, but didn't recall customers being billed for these items very often.

She then added that if Alan were "giving" oil and antifreeze away, that wouldn't surprise her, considering the way that customer bills were made up.

The regular procedure was to write up the customer service order (see Exhibit 2-1) when the car was brought in. The service order would then sit on Alan's desk. The work began as soon as a service bay became available and a mechanic was free to work on the car. When the work was completed, the car would usually be taken out for a brief road test, and then left in the parking lot.

The service order, meanwhile, would still remain on Alan's desk

EXHIBIT 2-1

until the customer arrived to pick up the car. At that time, Alan would (almost reluctantly) leave whatever job *he* was working on, and write down the charges for parts and labor on the same service order (see Exhibit 2-2), which then became the customer's bill.

To fill in the parts section, Alan would have to yell to the mechanic to ask what parts were used on the job. The labor section was billed at flat rate.

The bookkeeper's observation about how he normally made up customers' bills made Alan wince. She was right, of course. Alan was certainly well aware that his invoicing system was sloppy. He'd figured that the increased effort he'd have to put in, to "do it right," wasn't worth the cost of the occasional parts and supplies that never got billed. Now he wasn't so sure of this either. Maybe he'd been *extra* careless during the previous hectic month.

REPAIR ORDER

JOB NAME _GULLWING_

FOREIGN AUTO REPAIR, INC.
291 WEST CREEK RD.
VALLEY FALLS
Phone: 278-1091

NAME	DATE OF ORDER
WILLIAM HOUSE	3/8

ADDRESS _157 LUDLOW ROAD_

CITY	PHONE		
VALLEY FALLS	273-2226	N°	6202

CUSTOMER'S ORDER NUMBER	ORDER WRITTEN BY	DATE PROMISED
	Alan	3/10

YEAR, MAKE AND MODEL	SERIAL NUMBER	LICENSE NUMBER
1955 MERCEDES-BENZ 300SL		TF 7499

	MOTOR NUMBER	SPEEDOMETER
		57,592

QTY	PART NO. AND DESCRIPTION	AMOUNT		DESCRIPTION OF WORK	AMOUNT	
2 qvts.	Antifreeze @ $1.50 ea.	3	00	LUBRICATION ☒ .5 CHANGE OIL ☒ .2 OIL FILTER ☐ TUNE UP ☐	10	50
1	Fanbelt (GF-42)	9	50	TRANSMISSION ☐ DIFFERENTIAL ☐ WASH ☐ POLISH ☐		
1	Camshaft cover gasket	6	00	CHECK ANTIFREEZE ok. (Added 2 qts.)	1	50
	(MB-3046127-9841			ADJUST VALVES ok. 2.6 hrs.	39	00
1	Set shims	12	00	REPLACE FANBELT ok. .3 hrs	4	50
				NOT TO BE PARKED OUTSIDE OVERNITE		

				GALS. OF GAS @		TOTAL LABOR	55	50
(MAY BE CONTINUED ON OTHER SIDE) TOTAL PARTS		30	50	8 QTS. OF OIL @ $1.50	12.00	TOTAL PARTS	30	50
ACCESSORIES				.5 LBS. OF GREASE @ $2.00	1.00	ACCESSORIES	—	
						GAS, OIL AND GREASE	13	00

I hereby authorize the above repair work to be done along with the necessary materials. You and your employees may operate above vehicle for purposes of testing, inspection, or delivery at my risk. An express mechanics lien is acknowledged on above vehicle to secure the amount of repairs thereto. It is also understood that you will not be held responsible for loss or damage to cars or articles left in cars in case of fire, theft or any other cause beyond your control.

OUTSIDE REPAIRS		
	99	00
TAX	6	93

SIGNATURE _William G House_

TOTAL ACCESSORIES						TOTAL	105	93

FORM 650-3 - Available from NEBS Inc., Townsend, Mass. 01469

Thank You

EXHIBIT 2-2

"Well, your hunch on oil and antifreeze may be worth looking into," he conceded. "You got any other ideas?"

"Well, those are the two main areas where I'd *start* tightening up," she replied. "There's probably a lot of minor areas we can look at later, but I think you'll find a great improvement if you stop giving parts and labor away. We need to set up some controls, but not on *everything;* just on the most important things."

"What would you suggest?" Alan asked.

"Well, we probably should start by keeping the biggest problem items—like oil and antifreeze—in a storage area. Then when they're used, we *immediately* write it up on the service order. No more relying on memory at the end of the day."

"Yeah. We could do that easily enough," Alan conceded. "Come to think of it, there's lots of empty shelf space here in the office. We could use it for storage. What if I start by telling all the mechanics that they can't take a single can out of the office unless it's noted on the service order?"

"That's a good idea. But remember, oil and antifreeze might just be a start," the bookkeeper reminded him. "You may want to add other items later. For this size operation, it's probably best to stay flexible and control the items that are causing you the most grief—or costing you the most money!"

"OK," Alan agreed, "I'll do just that. Also, I'm going to tell my mechanics to mark down actual hours worked on a job as soon as they complete it. If they keep going over the flat rate, then it's going to be on *their* time!"

Alan initiated the new control procedures immediately. He was happy, and somewhat surprised, that the mechanics accepted the new sign-out system for oil and antifreeze without any fuss. In fact, one of the mechanics suggested that oil filters and fan belts be kept in the office, too.

On the other hand, the announcement that their pay would be docked if they exceeded flat rate too often got Alan into hot water. The mechanics told him if he was going to do *that*, then he should also give a bonus whenever they worked *faster* than the flat rate. . . .

CHECK YOUR PROGRESS

1. How can a supervisor tell when his department's operations are *out of control*?

2. How does the supervisor decide whether loose, rather than tight, controls are appropriate?

3. At what point should the supervisor take corrective actions?

4. How does a supervisor avoid having control standards become outdated?

ANSWERS TO PROGRESS QUESTIONS

1. When controlled items (such as labor hours and materials) have drifted beyond the *acceptable limits*, the operation is "out of control."
2. *Tight controls* should be set only when the anticipated *costs* of being out of control are large.
3. The supervisor should take action as soon as the system has drifted out of control; that is, *before* the problem has become severe.
4. By keeping standards *flexible*, and by constantly tailoring them to changing control needs.

Further Thoughts

How is a "flat rate" determined?

> *"Flat rate" is a standard (or "expected") time for doing a specific job. It is determined by a number of work measurement techniques. Basically, the steps include:*

1. *Motion study* to determine the best way to do the job, such as by eliminating unnecessary steps, delays in setup time, and so on.
2. *Time study* to arrive at a standard time, based on a "normal" work pace, and an adequate number of observations, with allowances made for fatigue, personal time, and contingencies that are beyond the worker's control.

> *Another way of defining "flat rate" is to consider it as a pay plan, sometimes called "measured day work," which presets standard output or time goals for specific jobs based on a large number of past observations and measurements.*

Are the mechanics justified in requesting a bonus whenever they work faster than the flat rate? Why or why not?

> *If the "flat rate" is a realistic and attainable standard, the mechanics' request for a bonus when they exceed flat rate is justified. Such a bonus would offer an incentive to compensate workers who perform above a reasonable standard. This is fair and proper. Also, it is in sharp contrast to the "Band-Aid" variety of incentive plans which ignore basic problems of bad management, and instead use incentives in an attempt to bring substandard performance up to reasonable levels. (For example, when inadequate supervision is producing poor results from workers, it is not a wise idea to "make it the workers' problem" by changing their pay from an hourly rate to a piece rate. To do so would be to fix the symptoms of the "disease" without doing anything about the cause.)*

To what degree is controlling dependent on planning?

Controlling and planning go hand in hand; the one cannot be done properly without the other. A plan that has no built-in measures of control is unlikely to be achieved. Likewise, a control procedure that is established with no plan in mind (as to its purpose and means of enforcement) is doomed to fail. The process may be visualized as circular; i.e.,

Planning

Controlling
(Feedback)

The "results" generated by control processes provide feedback that can be used to modify plans, and thereby keep them flexible and tailored to changing conditions.

1. Get to **know company policies** on staffing. There are probably restrictions on whom you can hire and how much you can pay them.

2. Match applicant qualifications with job requirements, and recognize that more skills are needed at the time of hiring if there is an urgent **need for performance** and **little time for training.**

3. Improve your hiring "batting average" by focusing on information that is **relevant to the specific** job. Also, **double-check** any questionable data you get on the application form and in the personal interview.

4. Recognize that the personnel department can provide valuable assistance in recruiting, testing, and interviewing job candidates, but **the line supervisor** is responsible for making the **final hiring decision.**

Staffing

3

A CRITICAL INCIDENT: A Tough Choice

Marvin threw the pile of papers on his desk and leaned back in his chair, looking dejected. Three of his accounting clerks were out with the flu. To make matters worse, the bookkeeping machine wasn't working, and he wouldn't be able to get it fixed for a couple of days.

But what was bothering him most was his indecision about whom to hire as the new credit analyst in his department. The position had been vacant for over a month, and Marvin was in a bind.

He soon realized that he wasn't getting anywhere by just sitting there and mulling over his problems, so he picked up the phone and called Catherine Weaver, Personnel Manager at Allied Industries. He told her he was having trouble deciding among the three candidates she had found for him. Catherine said she had to walk down by his area of the building anyway, and offered to stop by his office and talk it over with him.

When Catherine arrived, Marvin got right to the point.

"I've looked at the application forms and the test results, Catherine, and I've also interviewed each one of them. They've all got strengths and weaknesses—but then I realize we're lucky to find *anyone* in the tight labor market for credit analysts these days! I've got to hire one of them right away, since we're in a jam. I need your help. Could you save me a lot of headaches by telling me which one *you* would hire?"

Catherine laughed and said, "You've got to be kidding me! I'm not going to fall into *that* trap! I've done that before and got burned!"

"What do you mean?" asked Marvin, a little surprised.

"Our job in Personnel is to advertise the openings, and do some rough screening. *You* decide which one will suit your needs best. Then if the new employee doesn't work out, you can't pass the buck to us!"

"Come on, Catherine!" said Marvin, chiding her good-naturedly. "You know I wouldn't do that!"

"Well, that isn't the only reason, even though it's a good one," Catherine replied, smiling. "Look at it this way: The kind of information that *we* look at gives us clues as to who has the *basic* qualifications, and whether they're medically fit. Perhaps more important, we can usually tell whether an applicant is likely to be a problem employee. Beyond that, the supervisor is a better judge of which of the satisfactory applicants is likely to work out best for him in a specific job."

"That makes a lot of sense," said Marvin, nodding, "but I thought you were going to help me?"

"I *am,* Marvin," she scolded. "I'm just not going to make your decision for you!"

They both laughed, then Catherine opened up the folder she had been holding.

"Would it help if I read you my notes on the applicants that I rejected?" Catherine asked.

"Yeah," Marvin replied gratefully. "Quite honestly, I'm really stuck, and that would get me thinking along the right lines, at least."

"OK, but just realize that *I* have to use judgment, too, in deciding who isn't likely to work out," she warned. "You may not agree with my reasons for rejecting them."

"I understand," Marvin assured her.

"OK. Well, we had only seven applications, and here are the reasons why I rejected these four of them.

"The first is a guy with an unstable employment history. He's had three jobs—each in a different industry—in the past four years. The only reason he gave for changing jobs was that it was a chance to advance himself. He didn't look like a good bet in this tight labor market. I figured you didn't need turnover problems in your department!"

"You aren't just kidding!" Marvin agreed, wincing as he remembered the problems he'd had since the last credit analyst left.

"The second applicant," Catherine went on, "has had all his work experience in the building trades. As a matter of fact, his father and brothers are in the business too. For hobbies, this guy works on antique cars and his model railroad. His test scores were high in mechanical aptitude and interest, and average in clerical and mathematical. He indicated he's had two years of accounting, knows about credit, and wants to change to a job that isn't so hard or dangerous."

"By the way," Catherine added, looking up from her notes, "he told me during the interview how he almost fell from the roof of a building while he was working on a beam! He seemed sincere, but I figure the fear is only temporary. Given a little time, he'll be hankering to get back to 'his natural work environment' and his family loyalties. Again, I figure a high turnover risk."

Marvin nodded in agreement as Catherine dug out her notes on the third application she'd rejected.

"The third one's a woman who told me she's quite flexible because she's no longer married. She has a good formal education, but came across in the interview as a continual complainer." Catherine wrinkled her nose as she said this. "She seemed frustrated that she hadn't gotten any farther in life at the age of thirty. She admitted that she doesn't have much patience for errors or stupidity, and, reading between the lines, I sensed she's been having problems getting along with her co-workers and especially with people working under her.

"What bothered me most, though, was that I found a gap in her employment record that left a year unaccounted for (see Exhibit 3–1). She was very evasive and a little edgy when I questioned her about it. She mumbled something about a typographical error in the application, and said she couldn't be expected to remember exact dates *that* far back. It was only two years ago!

"Anyway," Catherine said in summary, as she closed the folder, "I tactfully suggested that she look somewhere else for a job."

"The fourth one is a guy who worked for his father-in-law, as credit manager in a private loan company. He said he quit recently because business was slow."

Catherine looked up at Marvin and added, "I don't know why he didn't find another job *before* he quit. I asked him, but he didn't really answer the question.

"In casual conversation I did find out that he has heavy personal debts and for the last couple of years, he's been working locally as a real estate salesman to earn extra money. He works five nights a week, plus Saturdays. I figure that means a lot of daytime phone calls on company time, a worker who's constantly tired—in an important position

ALLIED INDUSTRIES — EMPLOYMENT APPLICATION
Equal Opportunity through Affirmative Action

GENERAL:

Name: CLAIRE DEEZEE	Soc. Security No: 001-02-0003
Address: 1234 5TH STREET	Phone No: 999-9999
Have you worked for Allied Industries: ☐Yes ☒No	If Yes, Dates & Dept.: —	Birthdate, if under 18 or over 65:
Are you a veteran? ☐Yes ☒No	If Yes, Give Date and Type of Discharge: —	U.S. Citizen? ☒Yes ☐No

Explain any Physical Limitations: NONE

Have you ever been convicted of any criminal offense? If so, please explain NO

POSITION:

Type of Position Desired: CREDIT ANALYST

Preferred Hours: 8:00 5:00   Salary Expected: OPEN

Source of Referral: SELF

EDUCATION & TRAINING:

Name of School	City and State	Dates Attended	Graduate Yes	Graduate No	Major Subject
High School	LINCOLN H.S.	1962-66	✓		LANGUAGES
University or College	RAH UNIV.	1966-70	✓		ARTS
Technical or Other	—	—			

Skills, Training, Hobbies: ACCOUNTING, FOREIGN LANGUAGES

Allied Industries, Inc. does not discriminate because of age, sex, race, religion or national origin

---

EMPLOYMENT RECORD: List most recent employment first

Employer: HI FI RECORDS		Address: WASHINGTON
Start Date: 4/15/76	End Date: 1/31/79	Final Salary: $10,000
Position Title: OFFICE MANAGER		Last Supervisor's Name: M. SMITH
Job Duties: KEEP BOOKS		Reason for Leaving: SEEK BETTER JOB

Employer: PDQ ADVERTISING		Address: WASHINGTON
Start Date: 1/2/73	End Date: 4/15/75	Final Salary: $9,600
Position Title: ACCOUNT SUPV.		Last Supervisor's Name: R. JONES
Job Duties: PREPARE FINANCIAL RECORDS		Reason for Leaving: SEEK BETTER JOB

Employer: ABC WHOLESALE		Address: LINCOLN
Start Date: 11/1/70	End Date: 12/5/72	Final Salary: $8,000
Position Title: SALES PERSON		Last Supervisor's Name: T. MILLER
Job Duties: SELLING BY PHONE		Reason for Leaving: SEEK BETTER JOB

Employer: —		Address:
Start Date:	End Date:	Final Salary:
Position Title:		Last Supervisor's Name:
Job Duties:		Reason for Leaving:

REFERENCES: List 3 persons, other than relatives or personal friends who have knowledge of your work

Name	Mailing Address	Phone
M. SMITH	✓	✓
R. JONES	✓	✓
T. MILLER	✓	✓

I hereby authorize investigation of all statements contained herein and certify all statements are true.

Date: 3/15/79   Signature Claire Deezee

EXHIBIT 3-1

—and a guy who won't be able to work overtime when we're in a jam. What do you think?''

"I agree with you. I'm looking for more commitment to the job than he'd be likely to give,'' Marvin replied. "Furthermore, I think you did a terrific job of sorting through a mountain of disorganized information and picking out the most important points.''

Catherine smiled.

"Are you quite sure you don't want to tell me which of these three you think has the best chance of working out as a credit analyst in my department?'' Marvin asked hopefully, holding up the three folders.

"No, thanks!'' she answered. "I've already decided that they're in the 'suitable' range. But if you want to think out loud about them, I'll put in my two-cents' worth.''

"If you can afford the time, I'd sure appreciate it,'' Marvin assured her sincerely as he opened the first folder.

"The first one is Shirley Parker,'' he began. "She's a minority female . . . pleasant, bubbly personality, I thought. Let's see . . . she is quite young having just completed two years of community college, majoring in business. Tests show high clerical interest and aptitude. She's always been interested in a business career. Her father is a business manager and her mother works in a bank. She has no previous work experience, except for summer jobs, which didn't seem to be too

relevant to credit. Her references, I noticed, are all personal friends, and teachers from school.

"This woman feels sure she could do the job and would enjoy working here. I guess my major concern is her lack of experience. I really need someone who can do the job right away. I don't have time to train her right now. On the other hand, I'd like to be able to go along with the company policy of increasing the number of minority and women workers."

"Sounds like you hit all the key points," Catherine assured him. "Let's try the next one."

"The next one is Phil Schwartz—he's had a clerical job in our Sales Department for two years. Wants a chance to advance. I know this job pays $50 more a month than his present one, and he figures it would be more interesting than what he's doing now. He doesn't have any experience in credit, but his contacts with Sales would be an advantage."

Catherine nodded, and Marvin continued his analysis.

"Let's see . . . he's a high-school graduate, he's sort of quiet . . . kind of a bland personality. Phil's boss has given him all 'satisfactory' ratings, and doesn't have any objections to his leaving. I guess this bothers me. He really hasn't distinguished himself in Sales. And he has only limited experience in credit. But at the same time, I know the company has a policy of promoting from within, wherever possible."

Marvin shrugged his shoulders and went on to the next application.

"The last one is Howard Beckman. He's about forty years old, and has been unemployed for one year. He was in an auto accident with no seat belt on. Had to have his leg amputated—above the knee— and also came out of it with a back injury. He was a field salesman, and had seven years of credit experience prior to that. He usually uses a wheelchair, and obviously can't go on the road anymore. And the company he worked for doesn't have a decent desk job for him.

"This guy's disabilities don't seem to handicap him, though. He's got a letter from his doctor saying he can do any kind of office work. And mobility isn't a problem. He drives a car and gets around by himself.

"Overall," Marvin summed up, "I'd say that based on my interview, the man seems fully qualified; he wants the job very much, and he'd be satisfied with the salary, even though it's less than what he was making as a salesman.

"I'm not sure how his disabilities square with company policy on hiring the handicapped. I know we try to do so whenever possible, but I wonder whether his injuries are so severe as to raise hell with our personal liability insurance. Other than that, I assume we could find him a special reserved parking space, close to the door."

"I can check out the personal liability insurance situation for you," Catherine said. "Howard Beckman did pass the standard medical exam, so I assume there'd be no problem."

There was a moment of silence.

"Well?" Catherine asked.

"I guess I'm sort of leaning towards Howard Beckman—the disabled guy—as my first choice," Marvin decided.

"On what basis?" Catherine probed.

"Well, I guess I could work with any one of the three, but Howard Beckman is the best qualified, really. He'll need the least training.

"The real reason, though," Marvin confessed, "is that I figure he needs a break. And I'm sure he'll knock himself out to do a super job. Come to think of it, I guess I've sort of had a feeling in the back of my mind all along that he'd be my first choice. I just haven't been able to make a conscious decision. Thinking out loud sure helped."

"I'm glad," Catherine commented, smiling.

"Which one would you have chosen?" Marvin asked her bluntly, cocking his eyebrow.

"I think you made a pretty good choice," she replied, and got up to leave. "Now help me figure out what I can say to the applicants that you rejected."

CHECK YOUR PROGRESS

1. What should a supervisor know about company policies on staffing?

2. What are the two basic choices that a supervisor has when considering qualifications of job applicants?

3. An employment application contains a large amount of information. How can a supervisor decide what's useful? Also, can he (or she) get more information if it's needed?

4. *Who* should make the final hiring decision, and why is this a good idea?

ANSWERS TO PROGRESS QUESTIONS

1. A supervisor should know the company guidelines and restrictions that determine who can be hired. These may include preferences for promotion from within, quotas for minorities, and starting pay rates.
2. A supervisor can either hire someone with *potential,* and *train* that person, or hire someone *already qualified* (that is, previously trained by someone else). If time is short, the more qualified applicant should be favored.
3. A supervisor should focus only on what is *relevant* to the specific job that he (or she) is trying to fill. More information can be obtained by *double-checking* what's on the application, and during the personal interview.
4. The *line supervisor* should make the *final* hiring decision. This works out better because he (or she) has to live with the decision, and his judgment is usually better when it comes to who's likely to work out the best on a specific job in his department.

Further Thoughts

What are some of the major clues that you should look for to determine job applicants' relative strengths? Their relative weaknesses or risks?

Clues that can indicate relative strengths *include:*

1. Relevant and complete work history.
2. Good references—written and confirmed by telephone.
3. Desire to locate in community where plant is located.
4. Good scores on tests that relate to job performance.
5. Salary in line with applicant's needs and experience.
6. Applicant's strong and sincere desire for job.
7. Background that seems compatible with peers in work group.

Clues that can indicate relative weaknesses *or higher risks include:*

1. Erratic work history—no evidence of maturity or stability.
2. Incomplete or inaccurate information given (particularly if it appears something is being concealed).
3. Educational background not compatible with job being sought.
4. Outside jobs, hobbies, or other activities that could interfere with job under consideration.
5. References consisting solely of personal friends. (These are virtually useless.)
6. Temporary layoff with no evidence that the applicant won't return to old employer if given chance to regain seniority.

Was Marvin's decision in selecting Howard Beckman as the best prospect for the credit analyst position a good decision? Explain why or why not. Also, if Howard

Beckman is hired, how should Marvin handle notification of Shirley Parker and Phil Schwartz?

In light of Marvin's immediate need for an experienced worker, and on the assumption that there were no other applicants, Howard Beckman seemed to be the best choice. He was a "bargain" to the company, considering his high level of experience in comparison to the low salary offered. Had Howard not been at a physical disadvantage, it is unlikely that Marvin could have found his level of maturity and experience for the position in a tight labor market. Howard also seemed a low risk, since his physical disability apparently was not a vocational one; that is, it would not interfere with his ability to do a good job.

With regard to Shirley Parker and Phil Schwartz, the job candidates who were rejected, we must hope that Marvin explained to both of them during the personal interview that there was an urgent need to fill the position with someone as experienced as possible. If so, Catherine can use Howard's level of experience as the reason for the choice. Along with hiring a handicapped person, this could satisfy Shirley that the decision wasn't discriminatory. Marvin should also check with the personnel manager to determine if any other job openings exist for which Shirley and Phil qualify. Were it possible to give either or both of them a new alternative, it would make "breaking the news" much easier for her.

Critics of modern American business practice would interpret Marvin's decision making in a *different* light: They would say that what Marvin was really doing was figuring out which one of the applicants would be the *easiest to dominate—* that is, which one would just take orders and not give him any trouble. To what extent is this interpretation valid?

This critical view of the selection process has some validity. Critics maintain that the very nature of modern American business leaves workers feeling alienated. In other words, workers do not feel involved in the goals of the business, since the business itself is oriented towards making money for the owners (the stockholders), rather than primarily towards providing an important service to society.

According to the critics, when workers don't have the feeling that they are doing something useful—something that will make for a better world for themselves and their fellow man to live in—they won't naturally tend to cooperate, but will do so only when power is exerted over them. The goal of management under these circumstances is thus to find workers who can be forced to cooperate with the least managerial effort.

The most dependent workers tend to be the easiest to control. By contrast, someone who is a "high turnover risk" is likely to be a relatively independent person—someone who has many alternatives in the job market—and therefore is likely to be relatively more difficult to control.

"Turnover risk" was used in this case as an important factor in the selection decision. While both Marvin and Catherine talked in terms of the disruptive effects of turnover on the operations of the Accounts Receivable Department, the critics of modern American business would say that obedience was probably a more important factor than the risk of a temporarily unfilled position. As support for this argument, it would be pointed out that the credit analyst position had gone un-filled for some time, and the operations of the department had not ground to a halt; therefore, turnover couldn't have been too much of a problem!

A much stronger argument would be made by the critics concerning the specific case of Howard Beckman. This man would obviously be the easiest to dominate of all the applicants, since he is the most depen-dent. As a disabled worker, his alternatives in the job market are more limited. Obviously, Howard Beckman knows this, since we are told that he is willing to work for Marvin for less money than he made prior to his accident. The critics would charge that it is the resulting "vulner-ability to the supervisor's power" that would make this man an at-tractive employee in the eyes of the average American businessman.

Whether this was actually Marvin's foremost consideration in hiring Howard Beckman is a matter of guesswork. It is at least possible.

1. Conduct **regular** performance reviews, and keep them **objective and fair** by focusing on **actual results,** rather than on personality traits.

2. Recognize that generally it is **more difficult** for a supervisor to give **low ratings.** However, you must avoid using only the "satisfactory" category.

3. Have workers help you set **realistic performance goals.** This will increase their acceptance and understanding of what is expected of them.

4. Use the performance rating system to improve the effectiveness of supervision; be sure to **reward good performance** and **take corrective action** on undesirable performance.

Performance Rating

4

A CRITICAL INCIDENT: Paying the Price for Past Mistakes

Vince paced back and forth across his office in the Machining Department. He was racking his brains trying to figure out what to do.

Business had been slowing down at Precision Electronics. For the past few months, the regular customers had been cutting back their orders, and the Sales Department was unable to find new customers to take up the slack.

Faced with rapidly rising inventories, top management was forced to cut back production. This was to involve a layoff of 5 percent of the work force.

Vince's boss, the Production Manager, had told him privately that he would have to lay off one of his machinists. It was up to Vince to choose which one would be leaving, so long as his decision was consistent with company policies on layoffs.

What was upsetting Vince was that company policies were forcing him to get rid of one of his best workers, and keep his worst one!

Specifically, company policy provided that whenever there was to be a layoff, the worker with the least seniority would be the first to go. The only exception to this rule would be when a higher-seniority person had a less-than-satisfactory work record.

Seniority was determined on a plantwide basis. In other words, what mattered was how long the person had worked at Precision Electronics; it made no difference how long that person had worked in a particular *department* at Precision.

The person's work record was determined on the basis of an annual performance review. The supervisor rated each of his workers as being either "excellent, satisfactory, or unsatisfactory" on six general factors (see Exhibit 4–1).

After a while, Vince realized that he was getting nowhere by just pacing back and forth. So he went to see his boss, the Production Manager. Vince had always been able to level with his boss, so he decided to explain his dilemma, and see if his boss had any ideas. Vince outlined the situation as follows:

Raoul was the machinist in Vince's department with the least plantwide seniority. Thus he was first in line to be laid off. Unfortunately, things weren't that easy, because Raoul was an outstanding worker. Vince had hired him, eight months previously, straight out of trade school. Since that time, Raoul had worked hard, learned fast, and had taken extra courses in night school to add breadth to his education.

55

Worker's Name _____

PRECISION ELECTRONICS

ANNUAL PERFORMANCE REVIEW EVALUATION SHEET

Supervisors should rate the worker on each anniversary of joining the department using the scale below as a guide.

	Excellent	Satisfactory	Unsatisfactory
Personality (ability to get along with others)			
Motivation (drive)			
Self-confidence (poise)			
Character (honesty, forthrightness)			
Loyalty (trustworthy)			
Manners and Appearance			

Comments

Supervisor's
Last Name _____

Signature _____

Date _____

EXHIBIT 4-1

Raoul had been hired to fill one of two vacancies then existing in the Machining Department. The other position was filled by Ted.

Unlike Raoul, Ted was not "hired from the outside"; he was transferred from another department within Precision Electronics. Ted had actually worked for over five years in the other department before coming to Vince's Machining Department. Thus Ted had almost six years of seniority at Precision.

Vince recalled that he had wanted to get rid of Ted after the first week. Ted was careless and slow, and appeared to take very little pride in his work. And no amount of extra coaching by Vince seemed to make any difference.

But with the pressure of day-to-day problems over the past eight months, Vince hadn't gotten around to actually *doing* something about Ted, other than informally expressing his dissatisfaction. There was nothing in writing. Now that he again checked back on Ted's past record, Vince discovered nothing but satisfactory performance ratings from Ted's previous supervisor.

Vince knew he wasn't in a good position to bail himself out of his present dilemma. What really hurt, though, was that Vince had checked very carefully on Raoul's background, while hardly checking at all on Ted's!

At the end of this explanation, Vince added that he'd talked to Ted's former supervisor on the phone that morning. The supervisor agreed with Vince that Ted was "a dud," so Vince had asked him why he'd given Ted all "satisfactory" ratings.

"And I can tell you what he said," the Production Manager broke in. "He said that it just wasn't worth the hassle of giving Ted unsatisfactory ratings."

"Did you talk to him, too?" Vince asked, looking puzzled.

"No. I didn't have to. That's the answer I've been getting from lots of other supervisors. You see, Vince, you're not the only supervisor having this problem with the rating system."

"I had the Personnel Department do a survey of the performance review system a few months ago," the Production Manager explained. "And it turned out that about 99 percent of the ratings were 'satisfactory.'"

"Yeah, I was surprised too," the Production Manager continued, noting Vince's shocked expression. "So I did some digging, and found out that with the really vague categories we use—things like 'personality,' 'character,' and 'loyalty'—it's easy for supervisors to write 'satisfactory,' but a big hassle to write anything else."

"For instance, I found that supervisors hesitate to write 'excellent'—even when the worker really deserves it. This is because supervisors are afraid of being accused of favoritism. They're afraid that the

other workers will complain that the supervisors are giving merit increases to their buddies. There's really no way for supervisors to defend their ratings—how do you prove that the 'excellent' rating is justified?"

"It's harder still for them to give 'unsatisfactory' ratings. First, it's unpleasant when the supervisor goes over the annual performance review report with the worker. But secondly, the supervisor tends to see 'unsatisfactory' ratings as a sign of failure on his part—you know, if he's a good supervisor, why can't he straighten the guy out? Or if he *can't* straighten him out, then why doesn't he get rid of the guy?"

"Anyway, it's obvious what's happened here is that over the years, it's become *expected* that everyone will get a satisfactory rating, and the whole annual performance review has gotten to be a joke."

"Yeah, I see what you mean," said Vince. "but I'm gonna zap Ted with a low rating on most of those items when he comes up for annual review."

"That's fine, but that's four months away," the Production Manager pointed out. "In the meantime, I really don't see what we're going to do about Raoul. I hate like hell to lose a really good worker."

"There's gotta be *something* we can do," Vince pleaded. "This situation is ridiculous!"

"There's not a whole lot we *can* do in the short run, so don't get your hopes too high," his boss cautioned him. "I'll *try* to figure out some way of keeping Raoul on the payroll until business picks up again, but it isn't going to be easy!

"I'm more optimistic about the long run," he continued. "I'm going to try to replace the present annual performance review system with one that makes more sense. Here. Look at this."

He handed Vince a form. (See Exhibit 4–2.)

"This is the rating form we used at the last plant I worked at," he explained. "Everything is in objective, quantitative terms. The supervisor and the worker fill in the form together, so there's no misunderstandings about what's expected of them or how their performance measures up to the goals. It was tied into the merit pay increase system, and nobody ever griped about unfair treatment."

"This is just what we need here," said Vince, looking up after he had carefully read the form. "If we'd had a rating system like this, I wouldn't be in this jam with Ted and Raoul. I could have rewarded Raoul's good performance and taken corrective action on Ted's poor performance. But with our present system, my hands are tied."

The Production Manager nodded his head sympathetically.

"Since you've obviously got a better system here," Vince asked, holding up the form, "why don't you use it in place of the crummy system we're using now?"

"Just between you and me, I plan to, within the next six months," the Production Manager replied. "I've made a lot of changes already in this place in the twelve months I've been here. People can't take too many changes too fast; if you overwhelm them, all you get is resistance—you know, people trying to prove that the new system won't work. So I've been taking care of one thing at a time."

"Yeah, that's probably the best way," Vince agreed. Then he added, "Maybe you can do something with the seniority system too. It's about time we started rewarding merit instead of old age!"

"Oh boy!" the Production Manager muttered, shaking his head. "If you *really* want to generate resistance, changing the seniority system is the best way to do it."

CHECK YOUR PROGRESS

1. What are the characteristics of a good performance review system?

2. Why are worker performance ratings in the "satisfactory" category easier to give than in the "low" or "high" categories?

3. What is the best way to insure worker understanding and acceptance of performance goals?

4. How can the performance rating system be used to improve the effectiveness of supervision?

Worker's Name _____ Time Period_____

<u>WORKER RATING FORM</u>

This form is to be used to record the results of performance review conferences between the supervisor and the worker. The conferences should be conducted every 6 months, or sooner if there is an operating change which substantially affects the worker. Goals are to be recorded at the beginning of the time period; achievements at the end. The form should be signed by both supervisor and worker to indicate agreement.

Performance Area	Goal (record at beginning of time period)	Achievement (record at end of time period)
Productivity (quantitative increase in output)		
Waste/scrap (percentage)		
Quality (no. of defects, rejects, returns, complaints)		
Safety record (lost time due to accidents)		
Innovations (no. of suggestions, new ideas, etc.)		
Self-improvement (training, night school, etc.)		

Absences during time period _____

Disciplinary record _____

_____

Supervisor's overall rating and recommendations _____

_____
_____
_____

Worker's
Signature _____ Supervisor's
Signature _____

EXHIBIT 4-2

ANSWERS TO PROGRESS QUESTIONS

1. A good system involves doing the performance review on a *regular* basis, with emphasis on objective, actual *results,* rather than on vague personality traits.
2. Satisfactory ratings don't lead to confrontations. It requires extra time and effort by a supervisor to build and defend his (or her) reasons for a low or high rating.
3. It's best to have workers *help* the supervisor *set* their performance goals, and *ideal* if workers set their own realistic goals.
4. The performance ratings should be used as an objective basis for rewarding good performance, and for taking corrective action on poor performance (such as disciplinary action, retraining, or job transfer, whichever is most appropriate).

Further Thoughts

Vince's boss is planning to introduce a rating system that involves *worker participation* in setting goals, and *objective measurement* of actual performance. Clearly, there are advantages to this system. However, there are also some potential disadvantages; what are they?

Some of the potential disadvantages are

1. Participative decisions almost always *take more time* than using supervisory authority to make decisions "alone." Thus the supervisor can expect to spend more time on participative performance reviews—time that both the supervisor and the worker would otherwise be spending on actual production work. The benefits of this type of performance review must, therefore, be large enough to offset these additional "costs."

2. In order to be effective, the participative performance review requires that supervisors be *skilled in interviewing and listening.* Since this is not a normal job skill of most supervisors, specialized training is usually needed to make this kind of rating program work well. This training requires skilled instructors and an expenditure of time and money. Again, the benefits must be weighed against the costs.

3. It has been assumed all along that the worker and the supervisor can arrive at *mutually satisfactory goals.* This is not necessarily the case. Workers' goals may be so different from the supervisor's goals that agreement is impossible.

4. Because of the *extra time and effort* the participative approach requires, it is unlikely that the system could be made to work equally well throughout the plant. For instance, a department that constantly faces crises would be likely to give low priority to performance reviews. Furthermore, not all supervisors will be equally comfortable with having a participative relationship with their workers.

5. There is some variation between departments in the degree of *applicability of the rating categories.* The rating form seems to be well-

suited to Vince's Machining Department. In a research and development lab, for instance, where work is nonroutine and the whole emphasis is on creativity, some of the categories (such as productivity, waste, product quality, and safety) wouldn't be too useful, because results are so difficult to quantify, and goals may change constantly.

Conversely, in a department with steady routines, many of the categories would be inappropriate because the worker would not have any leeway to make choices that might influence the results. For example, picture an auto assembly line where workers are bolting wheels on passing cars. Productivity is fixed by the speed of the production line; there is virtually no waste or scrap because workers are attaching pre-assembled units; quality problems may be difficult to trace to the individual worker; innovations may be unexpected and unrewarded, being the responsibility of the "efficiency experts," or the research engineers.

In summary, it should be cautioned that although there are several potential problems, the system proposed by Vince's boss does represent an improvement over the previous personality trait rating procedure. While the new system may not be equally applicable to all work settings (at least not without modification), it is certainly worth considering.

If Raoul is laid off, he will feel that he is being treated unjustly, since he has tried so hard and has a good work record. If there were no company policy on seniority and *Ted* were laid off, would Ted think he had been treated unjustly?

The "feeling of injustice" has been studied by social scientists in terms of equity theory. The theory deals with the conditions under which people view their rewards as being equitable, or just (where people feel that they are getting what they deserve) or inequitable (or unjust, where people feel that they are not getting what they deserve).

Briefly, each worker makes an estimate of what he or she contributes to the job (time, effort, skills, knowledge, special training, etc.) and matches these "inputs" against the rewards he or she gets out of the job (pay, status, satisfaction, etc.).

This matching takes the form of a ratio of inputs to rewards. Workers compare their effort-to-reward ratios with the effort-to-reward ratios of other workers. On this basis, they decide if their rewards are in line with the rewards of others. If the ratio is about the same, workers will experience the satisfying feeling of equity or justice. If the ratio is out of line, workers will either change their inputs (e.g., work less hard) or try to manipulate their rewards (e.g., put in for a raise) to restore the balance.

Analyzing the layoff situation in Vince's Machining Department in terms of equity theory gives us some insight as to how Raoul, Ted, and Vince each perceived the situation quite differently.

Raoul, no doubt, saw his input contributions as being very high; he worked hard, and was making extra efforts to acquire additional skills (night school). He probably saw Ted's inputs as being much less, since Ted put in the minimum amount of effort and was doing nothing to improve his skills. Their (dollar) rewards were probably the same, since they were both doing the same work and had been in the Machining Department the same length of time (there was no merit pay system). Thus, Raoul probably felt that he was being inequitably (unjustly) rewarded for his inputs, as compared to Ted.

Thus even before the layoff, Raoul would probably have felt that he was being treated unjustly. Upon being laid off, his perceived rewards would have sunk to zero, and the feeling of inequity (injustice) relative to Ted would have been magnified many times!

If we look at the same situation through Ted's eyes, we may be surprised to find that even before layoffs enter the picture, Ted probably also felt he was being treated inequitably as compared to Raoul! How can this be?

Simply, Ted is likely to have put different values on the importance of various types of inputs, so that he could have made a good case to convince himself that he was being underrewarded while Raoul was overrewarded. More specifically, it is likely that Ted considered "doing an adequate job" as a basic input. From Ted's point of view, extra effort (like Raoul's) was just "for show" and didn't "count for anything" when figuring out what inputs should have been properly rewarded.

Seniority, on the other hand, was probably considered by Ted to have been an important input (whereas Raoul discounted its importance). Thus Ted probably figured he was underrewarded for his contributions because he wasn't making more money than Raoul, the "kid straight out of school" who had less "experience" at Precision and who hadn't "given up six years of his life to serve the company." In Ted's estimation, Raoul's extra effort was irrelevant, since he figured his productivity still met the acceptable daily minimums. Feeling underrewarded before the layoff situation arose, Ted would obviously have felt an overwhelming sense of inequality if he were laid off.

In trying to treat his workers fairly (i.e., equitably), Vince went through a similar mental calculation of Raoul's inputs and rewards as compared to Ted's. But Vince had his own values and priorities by which he would weigh the importance of each of their various types of inputs.

Vince thought of the importance of inputs in terms of "contributions toward effective departmental functioning." This added two dimensions not considered by either Raoul or Ted. The first input was "potential long-run contribution." Raoul scored high on this, because he learned fast and was working on self-improvement. The second input was "cooperativeness," which is less important among individual workers than it is to a supervisor running a department. Raoul was seen as being very high on this dimension also, while Ted was very low.

Thus Vince was upset that the rating system didn't let him keep a formal record of inequity—as a means of eventually restoring equity by increasing Raoul's rewards (via a merit raise) and decreasing Ted's (via a demotion). Recall that Vince had tried, unsuccessfully, on many occasions to raise Ted's inputs.

Vince was, in effect, being forced by company seniority policy to reduce Raoul's rewards to zero. This tipped the scales hopelessly in the direction of inequity.

Vince expressed the opinion that "it would be nice" to change the seniority system. His boss didn't disagree, but only commented that such a move would provoke resistance from workers. What are the *issues* involved in changing from a plantwide seniority system to a departmentwide seniority system, or to no seniority system at all? *Who* would resist the change, and *why*?

Eliminating the seniority system altogether isn't necessarily a good idea. Consider the hypothetical case of a person who has worked for the company for thirty years, is ten years below retirement age, and is "slowing down." Doesn't the company owe him anything?

Legally, perhaps not, but there is an "unwritten social contract" involved in the employment relationship. The terms of this informal contract say that if a person devotes most of his working life to an employer, then that employer has ethical obligations to the worker. These ethical obligations go far beyond the simple economic question of "can we get an energetic young man to do the same job for less money?" The seniority system tends to formalize this obligation, and thus it has value to the extent that it discourages the company from arbitrarily breaching this commitment.

A second reason for the popularity and prevalence of seniority systems is that seniority is easily quantifiable—that is, it can be expressed in factual numbers that can't be argued about. Because of this, seniority is often preferred by supervisors over merit as the basis for layoff decisions; the decision based on seniority is easier to defend. Unless merit is evaluated on the basis of very objective facts, the supervisor is hard pressed to defend himself against an accusation of favoritism. And workers facing a layoff often have nothing to lose by making the accusation, and pursuing it to the limit.

On the other hand, there are cases, such as Ted's, where the seniority system protects the worker who is not fulfilling his share of the social contract. This is not a fault of the seniority system, however; it is a fault of the rating system. To scrap the seniority system to pre-

vent similar problems in the future is like removing the appendix when the gall bladder is infected.

The less drastic alternative—changing from plantwide seniority to departmental seniority—has advantages and disadvantages. A departmental seniority system would clearly be an advantage in a case such as the one faced by Vince; if layoffs had been determined according to departmental seniority, Vince would have been able to choose between Ted and Raoul, since both had been in the department only eight months.

The main disadvantage of departmentwide seniority systems is that workers are hesitant to move from one department to another, even when such a move is to everyone's advantage. (The worker doesn't want the insecurity of being "low person" in the new department.) The result is a tendency towards inflexibility and stagnation.

Central to questions of seniority is the bumping system. "Bumping rights" allow the high-seniority worker to claim the job of a lower-seniority worker when the former's job is eliminated. While this may be the only way to make the seniority system work, bumping tends to have bad consequences for the department, if there is no recognition of ability. Where jobs are, in effect, assigned by seniority rather than ability or interest, mismatching is commonplace, and both the workers and the department suffer the consequences.

It is the older workers who will be most likely to resist changes in the seniority system. They tend to put up a fuss for two reasons. First, and most obvious, they usually have the most to lose; older workers usually have been around the plant longer than younger workers, and thus have vested interests in the seniority system.

Second, and not so obvious, older workers tend to have a view of the social contract between the worker and the company which is different from that of younger workers. Younger workers see merit as being their most important input. This is what they can best compete in; indeed, it is often their only way to get ahead.

Older workers, by contrast, tend to see seniority (years of service) as their most important input. Their career alternatives have shrunk as they have grown older, and they are more "locked in" to their current life style (friendship networks, credit obligations, homes, habits, etc.). Thus security is more important to the older worker, with the seniority system being their most effective device for ensuring it. Because older workers also tend to have more influence in the plant, as compared with younger workers, changing the seniority system can be very difficult.

The "resistance" to which Vince's boss refers actually becomes formalized at a later time when an attempt is made to change the seniority system at Precision Electronics. In Chapter 13 we will see this as an issue raised by the union in trying to organize Precision employees.

1. Give attention to each of the **four steps** involved in on-the-job training. These are: job breakdown, explanation and demonstration, supervised worker practice, and follow-up.
2. **Adjust training** to what each individual **trainee can handle:** People differ in their learning rates.
3. **Keep the closest watch** on trainees **during training** and **immediately after** it. Then you can slowly relax your attention.
4. Know the difference between a **good producer** and a **good teacher.**

On-the-Job Training (OJT)

5

A CRITICAL INCIDENT: Supervisors Have to Learn, Too

Vince was feeling more and more uneasy. He was sitting in a meeting called by his boss (the Production Manager of Precision Electronics), along with two other production supervisors. The topic of the meeting was delivery problems on the new government subcontract.

As the meeting progressed, Vince noted that everyone was starting to look at him! It was becoming increasingly obvious that *his* department—the Machining Department—was the weak link in the production process.

Vince's boss was very concerned because this was a very important subcontract for Precision Electronics. The profits were high. And the work was steady—a guaranteed order for 3000 units per week for the next two years. Since Precision Electronics had only recently recovered from a recession in which many good workers had to be laid off, no one wanted to lose such a good subcontract because of missed delivery deadlines!

The job itself was fairly simple: There were only three steps in producing the motor drive assemblies (see Exhibit 5-1), but special casting techniques were involved—which is why Precision Electronics got the subcontract in the first place—and great accuracy was required in drilling the castings. The big holdup was in this drilling operation.

The problem, Vince admitted, was that none of the three workers assigned to the drilling operation were turning out the necessary 200 units per day. And he didn't know why.

Before getting the big subcontract order, Precision Electronics had run a small batch of identical castings for development and testing. Vince had assigned two experienced machinists to this pilot run—Raoul (who had turned out 225 units per day) and Danny (205 units per day).

When the big order had come in, Vince felt the pressure for getting output fast, but he also realized that he couldn't spare *both* of these highly skilled lathe operators to do the simpler drill-press jobs. So he got approval to hire two new drill-press operators and then decided to assign Raoul—the higher producer—to train these people while also running the third drill press.

Vince figured this would be a good arrangement, since Raoul was enthusiastic and his most efficient worker. Raoul seemed appreciative of the new defense contract, because it kept him on the payroll after he had nearly been laid off a short while earlier. During the first day of

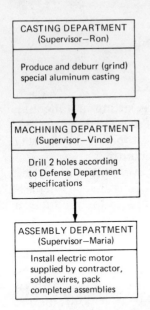

EXHIBIT 5-1 *Production Work Flow on Precision Electronics Government Subcontract*

work on the subcontract, it was obvious that some of Raoul's enthusiasm had rubbed off on the two new workers. By the end of the day, Vince felt confident that the training was going well and began to give most of his attention to other matters.

He had relaxed too soon. Production records showed that only 1200 units had been machined during the first three days. The schedule called for 1500 units to meet the first delivery deadline, and Vince's actual quota had called for 1800 units (200 units per day for each of the three drill-press operators)—which should have given Vince a buffer stock of 300 units. On the morning of the fourth day, the production manager had called the meeting, and Vince found himself in the hot seat.

When Vince got back to his department after the meeting, Raoul wanted to see him, having heard through the grapevine that the big boss was upset. Raoul didn't want to be the fall guy, especially since he'd gone out of his way to help the department on a rough new order.

Raoul pointed out that it would have been a lot easier for him to stay on his old job, alongside his friends, than to try to train two greenhorns. Although Vince was sympathetic to Raoul's concerns, he was anxious to figure out how to get the production output up to quota. The boss had told Vince to find a solution—fast—and report back immediately. So he asked Raoul what could be done.

Raoul said that he, himself, could easily turn out the 200 units per day if he didn't constantly have to stop and help the other two. However, he wasn't too optimistic about the others' *ever* reaching the quota.

Vince listened patiently, but Raoul wasn't much help in pinpointing what was wrong. He suggested that maybe the hiring decision was the problem—maybe the company should have paid a little more to get *experienced* operators. Raoul's only other point was that the two trainees seemed to be slow learners anyway. One of them, he said, "couldn't catch on after three days of me telling him what to do!"

By the end of the next day, Vince had figured out where most of the problems were. First of all, the job breakdown sheet (see Exhibit 5–2)—which listed the steps to be followed by the drill-press operator—was quite adequate. But the sheet had only been handed to the new operators to *read;* the steps were never *explained* to them, not even the more difficult steps 2, 5, and 9. Instead, Raoul had told the two of them to just *watch him* go through the process, then ask questions if they didn't understand.

In talking to the trainees, Vince also discovered that one of them found Raoul's explanations and demonstrations to be "OK," the other felt that Raoul "went too fast."

Both trainees complained that Raoul more or less deserted them as soon as he'd shown them what to do. He obviously was anxious to meet his own production quota. Consequently, no one was watching how they actually did their jobs, or gave them any further directions. The only feedback they got was at the end of each day, when Raoul told them they had to produce faster.

Vince spent considerable time trying to figure out how he got into this mess. In doing so, something dawned on him that should have been obvious, but which he'd overlooked under the pressure of making a fast decision.

Job Name: Drill Press Operator   *Dept:* Machining
Operation: Drill – Part #72 – Defense Dept. Casting

SEQUENCE OF OPERATIONAL STEPS	KEY POINTS AND ESSENTIAL INFORMATION
1. Pick up casting, checking deburring.	1. Give quick overall inspection to see if all rough edges have been removed.
2. Fix part in jig securely and place on work table	2. Show how to line up part with holes. Show holes to be drilled on blueprint. Explain where blueprints can be secured.
3. Apply cutting oil to tip of drill with brush.	3. On first part, check speeds. Drill speeds should be on position 2–500 rpm. Explain type of lubricant—where obtained, how often applied.
4. Start drill.	4. Safety precautions: Wear goggles and shop apron at all times. Remove all rings, and check for loose articles of clothing, particularly sleeves.
5. Lower drill with hand lever until it engages, then use steady pressure until hole is completely drilled.	5. Explain that with practice one can get the "feel" of the job. Explain where new drills can be obtained, and how much they cost.
6. Hold jig firmly on work table while drill is removed.	6. Illustrate the danger of lifting jig so that part spins out of hand.
7. Drill second hole.	7. Repeat steps 5 and 6 on second hole.
8. Turn off drill and remove part from jig.	8. Inspect the shavings, indicating how they *should* look if drill is properly sharpened.
9. Inspect part (every fifth piece).	9. Check to make sure holes are "clean." Demonstrate use of plug gauge to check dimensions. Demonstrate how to remove burrs with file. Check with set-up man if parts are out of tolerance.
10. Place work in shop tray with spindles all pointing forward.	10. Explain care needed in handling machined parts. Indicate number of parts expected per day on this operation.

EXHIBIT 5-2. *Job Breakdown Sheet*

Vince had thought back to *other* times when on-the-job training had been done in the Machining Department, and he remembered that about five years previously, he'd used *Danny*—quite successfully—to train new lathe operators. Danny, Vince recalled, had been patient with those trainees, and had showed he was good at putting into words the corrective action that each person needed.

Vince felt like kicking himself. He'd been so concerned with immediate, high production, he hadn't even considered Danny! He'd just picked Raoul, who worked slightly faster, and had completely ignored the issue of who would be better able to train the new operators.

In the process, Vince had made Raoul's life miserable. Looking back on what he'd done, Vince realized he should have established clear (and reasonable!) production expectations with a high producer like Raoul, *before* giving him the training responsibility.

Raoul had tried to achieve high production *and* good training, and as a result, hadn't done well at either. During the first three days, Raoul was producing only 175 units a day, while one trainee was producing 125 units and the other merely 100 units. Productivity had shown no sign of improvement, and the morale of all three had been going downhill fast.

Now that Vince knew how he'd got into the mess, he needed to know how to get out of it—and fast. After some careful thought, he figured he had four alternatives.

First, he could recommend to his boss that the two inexperienced trainees be terminated and replaced with experienced drill-press operators.

Second, he could have Danny trade places with Raoul—that is, use Danny as the trainer and drill-press operator, and return Raoul to his previous job as a lathe operator.

Third, Vince could step in and do the training himself, allowing Raoul to work full time at drilling the castings.

Last, he could begin instructing Raoul on how to be a good trainer, so that Raoul would be a source of help in future training.

Vince sat in his office racking his brains. He had to choose one of these alternatives and report to the boss in an hour.

CHECK YOUR PROGRESS

1. What are the four basic steps involved in on-the-job training?
2. What is wrong with training all workers in exactly the same way?
3. When should the supervisor keep the closest watch on trainees?
4. On what basis should trainers be selected to provide on-the-job training to new workers?

ANSWERS TO PROGRESS QUESTIONS

1. The four basic steps are job breakdown, explanation and demonstration, supervised practice, and follow-up evaluation of job performance.
2. Workers come to a job with different background knowledge. In addition, some learn faster than others. So training should be tailored to individual needs.
3. Trainees should be watched most closely during training and immediately after it. Then attention can be slowly relaxed as performance approaches standard and fewer problems arise.
4. Trainers should be chosen *not* on the basis of how well they *do* the job, but rather on the basis of how well they can *teach others* to do the job.

Further Thoughts

Which of Vince's four alternatives has the most promise? Why is that alternative better than the others?

Of the choices that Vince considered, the third one is the best. That is, the problem has become so serious that Vince should immediately step in and take over the responsibility for training the new workers. At the same time, by confining Raoul's responsibilities solely to working at his own drill press, Vince will soon receive Raoul's much-needed output of 225 units per day. With Vince doing the training, using good OJT practices (comparable to what Danny did earlier in training new lathe operators), the morale and output of the two new drill press trainees should recover rapidly.

If, beforehand, Vince had carefully thought about who should do the OJT, Danny would have been a better choice than Raoul. (This is the second alternative.) Instead, however, he chose the higher producer rather than the best teacher, and this proved to be a mistake. By the time he had realized this, it was too late to make the switch. Not only would such a move (at that point in time) be embarrassing to Raoul (it would dramatize his failure), but Vince couldn't afford to take Raoul off the drill press. Furthermore, by this time he couldn't afford to disrupt Danny's work on the lathe operation, either; otherwise, the productivity of both operations might fall behind!

Because of time pressures, Vince couldn't justify taking the extra time to train Raoul in how to be a better trainer (the fourth alternative). But even without the time pressures, it might not be wise to go to the trouble of training Raoul. Instead, it would be better to work with Danny, who has a talent for training. Raoul should be allowed to work at what he enjoys most, and where he can contribute most—as a machinist, not a trainer.

Finally, the first alternative (replacing the trainees with experienced workers) is poor for several reasons. The trainees' poor performance is a result of improper training, not a lack of effort on their parts. Therefore, to fire them would be unfair. It would also be likely to generate grievances, and would hurt morale throughout the department. Furthermore, even such a suggestion by Vince might be interpreted as being critical of his boss's judgment in hiring inexperienced workers in the first place; at the very least, it could be interpreted as "a cop-out," that is, an excuse for Vince's not being able to do his job properly.

A learning curve is one means of showing a worker's learning rate during OJT. An "ideal" learning curve looks like Exhibit 5-3. In Exhibit 5-4, the performance of

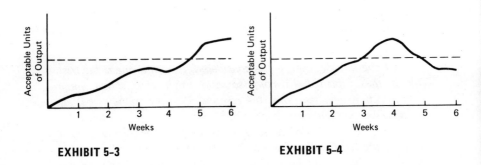

EXHIBIT 5-3   **EXHIBIT 5-4**

the trainee reached standard in three weeks, then exceeded standard for an additional two weeks before declining to a substandard level. What are at least four reasons that could cause such a drop in performance?

The following are possible causes of the drop in performance:

1. The trainer's *follow-up was relaxed too soon,* allowing bad work habits to develop.

2. The trainee became *overconfident or careless,* so that considerable rework was required (this is a consequence of bad work habits).

3. The *standard* was perceived as *too high* by the work group, so that the trainee came under pressure from his peers to slow down.

4. There were *inadequate incentives* (rewards) to motivate the trainee to continue production above the standard.

5. *External factors* beyond the trainee's control slowed down output, such as faulty materials, breakdown of equipment, bottlenecks developing in work flow, new layout or procedures, etc.

6. The trainee became *bored* as the job became more routine. Possibly the trainee was overqualified for the job, and lost interest after the initial challenge of learning the new job and beating the standard.

7. The trainee was *ill* but chose to come to work because he needed the money or hadn't yet earned any sick pay.

8. The trainee may have experienced sudden *stress,* such as a serious illness in the family, one of his kids getting in trouble with the police, etc.

Vince was providing special training to two people who would presumably *stay* in his department. Many times, however, supervisors train persons who perform well, then are *promoted out* of their departments. Training begins again with the same results. What can be done in such cases to keep supervisors from becoming frustrated and possibly unwilling to continue to devote efforts to training workers for the benefit of others?

Supervisors must be rewarded independently for their training skills and efforts. In other words, if they are rewarded only for the output of their own departments, they have no incentive to perform high-quality training, which helps increase the output of other departments.

One possible solution is to recognize good training accomplishments on their performance ratings, which could lead to a salary increase and promotion. Another solution is to allow more "slack" (e.g., man-hours) in the departmental budget of such trainers to offset the productivity loss that results when high-performance trainees are promoted to other departments where they can be of greater service to the company as a whole.

Perhaps most important is for the supervisor to see the "big picture"—that is, how his training effort is contributing to the overall good of the company, despite continuing disruptions in his department because of the promotions. Higher-level managers have a responsibility to present this "big picture" clearly and to see that a supervisor who makes such important long-range contributions (while making personal and department "sacrifices") is properly supported and rewarded.

POSTTEST QUESTIONS

Now that you've read the five chapters in Section I, you might want to try to answer the same questions that you answered in the Pretest. The correct answers are given on page 77.

By comparing your score on the Posttest with your score on the Pretest, you will be able to get an idea of how much your knowledge of supervision has improved.

Questions 1 through 6 are to be answered by circling T if the statement is **true**, and F if the statement is **false**.

1. Controlling is a distinctive process that needs to be kept separate from the planning process.   **T   F**

2. Supervisors can benefit from giving all of their workers "satisfactory" performance ratings, in order to demonstrate that they have a good work force.
T   F

3. The final decision to hire a new worker should be made by the line supervisor.   **T   F**

4. Tight controls should be used by a supervisor when there is the first sign of problems in meeting standards.   **T   F**

5. A good performance rating plan will focus on "ability to get along with others" and basic personality traits.   **T   F**

6. A supervisor should give preference in hiring to women and minorities even if they don't have perfect job qualifications.   **T   F**

For Questions 7-10, choose the letter from the five possible responses listed below which is the *best* answer, and circle the appropriate letter.

7. A supervisor's department is free of bottlenecks when there is:

   a. A source of technical help.
   b. A trained back-up staff.
   c. Smooth work flow.
   d. A preventive maintenance program.
   e. A number of workable standby machines or equipment.

8. A supervisor can help avoid *people bottlenecks* by having:

   a. A source of technical help.
   b. A trained back-up staff.

    c. A surplus of employees.

    d. A preventive maintenance program.

    e. A number of workable standby machines or equipment.

9. The four steps involved in on-the-job training are listed below, but they are not in the proper sequence. Indicate the correct sequence by writing the appropriate number (1, 2, 3, or 4) in the blanks provided.

    supervised work practice: This should be step ____.

    job breakdown: This should be step ____.

    follow-up: This should be step ____.

    explanation and demonstration: This should be step ____.

10. One of the following statements about on-the-job training is *false.* Which one is it?

    a. Trainees should be watched most closely during training and immediately after it.

    b. A good worker is not necessarily a good trainer.

    c. The *rate* of training should be adjusted to what each individual trainee can handle.

    d. An overqualified trainee can cause as many training problems for a supervisor as one who is underqualified.

    e. Trainees who reach an acceptable level of performance rarely decline from that level.

PRE- AND POSTTEST QUESTIONNAIRE—ANSWER SHEET

1. false

2. false

3. true

4. false

5. false

6. true

7. c

8. b

9. 3, 1, 4, 2

10. e

Here are ten questions. Try to answer them before you read the five chapters in Section II. You'll have another chance to try to answer the same ten questions in the Posttest (page 123).

An answer sheet is provided after the Posttest (page 124). You will be able to use this to score your Pretest and Posttest. By comparing the two scores, you will be able to get an idea of how much your knowledge of supervision has improved.

In Questions 11 and 12, circle the letter corresponding to the one statement which is *least* true.

11. a. Workers tend to "test" rules and stretch them to the limit.
    b. Rules create problems if they are applied too strictly.
    c. The biggest objection to rules is that they are impersonal.
    d. Rules tend to reflect experiences and problems of the past.

12. a. Rules can sometimes create problems if they are followed to the letter.
    b. Rules reduce the need for a supervisor to constantly give orders.
    c. Rules protect workers from arbitrary actions by supervisors.
    d. Rules can be used to "pass the buck" for unpleasant decisions.
    e. Rules make it harder for a supervisor to exercise authority.

GETTING
THE JOB DONE

In Questions 13 and 14, circle the letter corresponding to the *one best* answer.

13. In order for delegation to be effective, it is important that:

    a. Workers be capable of doing the work assigned.
    b. Workers who make some errors learn from them.
    c. Tasks delegated not need the supervisor's close attention.
    d. All of the above.
    e. None of the above.

14. When a worker has a preventable accident, the blame rests *mainly* on:

    a. The worker.
    b. The supervisor.
    c. The worker and the supervisor.
    d. The maintenance department.
    e. The personnel department.

Questions 15 through 20 are to be answered by circling T if the statement is **true**, and F if the statement is **false**.

15. The best time to get tough on safety rules is after an accident, when everyone will realize how bad the consequences can be.　**T**　**F**

16. To be a skillful communicator, a supervisor should not waste time by rephrasing or repeating what others say.　**T**　**F**

17. A supervisor who copies the leadership style of someone he or she admires risks being seen as a phony.　**T**　**F**

18. A supervisor should spend his (or her) time doing the things he knows best.　**T**　**F**

19. Spoken words usually tell more about what the communicator really thinks and feels than do nonverbal cues.　**T**　**F**

20. As a leader it is particularly important to maintain one's normal leadership style *during emergencies.*　**T**　**F**

A PREVIEW

The five chapters in this second section (Chapters 6–10) cover the skills that a supervisor needs to get *others* to help him (or her) get the job done. Although a supervisor is responsible for running his or her department, as noted in the first section, he (or she) cannot do it well without the willing support of his work group and his fellow supervisors.

Probably the most basic skill needed in working with others is being able to **communicate** ideas so that they are understood and followed. Getting through to people is the subject of Chapter 6. Particular attention is given to misunderstandings caused by making assumptions about what was said without checking what was really meant.

As desirable as it is to check every message, supervisors often are under such tight time demands that it just can't be done. One way out of this bind is through the use of written **rules**. By relying on rules that spell out what workers are expected to do (or not do!), the need for close supervision and constant face-to-face communication is greatly reduced. So too, should be the opportunities for misunderstandings. However, as Chapter 7 points out, rules that are followed strictly "to the letter" create problems by not allowing reasonable exceptions and by restricting worker creativity.

Many supervisors try to compensate for these undesirable problems by "bending" certain rules a bit. This practice, however, may cause another problem for the supervisor. Workers do not know exactly where the supervisor draws the line as to what is acceptable behavior. Such a case is the focus of Chapter 8, where a supervisor gets into trouble by trying to be a "nice guy" by relaxing his enforcement of **safety** rules.

Communication and rules are devices to get workers to help the supervisor get the work out. But all of this is of no use unless the supervisor asks for help! Chapter 9 deals with **delegation and time management**, looking at the plight of the supervisor who tries to do it all himself. The chapter tries to convey the notion that good supervision means that the supervisor does as little as possible. That is, the supervisor doesn't waste time doing what a subordinate can do equally well. Instead, he (or she) frees more time so that he can do things that really require his special talents and experience.

Once the supervisor has sorted out what the various members of his department ought to be doing, he must try to inspire or motivate them to do it. Supervisors differ in their styles of how they go about accomplishing this.

Chapter 10 points out that the chosen **leadership** style must be natural for the supervisor using it; otherwise, it will come across as phony. Furthermore, the style must be tailored to the occasion. For instance, "being a nice guy" may not be a good leadership style in an emergency!

The five chapters in this section cover the basics of getting others to help get the work out. This section is followed by a consideration of special problems that arise in the supervisor's dealings with people in the process of doing so.

1. Get into the habit of checking to **make sure you are being understood.** Don't just assume that the other person knows what you mean!

2. Improve your **listening skills** to make sure that you understand the messages you're receiving. Make a point of **restating other people's messages** in your own words, then asking them if that's what they **meant.**

3. Learn to be specific about the degree to which something is so, by **avoiding all-or-nothing terms** and by relying on **facts** and what you **observe,** more than on assumptions. Encourage others to do the same.

4. Allow people to vent frustrations, and be sensitive to people's needs to save face. Don't let pent-up **feelings block communications.**

Communication

6

A CRITICAL INCIDENT: "A Soft Word Turneth Away Wrath...."

Marvin felt bad after he hung up the phone. His department—the Accounts Receivable Department at Allied Industries—was in the doghouse!

An important customer had complained to the Industrial Sales Manager about the "bad service" he had been getting from Marvin's department. As supervisor, Marvin had assured the Industrial Sales Manager he would figure out what the problem was, take steps to make sure it wouldn't happen again, and also calm down the angry customer.

Marvin knew that Sylvia usually handled that particular account, so after pausing for a moment to collect his thoughts, he called Sylvia in to see what she knew about the situation.

Sylvia immediately became angry.

"I've had it!" she exclaimed. "That guy has stretched my patience for the last time! He doesn't listen to a *word* I try to tell him! You'd better get someone else to deal with him!"

Sylvia threw up her hands and slumped into the chair. But before a surprised Marvin could respond, she sat forward and began again.

"I don't even know why we do business with that creep," she continued. "The guy is a chiseler from the word go. He's probably got

cash-flow problems and is making excuses so he can delay payment 'til he can scrounge up another loan from somewhere."

Sylvia hadn't finished yet.

"And why did he go to the Sales Department and tell them that *I'm* not giving good service. Why is he out to get *me*?"

Before she could continue, Marvin interrupted.

"Hey, *come on*, Sylvia! You lost me! First off, how on earth did you find out he's got financial problems?"

Sylvia thought for a moment, then replied, "Well, I don't *know*. . . . It seems a pretty good bet to assume he does, though. Otherwise, why would he be so cheap? And why would he be trying to bully us into giving him discounts he's not entitled to?"

"Well, look, Sylvia," Marvin replied. "I don't think it's really fair to make assumptions like that. If you *really* think he's got financial problems, you ought to alert our credit people so we can get some *facts.*"

"Well, maybe he does, maybe he doesn't. But I still don't know why he's out to get *me*!" Sylvia replied, her mouth showing just a hint of a pout.

"I think you're *assuming* again, Sylvia," Marvin pointed out. "The report I got from the Industrial Sales Manager was that the customer had said the Accounts Receivable Department was giving him bad service. No particular person was mentioned in the department."

"OK, OK," conceded Sylvia. "But the guy really is impossible to deal with. I suppose you want me to call him and beg him to forgive me. I could also tell him he can disregard the invoices and pay whatever amount will keep him happy!"

"What I want you to do," said Marvin, ignoring Sylvia's sarcasm, "is to help me figure out what this complaint is all about so we can take some action to get Industrial Sales off our backs. Can we do that?"

"OK," Sylvia agreed, "let me get the records."

Having let off a little steam, Sylvia was able to quickly and efficiently bring Marvin up to date in her dealings with the customer. Marvin made three notes on a pad:

1. Only two invoices were in dispute. The totals on both invoices were correct. The customer was not entitled to a discount on the first because it involved special sale items not subject to a discount. The second was a replacement order for goods for which a discount had already been given.

2. Nothing special was written on those invoices to explain why the discounts were not allowed.

3. The customer had called the Accounts Receivable Department and had been "abusive." In return, Sylvia had *not* gone out of her way to be polite and cooperative.

As Marvin picked up the phone to call the customer, Sylvia started to leave.

"Come on, stick around!" Marvin said good-naturedly. "I might need some moral support!"

Sylvia was glad she did, because when Marvin got his first earful of abuse from the customer, a broad "I told you so" smile spread across her face.

"Every damn invoice I get from your department is screwed up," the customer was saying. "I'm tired of spending all my time straightening out other people's mistakes. I haven't dealt with *one* competent clerk in your department. I don't have this problem with other suppliers, and frankly, I can't think of a good reason why I keep doing business with your company. It's nothing but damn aggravation."

"Let me be sure I understand what you're saying," Marvin said calmly, now that the customer had paused in his tirade. "You're saying *all* the invoices you've received recently have been wrong, and that *all* the clerks in this department appear to be incompetent. Do I understand you correctly, sir?"

"Well, not *all* of them. I didn't mean *all* of them," replied the customer in a slightly less angry tone of voice. "But enough so that I have to spend a lot of time trying to straighten your people out. I'm a very busy man and I've got better things to do. . . ."

"Look, sir, could you please clarify something for me?" Marvin interrupted politely. "I was under the impression from talking to the

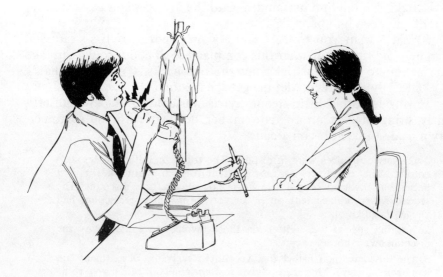

clerk in charge of your account that there are problems with only *two* of the thirty invoices you've received so far this quarter."

"Well, yes," the customer conceded, somewhat reluctantly. "But what the hell! Those were very important invoices."

"Yes, of course," Marvin agreed, "and I know you're a busy man, so let's you and I clear up these two discount questions that have been bothering you, so you can go on to something more important."

As Marvin was giving his polite, logical account of the two invoices, he paused frequently and asked whether what he was saying was making sense. At the end of his explanation, the customer seemed satisfied and obviously less angry, especially after Marvin thanked him for bringing to his attention the fact that explanations of special discount situations were not being written on the invoices.

As soon as Marvin hung up, his secretary brought in a message. His wife had called to report that his son had once again put a baseball through the picture window.

"Dammit," Marvin growled. "Every time I leave the house, I come home and *all* the windows are broken!"

Sylvia laughed and went back to her desk. She wondered how well Marvin would "practice what he'd been preaching" about good communication when he got home.

CHECK YOUR PROGRESS

1. Marvin seemed to spend a lot of time "repeating" what the other person said, using different words. Was this time wasted?

2. How can you, as a supervisor, improve your listening skills?

3. What is the advantage of distinguishing between what can be *assumed* and what is *specifically known* on the basis of actual observations?

4. Why did Marvin thank the customer for bringing it to his attention that the invoices didn't include explanations of special discount situations?

1. Probably not. What someone *means* isn't always the same as what you think you heard him say! It's usually best to rephrase the other person's point in your own words, and check to see if your understanding is accurate.
2. You can improve your listening skills by *restating* the other person's message *in your own words,* and then asking if that's what he or she meant.
3. If communications proceed solely on the basis of assumptions, there is no limit to where the discussion can go! Thus actual observations are more reliable in reaching a mutual understanding or agreement.
4. Marvin was helping the customer to *save face.* Instead of saying, in effect, "Look, you're wrong!" Marvin said, in effect, "Look, you're partly right, and you had a good reason for complaining. Now let's forget the whole thing." This is as important as allowing customers to "let off steam" in avoiding situations where *feelings block communication.*

Further Thoughts

Do you believe Marvin was a skillful communicator? If so, what did he do that seems to work well?

Marvin was skillful in that he was able to:

1. Ask good questions and listen well, both of which encouraged Sylvia and the customer to talk, and thereby give vent to some of their anger.
2. Probe for *factual* information and pinpoint faulty *assumptions* in locating the invoice problems.
3. Resist the temptation to challenge and embarrass an important customer who was reacting as a "know-it-all." Instead, he allowed the customer to *save face.*
4. Reach a *mutually satisfactory solution,* even though he was factually and perhaps legally in the right and could have forced the customer to back down. Marvin was thus smart enough to avoid "winning the battle and losing the war." (He made a friend out of the customer, instead of an enemy.)

What communication cues could Marvin pick up in his face-to-face interaction with Sylvia that he could *not* pick up in his telephone conversation with the customer?

Marvin was able to pick up nonverbal cues in talking directly to Sylvia. These may have included her body posture, facial expressions, hand or arm movements, other gestures, and eye contact. Such cues are very important to a communicator, as they often tell more about what the other person really thinks and feels than do the words being spoken.

What are the kinds of things that interfere with good communication?

The barriers to good communication are numerous, and include such things as:

1. Receiver of the message hears what he *wants or expects to hear;* that is, he or she ignores getting *feedback* to verify the meaning of what was intended by the sender.

2. Sender and receiver have *different perceptions* that are never sorted out, and thus they end up with *conflicting interpretations.*

3. Sender's message is not heard because of *poor timing* or because it is competing with many other *distractions* at the same time.

4. Sender and receiver use words without *checking* if they are clear and understandable to each other.

5. *Nonverbal cues* may be ignored or misinterpreted.

6. *Too much information* is given, so that the receiver is not able to absorb it and respond to it. (This is known as "information overload.")

7. Sender does not *check* (by asking questions or repeating the message in a different way) to be sure he is understood by the receiver.

8. Communication channels are too long, so that messages become *distorted* as they pass to various levels. (Remember the party game where people sit in a circle and a whispered message is passed from one to the next, finally returning to the source and being hardly recognizable?)

9. Senders and receivers *distrust* each other, leading to reinterpretation, distortion, and misinformation.

10. If bad communication continues over time, a "grapevine" (i.e., an *informal channel* of communication, or "rumor mill") will emerge. The grapevine messages will *compete* with formal communication channels, and block communication when there is a discrepancy.

1. **Evaluate rules** before you decide how to apply them. Figure out how they might **hurt** you as well as **help** you.

2. If you don't follow rules to the letter, **make sure that your workers know where you draw the line.** Realize that they will test out rules—to find out for themselves what will happen if they either follow or ignore them.

3. Use rules to **save your time, impersonalize orders,** and **reduce the need for close supervision.** But recognize that when rules restrict employee freedom, they also restrict creativity.

4. **Be flexible** in administering rules that are not spelled out or which don't give you any directions as to **when to make exceptions.**

Rules

A CRITICAL INCIDENT: All Work and No Play. . . .

During the morning coffee break, seven of the women at the first electronics assembly table had thought up a prank to pull on Irene, the eighth woman. They wanted to liven up the morning's work!

Before the coffee break was over, two of them sneaked back to the assembly bench and strung up an "instant mouse." The "mouse" was a fur-lined glove turned inside out. A piece of yarn was tied to the furry little thing and attached underneath the bench so it could swing over and brush against Irene's knee.

The plan called for Lucy, who sat across from Irene, to leave it taped to her side of the table until one minute before lunch time. Then she was going to let it swing!

At a quarter to twelve, Lucy began telling the other women stories about her cat's habit of bringing mice home. The other women joined in the conversation, with tales of their own pets, but Irene, who was not particularly fond of animals, just listened.

Just before twelve, Lucy recounted her "worst experience"—the time the cat brought home a rat. As she was describing in detail the "great big brown furry rat," she quietly released the end of the yarn.

The "mouse" silently swung through the air and brushed against Irene's bare leg.

Irene screamed and jumped backwards, knocking her chair over and sending a handful of electronic components flying.

Irene soon joined in the almost hysterical laughter of the other seven women at the assembly bench. As the lunch break buzzer sounded, she crawled under the table to inspect the artificial mouse apparatus, while the other women picked up the spilled components. They were all still laughing.

Meanwhile, Maria, the supervisor of the Assembly Department, had heard the blood-curdling scream, and had run over to investigate.

Maria joined in the laughter when she heard how Irene had been "set up." As the laughter was subsiding, she noticed that Vince, the supervisor in the nearby Machining Department, was hovering in the background, looking puzzled. He had also come over to investigate the scream.

Maria showed Vince the "mouse" and explained the prank, as the assemblers left in small groups for the lunch room. Vince, however, was not amused. He didn't even crack a smile.

Noticing that he was taking the whole thing very seriously, Maria kidded him.

"Hey, what's up, Vince? You afraid of mice?"

"Frankly," Vince replied seriously, "I'm surprised you didn't discipline Lucy. There's a company rule dealing with horseplay."

"Yeah, I know. There's a rule about *everything* in that book!" she replied good-naturedly, as they walked towards her office. "I read the whole thing when I was first promoted to supervisor. I noticed that some of the rules were pretty good advice. But others don't help you much. I never thought the one on horseplay was much good."

Maria reached up to the top shelf and took down a dusty book.

It was a thick loose-leaf binder, labeled *Precision Electronics: Production Rules and Procedures.*

She found the horseplay rule and read it aloud to Vince.

"Employees who engage in horseplay should be disciplined, since they increase the chances of accidents and personal injury, and damage to company property."

"So what's wrong with *that* rule?" Vince asked.

"Well, it's vague," she explained. "It doesn't set any clear limits to what workers can or can't do."

Not convinced, Vince asked her for an example of a good rule.

"I think the rule on waste is a good rule," she began, after thinking for a moment. "Three or four years ago, the rule just said that each production employee was responsible for helping to hold down the cost of waste. The rule obviously didn't work, because waste kept increasing. You remember, Vince, how we used to get pep talks from the old Production Manager!"

Vince nodded, remembering. He would have called it a "chewing out," rather than a "pep talk"!

"The rule was eventually changed," she continued, "so that employees were rewarded for keeping waste below specified limits. And they were penalized when it went 10 percent or more over the limits."

"Yeah, you're right," Vince agreed. "If we had more rules like that one, my job would be a cinch! I haven't had to spend *any* time on the waste problem since that rule was changed. My machinists know exactly what they have to do to fatten their paychecks. I never have to go down there and raise hell!"

"Yes, but don't forget the hassles we used to get into when that rule was first tampered with!" Maria reminded him. "People would stretch pretty close to those limits just to see what would happen."

"They sure as hell found out we meant business!" Vince commented.

"Yes. They did," she replied seriously, "but they had to test it out for themselves before they'd believe it."

Vince nodded thoughtfully.

"And you know what else?" Vince said, frowning. "I figure there's still a real drawback to that rule. Since they've been getting slapped hard for waste, the machinists don't experiment much any more. So I don't seem to be getting many new ideas from them."

"That could be a real problem in your department," Maria agreed.

The conversation soon returned to the horseplay incident. Vince told Maria that he *still* thought she should have disciplined the prankster.

"You have to enforce rules like that *before* someone gets hurt," he explained. "Irene could have fallen over her chair as she jumped back.

She could have broken something! I think rules ought to be enforced *consistently.* If anyone pulled a stunt like that in *my* department, I'd be all over them! And no one would get mad at me, either. They'd know I was only doing my job, enforcing the rules."

"Sure, Vince, consistency is important," Maria agreed, "but you have to use some *judgment* in applying the rules. I'd be a lot stricter on horseplay if I were supervising in your Machining Department! But assembly's a lot different. There isn't any dangerous machinery, and the work isn't as interesting. So when my girls pull a prank to break up the monotony, I'm pretty tolerant. There's a limit, of course, and they've got a good idea what it is. If they staged a karate match or started playing touch football. . . ."

"How you run your department is your business," Vince interrupted. "My only comment is that if you want to go to all the trouble of trying to work with flexible rules, that's your business. I just wonder whether it's worth it."

CHECK YOUR PROGRESS

1. What should a supervisor do before deciding how to *apply* rules?

2. How did Maria avoid being accused of making unfair and arbitrary decisions when she didn't follow the rule book to the letter? How does a worker usually find out whether a rule can be ignored?

3. When should a supervisor rely heavily on rules?

4. When should supervisors be *flexible* in administering rules?

1. Evaluate rules to figure out how they might *hurt* you (such as by being too strict where the job is boring and there aren't any hazards) or how they might *help* you (such as by reducing the risk of accidents or excessive waste).
2. Maria made it plain to all her workers where she *drew the line.* They all understood what was expected of them, even though they were occasionally allowed to depart from the written rules. Rules are usually "tested" anyway. The worker tends to *stretch* the rule close to the limits to see for himself what happens. Then the word is spread around.
3. When the need for saving time, impersonalizing orders, or reducing close supervision overshadows the need for worker independence and creativity.
4. Flexibility is wise when rules are not spelled out specifically or when there are no guidelines for making exceptions.

Further Thoughts

What are the major *advantages* of rules? The major *disadvantages*? Under what conditions would there be few rules? Lots of rules?

Some of the major advantages *of rules are as follows:*

1. Rules save time—employees don't have to consult their supervisor on routine matters.
2. Rules reduce the need for a supervisor to constantly give orders, thereby protecting the egos of persons who don't like to be "ordered around."
3. Rules make it easier for a supervisor to exercise authority—rules are consistent and impersonal. Thus they are harder to resist than are individual decisions.
4. Rules protect employees from arbitrary actions by supervisors (such as favoritism and ill humor).

Some major disadvantages *of rules are the following:*

1. In restricting employee behavior, they may thus limit creativity.
2. Employees can slow down operations and create an administrative headache for supervisors if they follow every rule to the letter.
3. Rules can be used to "pass the buck" for unpleasant decisions.
4. Rules may encourage certain workers to be aggressive and break rules to show independence, particularly if the rules are too rigid.
5. It is difficult to write them in such a way as to gain general acceptance. (For example, the horseplay rule was acceptable to Vince but not to Maria, who felt it didn't specify a definition of horseplay, nor define in what areas the rule should be applied).

Few rules would be expected when:

1. You have capable workers who are largely self-directed.
2. Workers feel highly involved with the mission of the organization (e.g., a group of volunteers working on the repair of a church).
3. Workers can be watched to see if rules are being followed.
4. Some external force (e.g., a union, a craft association, a profession) exerts control over workers.
5. The tasks are routine and spelled out.

Many rules would be expected when:

1. You have less than competent workers who need considerable direction and control.
2. Working conditions are poor; especially when workers feel alienated and do not care about the goals of the organization (e.g., an auto assembly line, or migrant workers).
3. Workers can't be watched most of time.
4. No external forces constrain what workers can do.
5. The job involves many risks that can't be left to chance.

It is sometimes said that rules generally tend to cover problems of the past, and therefore have limited value in guiding future-oriented decisions. To what extent is this true?

> *This statement is generally true. Rules tend to reflect experiences of the past, such as the rule at Precision Electronics on controlling waste. Only to the extent that future operations will continue in much the same way as in the past are such rules likely to endure and retain their value. Even then, such rules need constant review and updating if they are to have any chance of continuing to be relevant. Note that the book of rules Maria referred to was a loose-leaf binder. This would facilitate making the inevitable and frequent additions and changes.*

Laws are also rules. In what way are company rules like national laws, and in what ways are they different?

> *Laws are, indeed, just another type of rule. Thus we could compare a supervisor with the President of the United States (or any state governor).*
>
> *The President has two basic ways of getting citizens to do things. He (or she) can issue an executive order—a direct command—or he can make sure that citizens obey the law (the set of rules approved by Congress, including the Constitution).*
>
> *A supervisor has the same two basic choices. He (or she) can either issue an order (that is, tell the worker to do something), or enforce the set of rules approved by higher management. It is almost*

always easier for the supervisor to enforce rules than it is to give commands. This is because people basically object to losing their independence and autonomy, which is more or less what happens any time they have to do something that they wouldn't have done voluntarily. (If they were going to do what was desired by the supervisor anyway, there would be no point in issuing rules or orders.)

Thus, obeying rules or orders creates some resentment, by its very nature. It is much better for the supervisor to have workers resent "the rules" than to have them resent him personally. It makes his job considerably easier.

The President has much the same problem. If he wants to be re-elected, he can't issue too many unpopular executive orders. A better strategy is to ask Congress to pass unpopular laws. Then he won't be the target of citizens' resentment.

The biggest difference between national laws and company rules is that whereas citizens have a great deal of say in which laws will govern their "social" lives, workers essentially have no say in which rules will govern their work lives. Top management, the board of directors, and stockholders usually make up the rules without any worker votes, referenda, or even worker opinions. The same citizens who would not tolerate such totalitarian rulemaking in their outside lives for the most part don't question it in their work lives!

At first, it may appear that unions are an exception to this generalization. However, on closer examination, we find that few American unions (unlike their European counterparts) question management's right to make rules affecting workers' lives without ever consulting the workers. All the union typically does is try to change some of the unpopular rules so that they become more favorable to union members. The more basic question of democracy in the work place is rarely raised.

There is one form of business organization that creates its rules in the same democratic way that the citizenry creates the laws we live under. This is the self-managed company. Under this system, workers vote for rules (and changes in rules) affecting all levels of business decisions. The practice is not yet widespread, though, and has occurred mostly on an experimental basis. It may, however, be the basis of many business organizations in the future.

1. **Avoid joking around about safety.** Accidents aren't funny, and there's nothing heroic about taking chances.
2. Make regular inspections, and **get tough** on safety rules **before** there's an accident.
3. Understand that **being lax isn't a good way to become popular.** Respect comes from being fair and consistent. You won't feel too popular when you're explaining to a worker's family how an accident happened in your shop!
4. Take the view that all **accidents can be prevented.** Set a **perfect safety record** as the goal for your department.

Safety Management

8

A CRITICAL INCIDENT: The Oil Slick

The stamping presses made quite a racket, so Sam was almost shouting into the telephone.

He was still yelling when the press noises died down. Feeling a little foolish, he looked around to see if anyone was laughing at him. The men in the pressroom sure loved to tease him. Sam had been a press operator, too—for nine years—up until about twelve months ago when he had been promoted to pressroom supervisor at Globe Housewares. Now all his old pals would kid him every chance they got.

As it happened, no one was watching him. They were all over by Alex's press. Sam said into the phone, "Hey, I'll call you back. Something's up." Sam hung up.

Something was up, all right. There was a man lying on the floor next to Alex's press. He was bleeding from the back of his head. Alex, bending over him, looked up when Sam got there.

"He fell. Must've hit his head on the cement," said Alex, his face white and looking very scared. "You'd better call the doc!"

Fifteen minutes later, the injured man was on his way to the hospital.

What had happened was easy to figure out: Harold Shoop, a

60-year-old materials handler, was delivering a basket of small parts. Walking by Alex's machine, he had slipped on some oil.

Droplets of oil spattered out every time the press came crashing down. It needed to be wiped up every couple of hours.

Alex didn't like mopping up the oil. He figured, "What the hell does the sweeper get paid for anyway?"

Alex was a hard worker, but he was sloppy. Most of the time his overalls were just about saturated with oil, and there was usually a puddle around his press. The guys in the pressroom had nicknamed him "Alex the greaseball."

Sam had told Alex many times about the oil, but Alex would just kid him.

"Hey, look who thinks he's God, now that they've made him the boss!" Alex would needle. "I can remember not so long ago when you were working next to me. There was a few times I thought you'd struck oil and we'd all be rich! Don't ya remember how I used to bring an umbrella in to protect me from your spray?"

"Yeah, yeah, yeah," Sam would reply. "Very funny. But just try to clean up a bit around here, OK? You know the rules."

Sam had never really pushed the safety issue in his department. What Alex said was partly true. In his nine years as a pressman, before he got promoted, Sam *had* disregarded many of the safety regulations. He had often called them "sissy rules."

But now, things would have to be different. Within half an hour of the accident, the Production Manager had been on Sam's back. There was no excuse for the injury, and Sam had messed up the plant's safety record. It *had* been "318 days without an accident." Now it was all the way back down to zero.

In addition, everybody felt bad about poor old Harold Shoop. He had seven stitches, a concussion, and a sprained back, and he was going to be out of work for quite a while.

"From now on," thought Sam, "there's going to be no more fooling around when it comes to safety rules. Not in *my* department!"

CHECK YOUR PROGRESS

1. Why do some workers take chances with safety?

2. When should safety inspections be made?

3. Since strict enforcement of safety rules doesn't help a supervisor's popularity, what should a supervisor do to get workers to obey safety rules?

4. What safety record should a supervisor strive for in his (or her) department?

ANSWERS TO PROGRESS QUESTIONS

1. Many of them feel it is "heroic" to take chances or joke around. The supervisor must convince them that accidents are neither funny nor heroic.
2. Safety inspections should be made at regular intervals and *before* there's an accident.
3. The supervisor should enforce safety rules in a fair and consistent manner. Being lax will not earn a supervisor the workers' respect, which is more important than popularity.
4. A goal of a perfect safety record should be set, since virtually all accidents *can* be prevented.

Further Thoughts

What consequences can accidents have, beyond "messing up the plant's safety record?" What consequences do you think would be included?

The following are additional consequences of accidents:

1. Families dependent on the worker would also be harmed financially and emotionally.
2. Workers' compensation insurance costs would increase.
3. There could be a loss of production and quality, especially if the injured worker had to be replaced by someone with less experience.
4. In organized shops, there would be trouble from the union.
5. Violation of OSHA (Occupational Safety and Health Act) can lead to fines and in extreme cases, plant closings.

Note that supervisors need to have a basic familiarity with this law of job safety. The main implications of OSHA for supervisors are as follows:

1. The act "intends to stimulate employers and employees to institute new and to perfect existing programs for providing safe and healthful working conditions."
2. In compliance with the act, many companies have developed a cost effectiveness safety and health program designed, developed, and implemented for that particular industry.
3. The act will provide the supervisor with guidance, direction, and technical assistance to establish and implement a safety and health program.
4. Also in compliance with the act, many organizations have a SCAT or Safety Corrective Action Team. Supervisors will need to know their responsibilities regarding safety as to documentation, records, control, and internal management audits for judging the compliance of their own programs.
5. The important point to remember in the act itself is that its objective

is to "assure so far as possible every working man and woman in the country safe and healthful working conditions and to preserve our human resources."

The focus of the OSHA program is on industries and substances that are most hazardous as follows:

1. The target industry program is aimed at five industries with injury frequency rates more than double the national average. These are
   a. Longshoring (marine cargo handling)
   b. Meat and meat products
   c. Roofing and sheet metal
   d. Lumber and wood products
   e. Miscellaneous transportation equipment (primarily manufacturers of mobile homes, campers, and snowmobiles)

2. The target health hazards program is aimed at five of the most commonly used and hazardous of the more than 15,000 toxic substances, namely:
   a. Asbestos
   b. Carbon monoxide
   c. Cotton dust
   d. Lead
   e. Silica

Additional information can be found in a useful handbook for every supervisor, the OSHA 2056 pamphlet entitled "All About OSHA." This is a valuable resource of the who, what, where, when, why, and how of the Occupational Safety and Health Act of 1970.

Other information concerning this law may be obtained by contacting the nearest Regional Office, Occupational Safety and Health Administration, U.S. Department of Labor, or by contacting the Office of Information Services, Occupational Safety and Health Administration, U.S. Department of Labor, Washington, D.C. 20210.

What can be done with an "accident prone worker" (that is, a person who has a lot more accidents than others doing similar jobs)?

Certain workers tend to be "accident prone" for a variety of reasons. Usually they are persons who are having a difficult time adjusting to their jobs in one way or another. These may include people who are bothered because they are not meeting standards, people who are under considerable emotional stress, and those who panic easily when something goes wrong.

In some cases, discipline will help; in others, training could be of benefit; in cases involving stress, the supervisor will have to keep an especially close watch for signs of potentially dangerous behavior.

Another alternative—usually a last resort—is to transfer accident-prone workers to safer operations.

The supervisor sees safety issues differently from the worker's viewpoint. What is the difference, and what are the consequences of this difference?

Different organizational roles cause people to have different perspectives on safety. The worker thinks primarily in terms of his own safety, whereas the supervisor's thinking must be oriented more towards the safety of others. This point is important because one of the major problems encountered by freshly promoted supervisors is the reorientation of their view of the world of work.

This can be a particular problem in a situation where the worker's behavior constitutes a hazard only to himself. In such situations, the worker views whether or not he takes chances as a purely personal decision, whereas the supervisor, as part of his supervisory responsibility, seeks to eliminate all risk-taking. Thus what the supervisor views as "just doing his job" could be seen by the worker as an infringement on the worker's independence. It therefore becomes more difficult for the supervisor to discipline workers who take chances but are a hazard only to themselves (unlike Alex's leaving a puddle for Harold Shoop to slip on).

Note that this issue is not to be taken lightly. It is the same issue underlying the controversy over whether state law can require motorcyclists to wear crash helmets. Supreme Court decisions have ruled these laws to be a violation of constitutional rights, and thus the helmet laws are unenforceable in some states.

Finally, we have returned to the issue of rules being resented by the people who have to obey them. The argument "but this is for your own good" does not seem to carry much weight. People would, for the most part, rather decide for themselves, and not be told what's good for them.

What You Should Be Able To Do

1. Use delegation as a key strategy in **managing your time.**
2. **Avoid the do-it-yourself trap.** Constantly ask yourself, "Does this task I'm now doing **really** require **my** talents and experience, or can someone else do it?"
3. When you delegate an assignment, make sure the worker knows exactly **what you expect,** and how the task will be evaluated. Delegation doesn't relieve you, as the supervisor, of **your responsibility for results.**
4. As you delegate, expect your workers to make a certain number of **human errors.** Just be sure they **learn from them!**

Delegation and Time Management

9

A CRITICAL INCIDENT: The Sixty-hour Week

Marvin felt a knot in his stomach when he glanced at his watch. It was already after 9 P.M., and he figured he still had at least another hour of work to complete before going home. This was the third week in a row he'd been working overtime every night, and the pressure was getting to him.

Before diving back into his paperwork, Marvin decided he'd better call his wife and tell her he would be even later than usual.

The call got predictable results. His wife was already upset, and she let him know it.

"Who else is working there with you?" she demanded to know.

"No one," he admitted glumly, anticipating what was coming next.

"Why do *you* have to be the one who does all the work in that department?" she asked, sarcastically.

"It's not Accounts Receivable Department work I'm doing," Marvin protested. "It's work for a committee that is looking into buying out a competitor's company. I've got a deadline."

"You've also got a family," she reminded him, beginning to cry.

"Look, I'll come home in an hour or so and we'll talk about it. OK?" Marvin asked her, trying to be sympathetic.

"Yeah, sure," she said, and hung up.

Marvin tried to return to his financial reports, but couldn't concentrate. So he put all his papers away in his top desk drawer, turned out the office lights, and went home.

At home, his wife listened sullenly as he explained why the overtime work was so important. His boss had personally asked him to serve on the committee, which would make recommendations directly to the top management of Allied Industries.

"Look, Marvin, I *know* it's important work," she protested. "I just don't see why you can't do it during regular office hours."

"Because I *still* have to run the day-to-day operations of the Accounts Receivable Department," he said, patiently.

"But your department still runs when you're on vacation!" she reminded him. "Can't you pretend you're on vacation when you're working on this committee stuff?"

Marvin frowned deeply. His wife had made a good point. He thought for a while, then promised he would try to reassign some of his regular duties, starting tomorrow.

The next morning, Marvin made a record of everything he did. At lunchtime, he looked over his notes. He was amazed to find how many of the things he'd done really could have been handled by his office workers. He'd been "too busy" to pause and make the assignments!

That afternoon, he began delegating. First, he asked Sylvia to make a series of phone calls, which he'd originally planned to make himself, to sort out some inventory problems.

After she'd asked a number of questions to clarify what was expected of her, Sylvia seemed confident and agreed to make the calls. Marvin urged her to be sure to tell him if she needed any help along the way, since *he* was still responsible if anything went wrong.

Marvin was even more cautious before deciding to assign the sensitive credit rating reports to Jane. Information in these reports was highly confidential, since any leak could violate the privacy of customers. It could also result in a bad credit reputation for the customers before they'd had a final chance to make payments. Marvin had a lot of confidence in Jane, and had, in fact, shared confidential credit information with her in the past.

Despite his own time pressures, Marvin carefully explained to Jane the importance of the assignment, and was very specific about how he wanted it done. He encouraged her to ask questions to be sure she knew what was expected. Marvin also explained that he would evaluate how well she did the job by how carefully she kept the information confidential.

Jane assured Marvin that she fully understood her assignment, but would need a partitioned office for privacy, which Marvin arranged.

At 3 o'clock Marvin's secretary came into his office with her dictation notepad, and reminded Marvin that he'd been putting off writing several letters.

Marvin's mind, however, was on the committee work, so he asked her, irritably, to remind him what the letters were about.

After the secretary had outlined what each letter ought to say, Marvin realized that the secretary could compose such routine correspondence as well as he could! He asked her if she would mind writing the letters.

"I wouldn't mind at all. I often have to sort of rewrite them anyway, especially when your mind's on something else while you're dictating," she confessed, grinning.

"Then why have I been wasting my time dictating them in the first place?" Marvin asked.

"Beats me," she replied. "I guess you just got into the habit."

"Well, from now on, I don't want to be bothered with routine correspondence, since you probably do it better," he told her. "Don't even bring it to my attention unless there are special circumstances." Marvin felt like kicking himself.

He also felt relieved as he dove back into his work for the committee. At ten minutes before five, the secretary brought in six letters for his signature. She wanted to get them in the evening's mail. Marvin hurriedly glanced through the first letter and signed it, then automatically signed the others. He was out of the office by 5:30 that day.

However, several days later Marvin received an angry telephone call from a long-time customer who had received one of the six letters.

The secretary had made a mistake that Marvin hadn't caught.

The letter she had drafted implied that the customer was becoming a poor credit risk, while in fact there had been an agreement to delay payment until the insurance company had settled a claim for a fire in his store. There was actually a note to this effect in the file, but obviously the secretary hadn't checked the file. Rather, she had merely looked at how long the debt had been outstanding.

After explaining the error to the customer, amid many apologies, Marvin told his secretary what had happened. He wanted her to understand that the mistake could have been very costly. He also wanted to be sure that she, like himself, would learn from the mistake.

"In the future," Marvin told her, "I'll be sure to read each letter before I sign it if you'll be sure to check *all* customer correspondence and credit information before drafting a letter. Is that agreeable?"

"You mean you *still* want me to write all your routine letters?" she asked weakly.

CHECK YOUR PROGRESS

1. How can you study how well you are using your time during the working day?

2. Many people say, "If you want something done right, you have to do it yourself." As a supervisor, would you agree?

3. Even if a subordinate is *capable* of doing a delegated task, there may be mistakes due to misunderstandings. How do you avoid them?

4. What do you do when a worker makes an error in doing a delegated task?

ANSWERS TO PROGRESS QUESTIONS

1. Make a list of everything you do, and how long it takes you to do it. Then decide whether each individual task is worth the time *you* are spending on it.

2. This is the do-it-yourself trap. As a supervisor, you have to constantly ask yourself, "Does this task I'm now doing *really* require my talents and experience, or can someone else do it, or be taught to do it?"

3. It helps to make sure that the subordinate knows *exactly* what is expected of him (or her), and how the task will be evaluated by you. Then you check to see that the agreement is fully understood.

4. You must expect a certain number of human errors. Discuss the mistake with the worker to be sure that he (or she) knows what went wrong and how to avoid a similar error in the future. This way, you'll turn the error into a learning experience.

Further Thoughts

Under what circumstances does delegation work best?

Delegation, as a strategy, works best where:

1. The job to be delegated provides workers with a sense of self-satisfaction; i.e., it is seen as challenging, worthwhile, providing a break in routine, etc.

2. The workers and work groups trust the supervisor to reward good performance and not use them as scapegoats if they make mistakes.

3. The work to be done (the technology) allows workers to perform *independently,* such as a typist, rather than *interdependently,* such as an assembly line worker.

4. The workers desire responsibility and an opportunity to work on their own.

5. The workers are capable of doing the work assigned, or the supervisor is willing to take time to train them.

6. The supervisor provides adequate lead time to explain what is expected and how results will be evaluated.

7. The supervisor is not a "workaholic," nor is there any reward in the organization for being perceived as one.

At times, a supervisor may have so many things to do that even with delegation, some matters must wait. In such cases, what factors need to be considered in setting priorities?

The time-management factors to be considered for setting priorities in this crisis situation are:

1. *Impact.* What would be the effect of delaying a decision on the total operation of the company? Of the department? On the supervisor's career?

2. *Search.* How reliable are existing data? Also, how much additional information would be needed to make a sound decision, and how long would it take to obtain it?

3. *Social consequences.* How many persons would be affected by a decision to act immediately? To defer a decision until later?

4. *Political consequences.* How many influential parties (e.g., individuals, groups, union leaders, etc.) would be affected by a decision to act immediately? To defer the decision?

5. *Precedent.* What guidelines, if any, exist from past experience regarding deadlines for making specific decisions?

Should the supervisor accept *every* assignment delegated by his or her boss?

Accepting all assignments that the boss decides to delegate to you can be beneficial. You may learn about new aspects of the business, and this may help you if you should later want to move up in the organization. At the very least, your cooperation and helpfulness should put you in a favorable position when it's time for raises, annual performance reviews, or even letters of recommendation if you should decide to leave the organization.

However, there are pitfalls involved in accepting all delegated assignments. First, the boss may delegate more work than you can handle. Everyone has only a limited capacity!

Second, if the boss hasn't made it clear as to what is really wanted, and he (she) is too busy to take the time to explain, then you know the chances of "messing up" a delegated assignment of this kind are fairly high. It would be better for your record not to risk trying to do it.

Third, the delegated assignment may require coordination with other individuals or departments with whom you do not yet have a good working relationship. This can make the assignment twice as tough.

Last, tasks may be delegated that are more complicated than you can handle. In other words, you may be given new tasks that must be completed sooner than it takes you to learn how to do them properly. This has been joked about in the management literature—as a variation of the "Peter Principle."* Unfortunately, it is not very amusing for the supervisors involved. A feeling of incompetence is not very pleasant.

Thus, sometimes it is necessary to say "no" to the boss. A good boss will respect your judgment if you explain your reasons in terms of not being able to do the assignment well.

*The "Peter Principle" states that employees who do a good job will be continually promoted until they have risen to a level of management at which their skills are no longer suitable for the new kinds of tasks required. Thus, all employees rise to their "level of incompetence," where they are of no further use to the organization and need to be bypassed.

1. As a general rule, **use the style of leadership that seems most natural** to you. Don't try to copy a style that doesn't fit you.
2. **Be flexible** in your style, so that you can adapt to special circumstances, such as emergencies.
3. **Encourage creativity** by letting workers use their own judgment as much as possible. Motivate them by giving them more than their share of credit for successes.
4. **Be constructive** in the way you lead your work group. **Teach** them to do things better. **Don't police** their mistakes.

Leadership and Motivation

10

A CRITICAL INCIDENT: No Time for Discussion

Alan looked anxiously out of his office window. The sky was very dark over the nearby hills, and seemed to be advancing rapidly towards the valley where his auto repair shop was located.

Just to be on the safe side, Alan went out and rolled up the windows of the customers' cars in the parking lot. He noticed the creek was already running high, the result of melting snow during the warm spring days.

Before he could get back into the shop, a sudden downpour of huge drops of rain soaked his clothing. His mechanics laughingly teased him for "not having enough sense to come in out of the rain."

After fifteen minutes of the pelting rain, however, Alan realized that this was no ordinary rainstorm. The creek had already risen to almost the height of its banks, and Alan figured it wouldn't be long before the muddy water would flood the parking lot and come swirling around the shop doors.

He leapt into action. First he told three of his mechanics to drop everything and start moving cars. The cars that were parked next to the creek needed to be driven, pushed, or towed up to the high ground across the road.

Next Alan told the others to put tools away and help move all the many boxes of parts and supplies off the floor and into the storage racks in the storeroom and the office.

Nobody seemed to be moving, however, despite Alan's yelling for action. If anything, the mechanics seemed to be amused. Kirk strolled over to Alan with a tolerant smile on his face.

"Come on, Alan," he said. "There's no sweat. The water's never been more'n an inch deep in the parking lot. We've never had any inside. . . ."

"Listen, Kirk, and listen good!" Alan interrupted him, looking him right in the eye. "You and the rest of the crew are going to do what I say. And you're going to do it *now*! We can talk later about whether it was a good idea."

This time, the mechanics dropped everything and began preparing for a flash flood. Alan barked instructions as he helped them move everything that could be damaged by water.

All the boxes were off the floor before the first trickle of water came under the door. By the time the water was ankle-deep, all the cars inside the shop had been jacked up and were sitting on cement blocks.

At its peak, the water was ten inches deep in the shop, but by this time, the rain had stopped and the sun was already shining. The water level soon started to slowly recede, but didn't drop below shop-floor level until after 9 P.M.

At 10 P.M. the mechanics voluntarily returned to the shop to help with the cleanup, which wasn't complete until 3 A.M. Alan personally thanked each one, and gave them all the next morning off.

The next afternoon, Alan gave an informal "speech" during the coffee break.

He gave the mechanics all the credit for avoiding thousands of dollars of property damage. He even went to the trouble of pointing out particular contributions each one of them had made. For instance, he thanked LaMont for his quick thinking in throwing the master switch before the water reached the electric outlets. He thanked Kirk for the idea of jacking up all the disabled cars inside the shop. And so on until everyone's contribution, no matter how minor, had been recognized.

At 5 o'clock, everyone left but Gil, the oldest mechanic. He decided to stay and chat with Alan.

"You really surprised us yesterday!" Gil told Alan. "We could hardly believe it was you."

"Whaddaya mean?" Alan asked, pretending to be offended.

"You sounded like my old drill sergeant!" Gil chuckled. "Usually, you're so mild-mannered we forget you're the boss!"

"Maybe I'm a little *too* mild mannered," Alan retorted. "When I told you guys to 'jump', you all laughed at me!"

"Seriously, Alan, since I first started working here, I've been watching the way you get people to do things. You almost never actually *tell* someone to do something—except for emergencies like yesterday. Instead, you sort of *suggest* things. I guess usually you leave people alone unless they're having a problem. Then you show them how *you* would've solved it. That's the *real* you. So, maybe that's why we all thought it was funny when you started giving orders."

Alan grinned.

"Personally, *I* don't think I'd run the shop like that," Gil added. "I'd probably give more direct orders."

"How come?" Alan asked.

"I dunno," Gil replied, shrugging his shoulders. "I suppose it's got something to do with the way I was brought up. My old man was very strict. We *never* talked back to him. Then I went into the Army for ten years and took orders. Now I'm married and try to make up for lost time by giving orders to my wife and kids!"

They both laughed.

"So after all these years, I don't think I could run a shop quite the way you do," Gil concluded. "It's really not my style and it'd come across phony."

"What if all your mechanics were as old and experienced as you are?" Alan asked him. "Do you think maybe you might change your mind?"

CHECK YOUR PROGRESS

1. Why is it important to use the style of leadership that seems most natural to you?

2. When is flexibility important in your leadership style?

3. How do you motivate workers to be creative in the way they do their jobs?

4. What's the difference between a supervisor who leads his workers as a teacher, and one who leads them like a policeman?

1. If you try to copy a style of leadership that really doesn't fit you, you'll come across as a phony.
2. Flexibility in leadership style is important in *special circumstances,* such as emergencies, or when your workers are very highly skilled.
3. Workers should be allowed to use their own judgment as much as possible. The smart supervisor will give them more than their share of credit for successes.
4. As a *teacher,* the supervisor shows workers how to do their jobs better, rather than policing their mistakes.

Further Thoughts

Telling workers what to do is an *authoritarian* leadership style. Letting them help in making decisions is a *democratic* or *participative* leadership style. When is a democratic approach likely to work better than an authoritarian one?

The democratic style of leadership is likely to work out best under the following circumstances:

1. When workers have as much expertise and status as the supervisor (this is the point Alan was suggesting to Gil, at the end of the case), such as college professors and their department chairman, master craftsmen working together on a project, or volunteer groups that elect a leader.

2. When a democratic style best suits the supervisor's own "natural" style (and when lack of extreme time pressures permits such a style).

3. When a very unpopular decision has to be made, such as assigning workers to disliked shifts, weekend and holiday work, or unpleasant jobs. In such circumstances, the supervisor can often avoid the workers' hostility by letting them try to come to an agreement among themselves as to how the assignments shall be made. If the workers are unable to decide among themselves, the supervisor can impose a decision on them without being seen as "the bad guy."

4. When it is important to avoid being accused of favoritism or self-interest, it may be wise to have workers go through the more time-consuming process of voting on a decision. (It should be noted, however, that the supervisor is still responsible for the outcome of the decision; his/her responsibilities do not change just because he arrives at the decision by using a democratic procedure!)

5. When there is a great need to have the decision accepted, workers who have participated in a decision are less likely to fight it.

116

6. When the supervisor genuinely needs a variety of viewpoints to solve a problem, worker participation may be very helpful. Workers have many good ideas; often they have more production know-how than the supervisor. Yet they are seldom allowed to contribute. Thus worker creativity and knowledge are usually a great untapped resource in modern organizations. (Note that the supervisor must genuinely desire their inputs. Too often, workers are asked for their ideas in order to manipulate them into going along with a decision that has already been made. We will see this in Chapter 11 on loyalty. Once this is used as a manipulative strategy, workers are unlikely to ever again want to participate in giving management their ideas; they will have become alienated.)

7. When there has been a tradition of worker participation in decisions, it is often unwise to make changes towards authoritarianism, since the likely result will be resistance and alienation.

8. When management believes that workers have a moral right to participate in decisions that affect their lives.

Consider the following three requests that Alan might make:
1. "Please work on the Volkswagen first."
2. "Please empty the wastebasket in the men's room."
3. "Please shave your moustache off."
What kind of motivational problems are involved in each of these requests?

Each of the three requests differs in its acceptability—that is, the degree to which workers perceive the request as being reasonable for the supervisor to ask. The first is clearly acceptable; few mechanics would reject the supervisor's right to decide the order in which cars are worked on. The second request is more questionable, since it is not part of a mechanic's normal duties to empty wastebaskets. The third request is clearly unacceptable, since the choice between wearing a moustache and not doing so is a personal decision over which the supervisor should have no say. Thus the mechanic is likely to freely accept the first request, reject the third request, and "think about" the second one—go along with it if he feels like being cooperative; refuse to do it if he does not.

This discussion is based on the work of Chester Barnard (The Functions of the Executive), who viewed commands as falling into three categories:

1. The zone of acceptance (e.g., first request)

2. The zone of indifference (e.g., second request)

3. The zone of rejection (e.g., third request)

Barnard pointed out that it was in the interests of management to

*minimize the worker's zone of rejection so as to maximize manage-
ment control. (That is, to make management prerogatives as broad as
possible.) This involves a long-term persuasion process.*

*It is interesting to note that a union is interested in just the
opposite. The union wants to minimize the worker's zone of acceptance, because every task within the zone of acceptance is "expected"
of the worker. Everything within the zone of indifference represents
extra work to the union, so the union has grounds for bargaining for
extra compensation; otherwise workers can rightly refuse to do it.
This also involves persuasion, this time by the union.*

In exercising leadership power, the supervisor tries to motivate workers to carry
out an assignment in a certain desired way. Suppose Alan knew just how he wanted
a particular auto repair job done. The table below shows five different ways that he
could try to get one of his mechanics to do it exactly that way. What are the advantages and disadvantages of each approach?

MOTIVATIONAL POWER	SUPERVISOR'S APPROACH
Authority	"I'm the supervisor, and I'm telling you to do it *this* way!"
Professional pride	"Any *good* mechanic would do it this way."
Reward	"Do it this way, and I'll see you get a bonus."
Punishment	"If you *don't* do it this way, I'll dock your pay."
Expertise	"Listen to me. I've had years of experience, and I've found that this is the best way to do it."

*The advantages and limitations of using each type of power are
as follows:*

Authority

*The advantage of this source of motivational power for the super-
visor (the leader) is that little effort is required to exercise it. Workers
have been socialized throughout their lives to accept authority without
questioning the supervisor's right to give orders.*

*There are some limitations, however. The supervisor who relies
too heavily on this type of power may "pull rank" too often, so that
workers start questioning whether it is really legitimate for him to be
giving orders. Note that this is exactly what happens when workers*

reduce their "zone of indifference," as was pointed out in the second question. On a broad scale, this can produce a crisis of legitimacy (an environment in which union organizers thrive!), where every "management prerogative" becomes called into question. This has actually occurred in some European countries, but there seems little chance of the same thing's happening in the United States in the foreseeable future.

Professional Pride

The advantage of this form of motivational power is that the workers maintain high standards without being watched by the supervisor; they watch themselves, and they watch each other.

*As in the case of authority, there are limitations to how often the supervisor can exert this kind of power without a loss in effectiveness. Reminding workers of professional standards is a delicate per-*suasion *process, and if it is overused, workers are likely to become cynical about the supervisor's being more interested in his own production schedules than in their professionalism.*

Reward

According to the behaviorist theory of learning, rewards are the best motivators, because they directly reinforce the desired behavior. Furthermore, rewards are consistent with workers' feelings about equity—that extra effort to do a job just as the supervisor asks is generally felt to deserve a higher payoff to the worker. (Recall our discussion of equity in Chapter 4.)

An obvious disadvantage is cost: Tangible rewards (the worker will accept only so much praise before he/she wants something more substantial) cost money! A less obvious limitation is that after continued "extra" rewards, workers may come to expect *them, so the rewards lose some of their novelty, and thus their impact. This can be a particular problem if the supervisor becomes faced with budget cuts, and can no longer give out expected "extra" rewards (and no supervisor can do it indefinitely!). Then the reward system can backfire very badly.*

Punishment

This form of motivational power can have the advantage of working immediately (learning theorists say immediacy is best) and being generally inexpensive (docking pay, for instance, doesn't cost the company extra money, as bonuses do).

The big disadvantage of punishment power is that a lot of the supervisor's time is needed to "police" his workers—to catch them doing something "wrong." Workers tend to respond by being secretive rather than cooperative; they resent the supervisor, since he has cast himself in the role of an enemy; and furthermore, workers tend to become alienated from "the system," which comes to represent a hostile working environment.

Expertise

The advantage of this kind of motivational power is that it doesn't cost anything extra, and it always operates constructively (since, in effect, the supervisor has assumed the role of teacher).

Its limitation is that the supervisor must maintain a level of knowledge higher than that of his or her workers: over time he cannot become "rusty" through lack of practice or obsolete as technology changes. Furthermore, the higher the supervisor goes up the managerial hierarchy, the greater the demands placed on expertise as a source of power, since different skills are called for at higher levels (this point is amplified in Chapter 25).

In regard to the question, "which approach would you recommend?", the wise supervisor will develop several bases of leadership power rather than depending on any single one. However, professional pride and reward should generally be favored, while punishment should be avoided as much as possible.

What kind of a leadership style is likely to work best for a female supervisor in charge of male factory workers?

Being a supervisor in charge of male factory workers can be very difficult for a woman. *Because of history and traditions, the odds are stacked against her.*

To understand just how difficult it is, we need to explore the concept of social role. *The point here is that we don't just deal with a person as an individual. Rather, we must deal with the social role that the person takes on. And the same person can take on different roles in different situations, or even at different points in time. The specific role chosen in a particular situation depends on what the person* intends *to accomplish, and the* expectations *of others.*

For instance, a man who happens to be a father can also assume several other roles, depending on the circumstances. He can be a friend, a neighbor, an advisor, a creditor, a visitor, and so on, in addition to being a father. In this case, the several roles occupied by the same person probably mix well—there is no conflict between one role and another.

Now, in the case of the woman who is supervising male factory workers, we find there are two roles that don't mix well at all. The workers can respond to her as a woman, or they can respond to her as a supervisor. *But not both at the same time!*

Unfortunate as it may seem, particularly to supporters of the "Womens' Liberation" movement, the fact is, male factory workers are likely to view the woman's role as one of subordination. That is, in their eyes, the woman is typically seen as a "follower," not a leader.

In the supervisory role, however, the woman needs to be seen as a leader rather than a follower. Thus there is a conflict between the two roles. Since the "woman" role is likely to be the one more deeply ingrained in the minds of the workers, the men are probably going to respond to her as a woman rather than as a supervisor. As a result, she's going to have problems in getting the men to recognize her as a leader. And the more attractive she is to the male workers, the more problems she's going to have in getting them to forget that she's a woman, and start treating her as a supervisor.

With the odds thus stacked against her, the style of leadership that the woman supervisor chooses is often crucial to her success. Let's look at the options open to her.

Choosing a participative leadership style may actually undermine her supervisor role, since the men may interpret it as a sign of weakness. (Even though in fact it is often a sign of strength and security.) In other words, the men may think that she must be too timid to give direct orders, and therefore that she is not to be taken very seriously.

On the other hand, an authoritarian style may also cause problems. This style, even when used by a male supervisor, may arouse resentment purely because some workers don't like being told to do things. Thus it is easy to see that a female supervisor would likely arouse even more resentment: If the men already feel uneasy about the conflict between the social roles of "woman" and "supervisor," the added resentment of having to take orders may be the last straw.

With these difficult problems facing her, how can a woman be effective as a supervisor of male factory workers? It seems that the only way she can hope to be effective is to earn the workers' respect. This is probably best accomplished through a middle-of-the-road leadership style, which calls for careful judgment on her part.

She must be polite but firm in insisting that she be treated as a supervisor, and not as a woman. In other words, she must be consistent in getting her workers to deal with her in her primary role (the supervisory role). This means that she must be firm in correcting any of her workers who treat her differently.

Second, she must be able to handle any heckling gracefully—that is, without "losing her cool" when being "tested" by the men. Otherwise, she'll be stereotyped as a hysterical female. In surviving this testing, she must be very sensitive to the men's need to save face. A wounded pride may result in a permanent enemy. Thus egos must be protected wherever possible.

Third, the woman supervisor must avoid the temptation to try to "buy off" her male subordinates by relaxing performance standards. This strategy will always fail, because it will lead to a loss of respect, since it really represents admitting defeat; in any case, is hardly the route to take to become an effective supervisor! Therefore, the woman supervisor needs to be firm about maintaining (or even slightly exceeding) the performance standards that a male supervisor would use.

Finally, the female supervisor should expect to have more of a problem if she is younger than the men (because youth produces the same sort of role conflict with supervision as does womanhood). She can also expect to have more of a problem if she is seen as better educated ("snooty") than the men, or if they believe she got the position not because of merit, but because of favoritism or Affirmative Action pressure.

All of the above discussion concerned the case of a female supervisor in charge of male factory workers. In some other work settings, there may be fewer problems. In an office or a health-care facility, for instance, the female supervisor is a more accepted role. That is, there is more of a tradition of women supervisors in these organizations.

It is also worth noting that the supervisory dynamics are quite different when there is the opposite situation—a male supervisor in charge of female workers. There is usually little role conflict for the supervisor in this type of situation (no matter what the work setting is), because the man's work role as a supervisor is not in conflict with his "traditional" social role as a man.

POSTTEST QUESTIONS

Now that you've read the five chapters in Section II, you might want to try to answer the same questions that you answered in the Pretest. The correct answers are given on page 124.

By comparing your score on the Posttest with your score on the Pretest, you will be able to get an idea of how much your knowledge of supervision has improved.

In questions 11 and 12, circle the letter corresponding to the one statement which is *least* true.

11. a. Workers tend to "test" rules and stretch them to the limit.
    b. Rules create problems if they are applied too strictly.
    c. The biggest objection to rules is that they are impersonal.
    d. Rules tend to reflect experiences and problems of the past.

12. a. Rules can sometimes create problems if they are followed to the letter.
    b. Rules reduce the need for a supervisor to constantly give orders.
    c. Rules protect workers from arbitrary actions by supervisors.
    d. Rules can be used to "pass the buck" for unpleasant decisions.
    e. Rules make it harder for a supervisor to exercise authority.

In questions 13 and 14, circle the letter corresponding to the *one best* answer.

13. In order for delegation to be effective, it is important that:
    a. Workers be capable of doing the work assigned.
    b. Workers who make some errors learn from them.
    c. Tasks delegated not need the supervisor's close attention.
    d. All of the above.
    e. None of the above.

14. When a worker has a preventable accident, the blame rests *mainly* on:
    a. The worker.
    b. The supervisor.
    c. The worker and the supervisor.
    d. The maintenance department.
    e. The personnel department.

Questions 15 through 20 are to be answered by circling T if the statement is **true**, and F if the statement is **false**.

15. The best time to get tough on safety rules is after an accident, when everyone will realize how bad the consequences can be.   T   F

16. To be a skillful communicator, a supervisor should not waste time by rephrasing or repeating what others say.   T   F

17. A supervisor who copies the leadership style of someone he or she admires risks being seen as a phony.   T   F

18. A supervisor should spend his (or her) time doing the things he knows best.   T   F

19. Spoken words usually tell more about what the communicator really thinks and feels than do nonverbal cues.   T   F

20. As a leader it is particularly important to maintain one's normal leadership style *during emergencies.*   T   F

PRE- AND POSTTEST QUESTIONNAIRE - ANSWER SHEET

11. c
12. e
13. d
14. c
15. false
16. false
17. true
18. false
19. false
20. false

Here are ten questions. Try to answer them before you read the five chapters in Section III. You'll have another chance to try to answer the same ten questions in the Posttest (pages 171–172).

An answer sheet is provided after the Posttest (page 172). You will be able to use this to score your Pretest and Posttest. By comparing the two scores, you will be able to get an idea of how much your knowledge of supervision has improved.

21. Choose the ending that describes the *best* long-run strategy for the supervisor, and then circle the corresponding letter.

Conflicts between loyalty to the boss and loyalty to subordinates should be resolved:

a. By explaining to the workers the dilemma being faced.
b. On the basis of what will keep the most people happy.
c. On the basis of what the boss desires.
d. On the basis of what is the fairest thing to do.
e. As quickly as possible.

22. Choose the *least* appropriate ending to the following statement by circling *one* of the five choices.

DEALING
WITH PEOPLE

A supervisor's role in running a meeting is to:

a. Encourage group discussion.
b. Remain neutral as much as possible.
c. Help sort out controversial issues.
d. Stick to the agenda.
e. Take sole responsibility for handling disruptive persons.

23. Choose the answer that *best* completes the sentence, and then circle the corresponding letter.

A union contract usually _____ what supervisors are allowed to do in their departments.

a. Restricts
b. Avoids any mention of
c. Broadens
d. Is unclear about
e. None of the above

Questions 24 through 20 are to be answered by circling T if the statement is **true**, and F if the statement is **false**.

24. Workers vote for a union *primarily* to improve wages and fringe benefits.
T   F

25. Supervisors can avoid conflicts between loyalty to their bosses and loyalty to their workers.   T   F

26. In order to be as fair as possible, a supervisor cannot afford to permit any exceptions to established rules.   T   F

27. Nearly all worker grievances can be resolved at the supervisor level.
T   F

28. A supervisor should always try to remain "neutral" when running a meeting, even if others have difficulty in pinpointing to what position the supervisor is committed.   T   F

29. Fairness basically requires that a supervisor must not be too strict with his or her fellow workers.   T   F

30. There are really no important differences between the effectiveness of a grievance procedure in a nonunion company, compared with a unionized shop.
T   F

A PREVIEW

The five chapters in this third section cover what a supervisor must know and do to gain the cooperation and continued support of other people. Although an understanding of motivation and group behavior is important (we discussed these in the previous section), there are some even more subtle factors that determine whether the supervisor will succeed or fail in dealing with people.

A crucial consideration is how the supervisor decides to make tradeoffs between loyalty to the boss and loyalty to the workers. Chapter 11 deals with being caught in the middle of such *loyalty conflicts*. A supervisor can't always please both sides and sometimes has to "bite the bullet" and make a choice based on what is honest and fair.

A reputation for *fairness* gives the supervisor a big advantage in gaining workers' support and cooperation. However, just as with gaining the loyalty of others, gaining the reputation is easier said than done. Not only does it require being consistent and not playing favorites, but the supervisor must set a *personal example* of what is acceptable. This is the focus of Chapter 12.

A good reputation between the supervisor and his (or her) workers can be built upon loyalty and fairness, but the relationship can come under fire during a *union organizing drive*. Previous good relationships are often strained, particularly if top management conducts a propaganda campaign that involves the supervisors for the purpose of keeping out of the union. Actions taken at such times, while emotions are high, can lead to some hard feelings, which can return to haunt the supervisor in the future. Besides, there may even be legal consequences if the supervisor is not careful. A supervisor must be especially sure that he does nothing that will hurt his workers' rights to democratically choose a bargaining representative. This is the only way to avoid the "traps" that can lead to unfair labor practice charges, as Chapter 13 points out.

One way for workers to express hostility against their supervisor is by filing large numbers of *grievances*. It keeps the supervisor busy and on the defensive, since he now has to worry about how his boss will react to all the commotion. Skills in handling grievances under such circumstances are obviously quite important, as noted in Chapter 14.

However, even if there are only a few grievances to deal with (and there are always some), the wise supervisor will try to handle as many of these as he can *informally*. The trick here is to find the *real* issue; what the worker complains about may not be what's actually bothering him. If the supervisor can't pinpoint the problem, he obviously can't hope to solve it!

Another area where the real issues are often not clear is in *running a meeting*. It is quite common for people to complain that they are more confused *after* a meeting than they were before! Part of the problem is that people have their own "private agendas." Chapter 15 deals with this and other problems in running a meeting.

These are five key situations requiring supervisory skills for *dealing with people* fairly and openly to gain their cooperation. Such skills form a foundation for advancing to the even more complex and sensitive "people problems," which are covered in the section that will follow this one.

1. **Expect to have loyalty conflicts.** As a supervisor, you'll often find yourself **caught in the middle**— between loyalty to workers, and loyalty to your own boss.
2. **Take a long-run perspective.** Don't please your boss in the short run, if it means sacrificing the trust and support of your workers in the long run.
3. When you have to "side with your boss," try to **explain** to your workers the reasons why you're caught in a dilemma. They'll be more likely to **respect your decision,** even if they don't like it!
4. Try to resolve loyalty conflicts in favor of what you feel is the right thing to do, in terms of **fairness and honesty.**

Loyalty Conflicts

11

A CRITICAL INCIDENT: You Can't Always Sit on the Fence

The Production Manager for Precision Electronics began the weekly supervisors' meeting by unrolling a flip chart. The chart showed a slow but steady decline in the company's share of the total market for its products.

Vince, the Supervisor of the Machining Department, exchanged uneasy glances with some of the other supervisors. They were all a little fearful of what the "punch-line" was going to be.

New competitors—especially those from overseas—were muscling in on the market, the Production Manager pointed out. In order to win customers away from competitors, Precision would have to lower the price of its products.

"The purpose of this meeting," the Production Manager explained to the supervisors, "is to have you help us figure out ways to lower prices."

Since no one offered any immediate comment, the Production Manager added, "We really need your suggestions. Let's think through this problem together."

In the "discussion" that followed, the Production Manager did most of the talking. He very smoothly led them into "agreeing" that there was only one solution to the company's problem. Each department had to increase its output while holding the line on costs.

"I don't see how we're going to do that in *my* department," Vince said. "There'd have to be some major equipment changes—like automatic controls on the lathes and milling machines."

"Well, we can certainly look into that," the Production Manager replied. "But that's a long-run strategy. It would require a lot of capital investment and would take time. We need to do something *quickly*. For instance, in your department you could change the piece-rate* so that workers would have to produce more for the same pay."

Vince frowned "You mean we should have a 'speedup'?" he asked.

"Let's not call it a speedup," the Production Manager replied irritably. "Let's think more in terms of taking some of the slack out of the system."

Piece rate is a method of calculating a worker's wages. Under this system, the worker gets so much pay for each "piece"—or unit—that he (or she) turns out. This is different from an *hourly* wage, where the worker is paid for the hours worked, regardless of how many pieces are turned out during that time.

"My machinists are going to call it a speedup!" Vince pointed out. Some of the other supervisors nodded in agreement. "Their piece-rate was already set pretty tight last spring," Vince added.

"Well, Vince, maybe you'd better look at the rate again," the production manager said, firmly. "By next week's meeting, I want all of you to have figured out how to increase productivity by 10 percent."

A murmur went through the room. Ten percent was a lot. But no one argued. The Production Manager's tone of voice in answering Vince indicated that he didn't welcome any questioning of his judgment!

The meeting closed abruptly, with a warning from the Production Manager not to leak word to the workers about the discussion.

Vince was upset all that day. He believed that his machinists worked hard, and that the price cut shouldn't have to "come out of their hides."

At the end of the day, Zeke, one of Vince's machinists, came into his office, and told him that rumors were running wild about layoffs and speedups. It soon became obvious that the story *had* leaked.

Vince told Zeke that he didn't want to talk about it until he'd had a chance to think it through properly.

The next morning, Vince went to see Maria, Supervisor of the Assembly Department, to talk over the issue. She confirmed that the rumors were widespread, and also quite accurate. Vince explained the situation, as he saw it, to Maria:

"If I go along with the speedup, I'll please management, but I'll also be cheating my machinists out of a fair day's pay. On the other hand, if I back up the workers, then I'm risking my job. The Production Manager isn't too pleased with my comments as it is!"

"Yeah. We're really caught in the middle," Maria agreed. "If we side with management in the short run, we'll be losing a lot of the workers' goodwill, and it's taken us years to build that up. On the other hand, if we *don't* side with management, I think you're right: We may not be around in the long run!"

"So what do we do?" Vince asked helplessly.

"I honestly don't know," Maria replied. "I think I'm gonna have to talk it over with my assemblers. They already know what's going on, so I wouldn't be leaking any secrets."

"Yeah. Getting it all out front may be the best thing to do," Vince agreed. "Let me know how things work out."

That afternoon, Vince decided that he, too, should talk it over with his workers. He met informally with them during the coffee break. He explained his dilemma in full, and admitted that he thought they were already working as hard as could reasonably be expected.

The machinists trusted Vince, and respected him for leveling with them. They decided to level with him, too.

Zeke, as their spokesman, told Vince that the machinists had been doing some experimenting since the rumors started flying. They figured that if the chips were down, they could squeeze out another 5 percent productivity, but no more.

This meant that management *could* lower the piece rate by 5 percent.* However, if management insisted on reducing the piece rate by more than 5 percent, the machinists would have less take-home pay each week.

Vince trusted them enough to believe that what Zeke said was true. So he decided to "go to bat" for his workers. He felt it was the only fair and honest thing to do.

Meanwhile, Maria was having less luck. She wasn't able to come

*Lowering the piece rate by 5 percent means paying workers 5 percent less for each unit produced.

up with any kind of acceptable plan for her department. It seemed there was no cost-cutting alternative but to lay off one of her assemblers.

The atmosphere was tense in the next weekly supervisors' meeting. One by one, each supervisor presented his or her plan for increasing productivity or cutting costs. Vince and Maria were left until last. This just added to their nervousness.

When it was Vince's turn, he presented his plan for a 5 percent increase in productivity. He explained that 10 percent was impossible without hurting quality standards.

"I asked you to come up with a plan for a 10 percent increase," the Production Manager reminded him icily.

"You also granted me some discretion when you made me supervisor of the Machining Department," Vince pointed out, bravely. "I have to exercise judgment based on my expertise as a machinist. My judgment is that 5 percent is all there is."

"Then it looks like you'll have to lower the piece rate more to get the other 5 percent," the Production Manager said, his penetrating eyes focused on Vince.

"I *can't* do that. They'll quit!" Vince protested. He was sweating.

"Like hell they'll quit," the Production Manager retorted. "They know damned well I could replace them tomorrow. There's lots of machinists roaming the streets looking for jobs since the Fraser Bearing Company moved out of town."

"Maybe they won't quit right away, but as soon as they get another opportunity, they'll be gone," Vince said firmly. "Then all the work I've done specially training them and building up a team will go down the drain. As I said, you gave me discretion to make decisions. My decision is to limit the change to 5 percent."

There was a silence.

"OK, Vince," the Production Manager conceded, rather reluctantly. "I'll go along with your judgment, at least for now.

"How about the Assembly Department?" he said abruptly, turning to Maria.

"I can't come up with a plan that won't destroy the morale of my assemblers," Maria said, looking down. "In the long run, cutting their pay by ten percent is going to put the company in an even worse competitive position."

"And just how do you figure that?" the Production Manager asked, a little sarcastically.

"Because *unions* thrive where workers have been kicked around," she replied, looking him in the eye.

"Don't ever mention unions around here again!" he said angrily, dismissing the meeting with a gesture.

As the Production Manager hurried out of the room, Vince and Maria exchanged nervous glances.

CHECK YOUR PROGRESS

1. In what sense is a supervisor "caught in the middle?"

2. What is meant by taking a *long-run perspective* in resolving a problem affecting your boss and your workers?

3. How can the supervisor try to maintain the trust and respect of workers if in a loyalty conflict he (or she) decides to take sides with his boss?

4. What's a good rule of thumb for resolving a loyalty conflict when there seems to be no one best solution?

ANSWERS TO PROGRESS QUESTIONS

1. A supervisor often finds that looking out for the interests of higher management *conflicts* with looking out for the interests of the workers.

2. It's often possible to "win the battle but lose the war." Thus the supervisor should always consider if the *long-term consequences* are worth the short-term benefits when solving a problem.

3. It often helps to *explain* the dilemma to the workers. If they know the basis of the supervisor's decision, the workers will tend to be more understanding, even if they don't agree with the decision.

4. Supervisors should always try to resolve such a loyalty conflict in favor of what they feel is the *fair and honest* thing to do.

Further Thoughts

How often could Vince afford to take the workers' side and buck higher management before there would be some unpleasant consequences for him?

> *It's not so much how often Vince resisted management, as it is a matter of how he went about it. This point was hinted at in the "critical incident," in which Vince and Maria both bucked the Production Manager's direct order to increase productivity or cut costs by 10 percent. Simply, Vince pulled it off better than Maria did. Vince's approach contains three strategies that you can use to "take the edge off" an act of resistance:*

1. Always allow the boss to *save face*. Vince did this by saying, "I'm using the discretion you entrusted in me." If Vince's resistance were phrased so as to make the boss look stupid—in front of the other supervisors—for issuing the order, then Vince would be asking for trouble.

2. Always try to arrive at a *compromise* instead of an outright victory. Vince's offer to increase productivity by 5 percent was much easier to swallow than Maria's refusal to give in at all.

3. Present your case in terms of the *interests of the company*. This is likely to be more persuasive than an argument based on what's best for the workers, or even on ethics. Interestingly, *both* Vince and Maria adopted this strategy, but Maria brought up a sore subject—the union—in making her point, and the "diplomacy" went out the window.

If workers see their supervisor as being loyal *to them,* how does this benefit the supervisor?

> *If workers perceived the supervisor as being loyal to them, they would be likely to respond in the following beneficial ways:*

1. Since the relationship would be founded on trust, worker behavior and performance would tend to be more stable and predictable.

2. More information would be shared by workers, to which the supervisor would normally have difficult access.

3. Less worker resistance would arise in response to "unfavorable" decisions.

4. A strong informal group would help "back" the supervisor in his dealings with superiors, peers, competitors, etc.

Throughout this chapter, there was a focus on the loyalty *of* the supervisor. Now regarding loyalty *to* the supervisor:

1. What are the disadvantages of workers' being 100 percent loyal to the supervisor?

2. What are the disadvantages of higher management's being 100 percent loyal to the supervisor?

There are dangers in blind loyalty to the supervisor, since it assumes that the supervisor can do no wrong:

1. Since no supervisor can be expected to possess 100 percent wisdom, 100 percent loyalty may be bad when the result is that no one cautions the supervisor about bad decisions. After all, everyone makes mistakes, and a little resistance is a good way to catch them! (The two-party system of government, the prosecutor-defense system of law, and many other institutions are based on this principle.)

2. Higher management's 100 percent backing of the supervisor can also create problems. Workers occasionally question the supervisor's decisions or actions by filing a grievance (formal or informal). If higher management always backs the supervisor, even when the worker has a good case, then workers will be forced to resort to the power of a union to protect themselves from the errors or misjudgments of even a well-meaning supervisor.

It should be further noted that a formal grievance procedure won't work as well, even with a union, when higher management backs its supervisors 100 percent, because all grievances would have to be settled by an arbitrator. This is time-consuming and costly.

Supervisors can do wrong; they're only human. Loyalty to them should therefore remain within reasonable bounds.

1. **Let your workers know what's expected of them.** Give specific warnings if these expectations are not met, and if the problem continues, do exactly what you promised.

2. **Stay away from extremes:** If you punish too severely, your workers will see you as cruel. If you are too lenient, you will lose respect. There's a **happy medium,** just as there is for rewards.

3. Avoid playing favorites: **Gain a reputation for being consistent,** but have the sense to **know when to make an exception.**

4. **Set a personal example** for your workers to follow.

Fairness

12

A CRITICAL INCIDENT: Accepting the Exception

At exactly noontime, Brian and Neil left their desks in the Accounts Receivable Department at Allied Industries and went down to the cafeteria. While they were eating their sandwiches at a small table off in the corner, Brian started complaining about Marvin, the department supervisor, and all the "breaks" he was giving to Tony, another clerk in the department.

"If Marvin's going to make these rules, he's got to stick by them," said Brian. "He can't make exceptions for Tony and not for me."

"Come on, Brian," said Neil patiently, "you've got to admit the situation's a bit different for Tony."

Tony's wife was in the hospital. She had a tumor and was about to undergo surgery. Tony had been worried sick that she might have cancer, and he had been unable to concentrate on his job. The hospital was only a twenty-minute bus ride from the office, and Tony had been going to see her at lunchtime each day.

Tony had frequently been late in getting back from these lunchtime visits, sometimes a half-hour or more. More seriously, in his anxiety Tony had twice forgotten to punch out on the time clock when he had left. Marvin had deliberately overlooked these infractions of the company rules. Furthermore, Marvin himself was helping Tony with his work, and was also reassigning some of it to the other clerks.

What made Brian so upset was that three weeks earlier, Marvin had docked *his* pay for repeatedly overshooting the lunch hour.

"Look," said Neil, "Marvin was fair with you. You were coming back from lunch late because you were playing cards, and you always played one hand too many. You told me that yourself! Marvin warned you he'd have to dock your pay if you kept on doing it, and you did it *again*!"

"I know, but it shouldn't make any difference *how* I was spending my time: That's *my* business!" replied Brian. "If it's wrong for me to come back late while I'm still on the clock, it's wrong for Tony, too."

"Tell me honestly," said Neil, "if *your* wife, or mine, or anyone else's was in the hospital, and *we* were going out of our minds worrying about cancer, don't you think Marvin would relax the rules a bit for any one of us?"

"Yeah, I guess your're right," Brian admitted.

"I'm not sticking up for Marvin, particularly, except I don't think you're being fair to him. Marvin's not out to *get* you," Neil went on. "Remember last year, when you reorganized the entire Paid-Accounts Receivable system in the department? Well, Marvin took good care of you then, didn't he? He saw to it that you get a special bonus at the end of the year. And when you were working a lot of overtime, he got you a parking space in the supervisor's lot close by the door, which I noticed you hung on to!"

"Yeah, I guess so," said Brian.

"And besides, Marvin never abuses the lunch hour himself, even though he doesn't have to punch a time card," Neil added.

"OK, OK! You already made your point!" Brian interrupted him.

When they got back to the department, Brian went over to Tony's desk. A thick stack of routine paperwork had piled up in Tony's in-basket file. Brian grabbed a handful and took it over to his own desk.

Tony looked very upset when he came back from the hospital. He was forty minutes late. Marvin called Tony into his office. Brian and Neil exchanged grim glances, then went back to their work.

CHECK YOUR PROGRESS

1. Do you think that it made a difference that Marvin, the supervisor, had warned Brian about abusing the lunch-hour rule before punishing him?

2. Why does a supervisor who wants to be fair need to stay away from extremes?

3. How can a supervisor avoid being accused of playing favorites?

4. What is meant by "setting a personal example"?

1. You've probably heard the expression, "Ignorance of the law is no excuse." The same principle generally applies to office rules. However, people don't like surprise punishments, so it's always a good policy for the supervisor to spell out exactly what's expected of workers, and to warn them of the consequences when they step over the line.
2. Extreme action causes problems; if it is too severe, it will be resented and resisted. If it is too lenient, it may lead to a loss of respect.
3. The supervisor can avoid charges of favoritism by being *consistent* with all workers, making exceptions only when there is strong evidence that workers deserve special consideration.
4. A supervisor who sets a "personal example" acts as a "model" for how he (or she) expects his workers to act.

Further Thoughts

How long can Marvin continue to make an exception for Tony? What factors should Marvin consider in making this decision?

Obviously, Marvin, a supervisor, cannot allow Tony to continue to violate the lunch-hour rule indefinitely. However, Marvin is in a better position to permit the exception to the rule to be continued if:

1. Tony's co-workers support the leniency policy, and particularly if they voluntarily help to make up for Tony's lost working time.
2. Tony will put in (at least) a token effort to offset the perceived inequity—such as by taking some of his work home with him, or working extra hours for no additional pay.
3. Tony has "money in the bank" at the office—that is, he has a long history of good performance and extra effort.
4. There is additional support for Marvin's leniency—such as the doctor's advising that Tony be at his wife's bedside frequently to minimize complications due to her anxiety.
5. Tony is a *salaried* employee. Note that if Tony were actually an *hourly* employee, punching the time clock, the Department of Labor's wage and hour laws actually do not allow Marvin the discretion to let Tony take time off without reducing his pay.

Should Marvin inform his boss about his giving Tony extra time off? What are the advantages and disadvantages of doing so?

This decision involves a trade-off. If Marvin tells his boss, there is the danger that the boss will say "no" because of the possible plant-wide precedent. If he doesn't tell the boss, Marvin is departing from company policy (and risking the boss's resentment) by not keeping his boss informed. Furthermore, he takes the chance that his boss will find out from another source, which would be embarrassing to both of them. In general, the boss will give each supervisor discretion in applying (and making exceptions to) the rules, and there shouldn't be any problems if Marvin applies them carefully and conscientiously, and there is trust between Marvin and his boss.

There are really *two* dimensions to fairness. First, there is the extent to which *the supervisor himself* believes he is being fair. Second, there is the extent to which his *workers* believe he is being fair. How does the supervisor handle each of these dimensions?

The extent to which the supervisor himself believes he is being fair depends on his own ethical principles. A good guideline for the supervisor to use would be to ask himself how he would feel if someone else was treating him in that manner. If the supervisor would honestly consider a certain act—such as an exception to the rule—as fair treatment of himself, then he can be satisfied that he is being fair.

How workers evaluate the same situation, however, may be quite another matter! It is more a question of perception (or even persuasion), rather than it is a question of ethics. In general, the workers are likely to accept an exception as being fair:

1. When the work group fully understands *why* the exception was made.

2. When the work group believes that the exception represents a carefully considered judgment, taking into consideration the injustice or hardship that might arise if the exception were *not* made (in other words, that the decision was not just an impulse).

3. Where the exception does not interfere with the rights of other employees.

4. Where it is not necessary to *order* other workers to do extra work caused by making the exception.

5. Where the supervisor's past history of fairness has created a generally *trusting* relationship with his workers.

1. **Avoid unfair labor practices.** Know what supervisory actions are illegal **infringements on workers' rights** to join or support a union.

2. Recognize that unions seek employee support by stressing **job security,** an effective **grievance procedure,** and **participation in decisions** affecting them. Wages are rarely the big issue.

3. **Expect restrictions** on what you, the supervisor, will be allowed to do in your department if the union's organization attempt is successful.

4. **Take a long-range perspective.** Remember that life must go on in your department after the union's organizing drive is over. If you generate unnecessary hostility, you'll have to live with it later.

Union Organizing Drive

13

A CRITICAL INCIDENT: A Difference of Opinion

Maria, supervisor of the Assembly Department at Precision Electronics, decided to drop in on Vince during the morning coffee break. She found him in his office in the Machining Department, studying a memo that he had received that morning from the Personnel Department. [See Exhibit 13-1.]

"Glad you came over," he said, as she sat down. "Maybe you can explain something to me."

"Like what?" she asked.

"Like what happens if I don't follow these guidelines? Does the union set up a picket line around my desk?"

"No, Vince," she replied, grinning. "The union will file a complaint with the National Labor Relations Board, and they will investigate what you've done, and determine if you've committed an unfair labor practice."

"Then what happens?" he asked.

"Well, if you have, next they'll figure out how it might have affected the election results, and then adjust the votes."

"You mean, if most of the workers in this plant voted *against* the union, the Board could reverse the results?" Vince asked.

"That's right," Maria replied. "And don't be misled about the union needing *most* of the workers voting for them. You'd be surprised how few votes they actually need."

Vince raised his eyebrows, so Maria explained further.

"The union only needs the signatures of 30 percent of the eligible people on those authorization cards that the union has been handing out. You've seen those, haven't you?"

"Yeah. I got one right here. One of the guys brought it in—to cheer me up!" Vince showed her the card. [See Exhibit 13-2.] "I thought a *majority* had to sign those."

"Nope," Maria replied. "Only 30 percent. Then the Board holds an election."

"Oh, I see," Vince said. "And *then* they need a majority."

"Not necessarily," Maria corrected him. "The union only needs more people voting *for* them in the election than against them, and people usually don't turn out and vote unless they *really* care one way or another."

"Well. I guess I didn't realize that's all they needed. How come you know so much about unions?" Vince asked her.

TO: All production supervisors

FROM: Personnel Department

As you no doubt already know, the Electronics Workers Union is presently engaged in a vigorous campaign to organize our production workers. We are in the process of hiring a Director of Industrial Relations who will begin working at Precision next Monday. A meeting of the supervisors will be held very soon to explain what supervisors can do to counteract the union's strategies. In the meantime, the company attorney has drawn up some guidelines as to what you, as supervisors must not do during the campaign:

1. Don't promise any sort of rewards to workers for opposing (or even "not supporting") the union.

2. Don't threaten workers in any way, where the objective is to interfere with the workers' legal right to support the union.

3. Avoid any action that may be interpreted as discrimination against union activists or supporters. However, you should insist that workers continue to do their own regular job properly, and allow others to do so, too.

4. Don't try to control what workers do during their nonworking time, which includes coffee breaks, lunchtime, and waiting in line to punch out.

5. Don't question or spy on workers engaged in union activities. However, you are free to listen to any information that is offered voluntarily.

6. While you may express your (and the company's) opinions of the union and its likely effects on the company, you may not call workers into your office to do so. Nor may you visit their homes for this purpose.

We urge all supervisors to be extra careful in avoiding violation of these NLRB rules. We are firmly opposed to the union and do not want anything to jeopardize a favorable outcome for the company.

If you are in any doubt as to what to do, please consult the Personnel Department before taking any action.

EXHIBIT 13-1

"I've been through this whole thing before," she explained. "The last place I worked at got itself a union. Deserved it too."

"What do you mean?" asked Vince skeptically.

"All the company cared about was profits. Didn't give a damn about the workers."

```
                    AUTHORIZATION CARD
_____

                    _____, 19_____
                    (Date of Signing)

I, _____, now employed by
          (Print your full name here)

_____
(Name of Company employed by, and location such as Street-City & State)

have voluntarily accepted membership in _____

_____ of the  ELECTRONICS  WORKERS
UNION    __ __ __ __ __ __ , and designate said Union as my bargaining
agency in all matters pertaining to wages, hours, and other conditions of employ-
ment. I hereby authorize my Employer (the above named Company) to deduct
from my wages my dues and initiation fee due to said Union. This authority to
make such deductions shall be irrevocable for the period of one year or until the
termination date of the collective bargaining agreement between my Employer and
the Union, whichever occurs sooner, and I agree and direct that this authorization
shall be automatically renewed and shall be irrevocable for successive periods of one
year each or for the period of each succeeding collective bargaining agreement
between my Employer and the Union, whichever shall be shorter, unless written
notice is given by me to the Employer and the Union not more than twenty (20)
days and not less than ten (10) days prior to the expiration of each period of one
year or of each collective bargaining agreement between my Employer and the
Union, whichever occurs sooner. If a new worker: this authorization becomes effec-
tive at the end of my trial period.
                                        Miss
                                        Mrs.
_____ Mr. _____
          (Operation & Dept.)                   (Sign here, do not print)

Social Security No._____  _____
                                          (Print here signer's home address)
```

EXHIBIT 13-2 *Sample of Union Authorization Card*

"Yes, but *our* people are pretty well paid," Vince pointed out.

"There's more to it than just wages," she replied. "Did you see the union's newsletter?"

"No. I heard there was one, but I haven't seen it yet."

"Here. Look at it," she said, handing him a copy. (See Exhibit 13–3.) "You'll see that money hardly even made the front page! They're playing up issues like job security, grievances, and participation in decision making."

Vince studied the newsletter for a couple of minutes.

 The ^ePRECISION **WORKER**
ELECTRONICS, INC.

NEWSLETTER OF THE ELECTRONICS WORKERS UNION

PRECISION ELECTRONICS MOTTO: LOVE IT OR LEAVE IT!

When the chips are down, that's what your alternatives are at Precision. When a supervisor decides to do something, you've got to go along with it — or else!

What if the supervisor is being unfair? or arbitrary? or acting on the basis of favoritism? Too bad, friends. Those are the breaks! You don't have any rights because you don't have any power. You're only one small voice!

Isn't it like that in every plant? NO. Other plants have grievance procedures, with a union representative to stand by your side.

But doesn't Precision already have a grievance procedure? NO. Precision has a rubber-stamp procedure. They call it a grievance procedure, but it really isn't! Look what happens: If the worker has been mistreated by his supervisor, the worker must first complain to the supervisor!! We all know what that does. It invites further mistreatment.

continued on page 2

THIS IS YOUR LIFE

This is your working life, at least, and many workers have spent most of their working lives at Precision.

There are a lot of decisions made at Precision that affect the lives of workers. But how much say do workers have in those decisions? NONE. Let's face it. If a worker wants to have some say in a decision at Precision, there's only the suggestion box, which some secretary is in charge of.

If a worker wants to say something to management, he tiptoes in with his hat in his hand. If there was a union, workers would march in, shoulder to shoulder!

Let's look at an example. Let's look at the Annual Performance Review system at Precision. Six months ago, the Plant Manager announced a change that would go into effect immediately.

There are problems with the new system. Problems that can affect the lives of workers. Problems that could have been worked out if management had benefited from the wealth of experience of its workers.

continued on page 4

MANAGEMENT PULLS RUG OUT FROM UNDER WORKERS

We all saw how easily management can ignore the rights of long-service workers. We saw it when the Plant Manager suddenly changed the seniority system from plant-wide seniority to department-wide seniority.

How did he do it? It was easy. Management had ALL the power; the workers had NONE. How can workers prevent management from pulling the rug out from under them again? — By standing together. By having a strong union to balance the power of management, and prevent management from wielding power irresponsibly in the future.

Many loyal workers — hard workers who have given good years of service to the company — had the ground rules changed on them. They had made their career decisions based on a standing agreement with management — that it was plant-wide seniority that mattered. Now we have long-seniority workers with low seniority in departments. Whatever happened to justice???

What's to stop management from pulling another switch on you? Only you can stop them. Sign an authorization card and vote for the Electronics Workers Union — YOUR UNION — when the election comes up.

PROFITS RISING FASTER THAN WAGES

The company profits have grown by 25 percent over the past 12 months. Yet wages have grown only 5 percent.

It is through the hard work of people like YOU that the company and its profits have grown. YOU'RE NOT GETTING YOUR SHARE!

In fact, sometimes the profits come out of YOUR hide! There was a layoff two years ago at Precision. Management said the layoff was necessary "to reduce inventories." But profits rose 15 percent that year! Why couldn't management have kept workers on the payroll during that time?

Workers at Precision are not yet in a position to ask such questions. It's none of their business! It's a matter between top management and the board of directors.

EXHIBIT 13-3

"You're right," he conceded, "and they do have a way of phrasing things to sound very convincing."

"Yeah. And it's working. There's a lot of people around here already convinced," Maria responded.

"Well, I don't know whether I agree with that. I know I'm going

EXHIBIT 13-3 *Continued*

to take a stand against the union in my department," Vince said. "I don't think a union is going to be good for this company, and I'm going to fight them as hard as I can—without doing anything illegal."

"Not me," Maria said. "I'm going to sit back and let the chips fall where they may. I think you're getting too uptight about the union."

"I don't see how you can have such a lackadaisical attitude," Vince said, irritated. "Don't you realize that the union's going to restrict what supervisors can tell their workers to do? And we won't be able to jump in and help any more, when there's a problem on the line."

"You're right," she admitted, unconcerned, "but I look at it this way: Workers won't vote for a union unless they really *need* one. The union costs them money. It costs them money to join, and then more money comes out of their paychecks each month in union dues. Workers are not crazy. Quite often they're just desperate. And if the union stops them from getting ulcers about things like job security, then maybe it's not so bad. . . ."

"I'm sorry. I just don't agree with you," Vince retorted. "There's a lot of troublemakers campaigning for the union—they figure they'll

be able to get away with a lot more, without being disciplined. I think *you* need to be a lot more realistic about the problems we're going to have."

"And I really think you should just *relax* more!" Maria replied. "In the long run, you'll be a lot better off. Just think what happens if you fight the union tooth and nail. If they win the election—and I figure they will—you're going to start out as an enemy."

Vince shifted uncomfortably in his seat. "Sounds like you're giving in without a fight," he said. "I'm beginning to wonder just whose side you're on, anyway."

CHECK YOUR PROGRESS

1. In general, how does the supervisor avoid being charged with an unfair labor practice?

2. What motivates workers to join a union, when they know it will cost them money?

3. How does the presence of a union change what supervisors are allowed to do in their departments?

4. Why is it important for the supervisor to think in "long-range" terms when deciding what he (or she) should do about the union's organizing attempt?

ANSWERS TO PROGRESS QUESTIONS

1. The supervisor must avoid doing anything that might interfere with a worker's freedom to choose whether to be represented by a union. Rewards, punishments, and threats are all considered interference.
2. Strong motivators include job security, a grievance mechanism, and participation in decisions that affect their lives. Increases in wages are generally of only secondary importance.
3. The union contract will probably restrict *which* workers can be told to do which tasks. It will probably also restrict what the supervisor may personally do on the production line, even during a crisis.
4. The supervisor must continue to work with the union supporters in his department long after the organizing drive is over (and no matter what the outcome is). Thus it's best to avoid making "long-term enemies," whenever this is possible.

Further Thoughts

What are the positive and negative impacts of a successful union organizing attempt on a supervisor?

The impacts of a union on supervisors that are usually perceived as negative *include:*

1. Union leaders are able to use the contract language to challenge a supervisor's decision, and, on occasion, to force changes. The supervisor, therefore, has *less freedom to take action* on matters regarding his (or her) workers.
2. The union competes for the loyalty of the workers. Frequently workers turn to the union steward for information or assistance, rather than the supervisor. The supervisor's relationships with workers can thereby become more *impersonal*.

The impacts that can be positive *include:*

1. The union's careful watching of all actions that affect workers forces a supervisor to think through and develop *consistent personnel practices*. Arbitrary decisions, favoritism, and unpopular "seat-of-the-pants" rulings, all of which are usually made as a matter of expediency, are no longer acceptable. Supervisors thereby are forced into following good management practices right from the start.
2. The union tends to force supervisors to find more efficient work methods to help offset wage increases realized by collective bargaining. As a consequence, new innovations often occur, because cost pressures discourage complacency.

Maria is unconcerned about the union. She evidently feels that the union will not affect her friendly relationship with her workers in the Assembly Department. Is it true that she has no cause for concern?

There is considerable evidence to suggest that industrial workers have a view of the worker-management relationship that is quite different from management's view of it.

Briefly, people in management positions visualize a hierarchy. The supervisor, for instance, tends to see himself (or herself) sandwiched in a pyramid, the second level from the bottom. Below him are workers; above him are higher managers. The pyramid is seen as functioning as a cohesive structure, with everyone "pulling together" in the direction of the company's overall goal.

Workers generally visualize the relationship quite differently: They see two sides lined up against each other and describe the worker-management relationship in terms of us and them. The supervisor, of course, is one of "them." a member of the other "camp."

This generalization needs to be modified to fit particular circumstances, such as in Maria's department. We saw in Chapter 9 that Maria gets along very well with the women in her department. We would thus expect that workers would not visualize her as falling neatly (or at least completely) into the "them" camp. To some degree, it is likely that Maria is seen as one of "us."

When the union comes on the scene, it builds solidarity among the workers by intensifying the workers' sense of "us and them." The union's power partly depends on how strongly it can polarize the workers against management. Thus there is a heavy propaganda campaign to paint supervisors as "bad guys."

How well Maria can survive the effects of this persuasion (in which her workers will be tempted to highlight her shortcomings and downplay her good qualities) depends partly on how she acts during the organizing campaign. The union, meanwhile, will continue to do its best to try to have her workers reinterpret her "good points" as merely being manipulative. Maria, therefore, really does have some cause for concern. It won't be easy to compete with the union to maintain friendly relationships with her workers.

How does a union affect what supervisors are allowed to *do themselves*, and what they may *tell workers to do?*

The union readjusts the authority relationship between supervisor and worker. To understand the change, we have to understand what the supervisor-worker relationship was before the union entered the picture, and then examine the more formalized union-management relationship.

In a nonunion company, the relationship between supervisor and worker is based on the social contract between the worker and the company. Briefly, the social contract is an agreement between the two parties to the effect that the company supplies wages to the worker, in exchange for the labor services that the worker supplies to the company.

This exchange is fairly explicit: There is a formal agreement about the amount of labor to be provided—in terms of the number of hours or units of output—and the wage rates that will be paid for that labor.

Many of the other terms of the social contract are not explicit; rather, it is assumed that both the company and the workers will go along with normal customs—that is, each party expects the other to do what is "common practice" in the culture, unless there is an explicit agreement to depart from these norms.

These "unwritten" aspects of the agreement are unwritten for good reason. To specify everything that each party expects would require an enormous contract—about the size of Encyclopedia Britannica *(the full set of volumes!). Examples of what would have to be specified are*

The employee expects the company to replace broken windows where the draft causes great discomfort in the wintertime.

The company expects the worker not to sing at the top of his lungs while at his work station.

Obviously, these things don't have to be formally agreed upon. The company does fix broken windows, because it normally expects to do so. Employees refrain from bizarre behavior because they are ex- pected *to refrain from doing so. ("It's just not done.")*

One of the key unwritten aspects of the social contract is the relationship between the supervisor and the worker. The worker expects (and is expected to comply with) reasonable demands by the supervisor. The society provides the worker with a good idea of what are reasonable demands and what are unreasonable demands.

However, there is a certain "gray area" in which it is not clear *whether or not the supervisor has the right to tell the worker to do things. A familiar example is telling one worker to pinch-hit for another, in the interest of departmental expediency. In a nonunion company, the social norm is to "do what the supervisor says" unless the demand is obviously unreasonable. Thus, the supervisor usually gets the benefit of the doubt in these "gray areas."*

Once the union enters the picture, much more of the unwritten social contract is formalized in a negotiated, written agreement. Many of the previous informal social expectations become formal *contractual obligations.*

More importantly, the "gray areas" are resolved through negotiation and bartering into specific decision guidelines. When this happens, the supervisor has to be very careful about telling one worker to pinch-hit on another's job, because "job jurisdiction" clauses may prohibit this practice. Similarly, those clauses may prohibit the supervisor from pitching in and helping with a problem on the line. Vince was well aware of these constraints, and he pointed them out to Maria.

The union-management contract, of course, cannot specify every aspect of the worker-supervisor relationship. To do so would incur the same lengthy constraints as with the informal social contract. Much of the union-management contract is written in vague, general terms, and is interpreted *(as to its application to particular cases) when a grievance must be decided. That process is covered in the next chapter.*

1. Make sure that you **know what the real issue is.** It may not be stated, but you **must** know what the problem is if you're ever going to solve it!

2. **Handle complaints informally,** where possible. This will save everyone's time—especially your own.

3. Process formal, written grievances (when you just **can't** handle the problem informally) with care. **Keep written records, stick to the issues** (don't let yourself get sidetracked), and try to settle the problem **as quickly as possible.**

4. **Learn not to take it personally** when a grievance is filed against you. Workers have a right to question actions by management if they feel that prior agreements have been violated.

Grievance Handling

14

A CRITICAL INCIDENT: Sometimes You Can't Win. . . .

Sam picked up the phone and called Walter Brooks, the Industrial Relations Director at Globe Housewares.

"Hey, Walter, this is Sam. There's something funny going on down here in the Stamping Press Department."

"Oh? What's up?" asked Brooks.

"I just got slapped with a grievance," replied Sam. "I know I'm supposed to try to handle it at this level, but the guy who signed the grievance doesn't want to talk about it. He just says, 'Talk to the steward.' So I ask the steward, "What's this all about?' and he says, 'You can read, can't you?' and walks away. I really don't know what I did wrong. The paper says I changed Stan Pulanski's job description in violation of the contract."

"Look, Sam," interrupted Walter Brooks, "why don't you drop by and we'll talk about it? Now's OK."

When Sam arrived at the Industrial Relations office, Brooks apologized.

"I meant to warn you about this," Brooks said, as Sam was handing him the grievance form, "but I've been busy as hell the last few days doing my homework for the new contract negotiations. Sorry about that." (See Exhibit 14-1.)

"You mean you *knew* I'd be getting a grievance?" asked Sam, a little confused.

"Well, not exactly. But I sort of *figured* you would, as soon as the first section of the conveyor was operational. Don't be surprised if you get nine more! People are starting to get pretty uptight around here."

Worker's Name: _STAN PULANSKI_   I.D. No.: _2465 - M_

Job Title: _PRESS OPERATOR_   Dept.: _STAMPING PRESS_   Shift: _DAY_

Date of Hire: _2/1/71_   Supervisor: _SAM_

Name of Employer: _GLOBE HOUSEWARES_

Nature of Grievance:
SUPERVISOR CHANGED WORKER'S JOB DESCRIPTION
IN VIOLATION OF THE CONTRACT

(use additional sheets of paper if necessary)

Adjustment Desired: _RESTORE WORKER TO PRIOR JOB_
WITH NO PENALTIES

Management Reply: _STILL PENDING_

Steps Taken: _____

Disposition: _____

Date: _3/15_   _Stan Pulanski_   _Mike Martinant_
                 Signature of Worker   Signature of Shop Steward

EXHIBIT 14-1

Brooks was referring to the new conveyor system that was being installed in Sam's department. It was the first step in automating the materials-handling system throughout the production operation.

Previously, the procedure had been for the stamping press operators to throw the stampings into a hand truck. When the hand truck was full, a person whose title was "materials handler" would wheel the hand truck over to the vapor degreaser and feed the oily stampings in by hand. Under the new system (see Exhibit 14–2), a continuous conveyor belt was to replace the materials handlers.

"Yeah, I know," Sam agreed. "I've been getting some bad vibes in the plant for the last couple of weeks. But that shouldn't have anything to do with grievances against me. Grievances go on my performance record. What the hell did I do?"

Sam didn't even pause for an answer before continuing.

"Remember the talk you gave on grievances at the Supervisors'

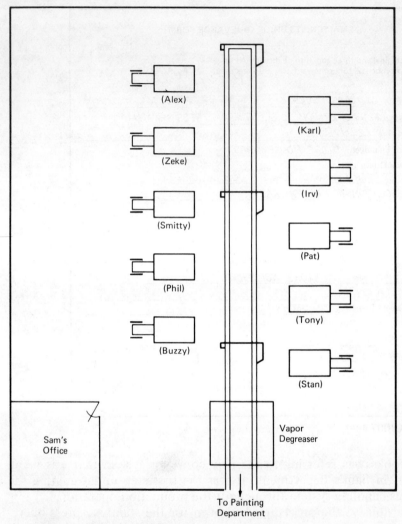

EXHIBIT 14-2 *Proposed Layout Change in Stamping Department*

Club meeting a couple of months ago?" he asked Brooks. Brooks nodded.

"Well, you said we should be patient, and listen to gripes. I always did that, anyway. Half the time, all the guy wants to do is get it off his chest, and that's the end of it. But if there's still a problem, and the steward gets involved, you gave us all those rules about sticking to the issues and not going off on tangents, keeping detailed records of what exactly happened, and so on. How the hell am I supposed to go by the rules when I don't even know what the issue is, and nobody wants to talk?"

"Well," Brooks reminded him, "don't forget I also told you that you've got to look beneath the surface, to see what the *real* issue is. I think that's what we've got to do in this particular case. Actually, it's my fault for not warning you beforehand that this was coming.

"You see the root of the problem is that the union doesn't like automation. Those conveyors are going to mean that materials handlers will be out of a job. The union *knows* we have to do more automation. They realize that our competitors are automated, and if we don't do it too, we won't be able to compete with their prices. And *that* would mean that the whole manufacturing operation eventually would fold, and all the union members would lose their jobs. The union sure as hell doesn't want that to happen, any more than the company does!

"On the other hand," Brooks continued, "the union isn't going to come out of this empty-handed, so they're turning the heat on, by stirring up grievances. You just happened to get the first one!"

"Lucky me!" Sam replied, dryly.

"Oh, just wait; it'll get worse!" Brooks assured him. "Look: You have to see things from the *union's* point of view. If the union did nothing when some of their people got replaced by machines, all the members would be up in arms! The workers pay a lot of money out in union dues so that their jobs will be protected. When something very *visible* happens, such as conveyor belts replacing materials handlers, then the union has to do something dramatic in response. That's why you'll be seeing plenty of hostility and grievances around this plant."

"Secondly," Brooks pointed out, "even though it's the contract negotiation that gets all the publicity, many of the *details* of dealing with the union are actually worked out on a day-to-day basis when the union challenges management's decisions through grievances. In other words, by means of grievances, we negotiate year 'round with the union. That's the way it has to be. A contract would have to be a thousand pages long to cover every tiny little detail that might come up. And we have enough trouble agreeing on twenty pages."

"Well, all right. I guess I sort of took it personally that the grievance was against *me*," said Sam, beginning to understand. "But I obviously can't do anything about this damn grievance! What do you want me to do with it?"

"Just follow the procedure: Write 'grievance denied' on it, sign it, and date it. Then give it back to the steward. He'll bring it to me and the games will start with the union president. I already know what he's after. He wants the workers to get a 'fair share' of the savings we get from increased efficiency. Nothing wrong with that; the workers *should* get some of it. My job is to fight with him about how much!"

Sam nodded, now understanding what was going on. As he got up to leave, Brooks added, "You know, I'll have to help figure out some acceptable way of transferring or terminating those materials handlers. If you've got any ideas, Sam, I'd sure like to hear them."

CHECK YOUR PROGRESS

1. Sam was advised to "stick to the issues written in the formal grievance." But he wasn't able to do so in this particular case. Does that mean the advice was worthless?

2. What are the major advantages of handling complaints informally, whenever possible?

3. What is the advantage of handling grievances promptly?

4. What should a supervisor learn to do when a grievance is filed against him (her)?

ANSWERS TO PROGRESS QUESTIONS

1. No. You only "stick to the issue" when you're sure that it's the *real* issue. The advice that he received from Brooks is good advice in most cases. If you don't stick to the issue, you may open up the floodgates for other gripes. If this happens, you won't be able to solve the original problem; it will simply get lost.
2. It saves time for everyone involved and builds more trust between the supervisor and grievant.
3. If the person who files the grievance is also frustrated because of slowness in the grievance process, he (or she) will be less cooperative, and the problem will become a lot harder to solve.
4. A supervisor should learn not to take the grievance personally and to encourage open, honest communication with the grievant.

Further Thoughts

Assume that Walter Brooks, the Industrial Relations Director, was the *third step* in a four-step grievance procedure. What does this mean in terms of his responsibility for handling plant-wide grievances?

> *Walter Brooks did not get involved in handling grievances unless the grievance was still unresolved after the first two steps, namely: (1) a conference between the first line supervisor and the shop steward, and (2) a second conference, this time also attended by the Production Manager. At the third level, the grievance would be "heard" by Walter Brooks, the Industrial Relations Director, along with higher union officials. If Brooks could not resolve the difference at his level, the grievance would progress to a fourth and final step—arbitration by a neutral, "outside" arbitrator acceptable to both management and the union.*

Should grievances be *recorded* on a supervisor's performance record, as was the case with Sam? Does a record of *no* grievances signify a better supervisor than a record showing a number of grievances?

> *Recording grievances as one measure of a supervisor's performance is acceptable, provided that a wide range of other measures of performance (such as quantity and quality of work, safety record, promotions, etc.) is also noted.*
>
> *A record of no grievances does not necessarily mean a superior record of performance. It is possible that such a record has been achieved by such means as:*

1. Intimidating workers so that they are afraid to file well-founded grievances.

2. Making "deals" with the union—at a cost to the company—to keep a grievance from being filed.

3. Giving in to worker demands, even if unreasonable, in order to remain a "nice guy."

However, everything else being equal, a supervisor who is able to skillfully resolve or minimize grievances is valued as superior to one whose inept performance with grievances requires managers at higher levels to spend considerable time in "bailing him out."

What are the major differences in a typical grievance procedure within a nonunion company, as compared with a unionized one?

The important difference between a grievance procedure in a unionized shop and the procedure in a nonunion shop is that the union processes the grievance and backs up the worker, whereas in the nonunion shop the worker has to "go it alone." (This point was brought out in the union's newsletter in Chapter 13.) The nonunion situation is less desirable for workers because:

1. The worker acting alone is usually not as knowledgeable about company rules (and his rights) as is the union, which processes grievances regularly.

2. The individual worker is usually not as good at *arguing* his case as the union steward would be (since this is a basic job qualification for union stewards!).

3. Without union backing, the individual worker tends to be easily intimidated by higher-status managers. He realizes that they can later arrange to "punish" him for speaking up.

4. Without the union to "keep them honest," there is a natural tendency for higher management to "back" their first-line supervisors, that is, to support their authority by giving them the benefit of the doubt wherever possible. (See the union's newsletter in Chapter 13.) A strong union counteracts this tendency for higher management to drift away from being neutral.

1. **Keep loose control** over what is discussed, unless the group needs strong direction.
2. Learn to **handle the difficult and disruptive person,** and encourage the creative thinker to contribute even in the face of heckling.
3. Let supportive group members help in **sticking to the agenda** and in maintaining **fair play** in group discussion.
4. Avoid wasting time and effort with a group meeting, unless you believe that it can help sort out a **controversial issue,** or that it is necessary to get **opinions and reactions** before making a decision.

Running a Meeting

15

A CRITICAL INCIDENT: It Wasn't "Just Another Dull Meeting"

Marvin, the supervisor of the Accounts Receivable Department at Allied Industries, stared in disbelief at the memo on his desk. It was a notice to all supervisors, advising them that as of the end of the month, half of the parking lot would no longer be available to employees. The State was building a new roadway over the area, and the company lawyers had run out of legal steps to save the parking lot.

All of the supervisors were directed to meet with their departments to work out alternative transportation arrangements that would reduce the number of cars using the parking lot. Now, at the peak of the company's busy season, there were plenty of things to attend to without bothering with a troublesome and time-consuming problem like parking! But Marvin knew he had to give it prompt attention.

Parking had always been a problem, and many people arrived quite early, with no extra compensation, just so they could find a place to park in the company lot. The alternative was to park on the streets surrounding the plant, but employees generally hated doing this.

The plant was located in an older section of the city, and the streets were narrow and busy. Most of the streets had one-hour parking meters, and stiff fines for violations. The no-parking areas were tow-away zones, and the police patrolled the area very efficiently, and without mercy.

Because the streets were so narrow, cars were frequently scraped or dented by people backing carelessly out of driveways. To make matters worse, there was a high rate of theft and vandalism in the neighborhood.

If there was *anything* that would get employees riled up, it would be to make the already "hot issue" of parking an even bigger headache!

Marvin called a meeting right away and read the memo to the people in his department. Amid groans, they agreed to meet the next day during the noon hour to figure out what to do about it.

Everyone arrived promptly in the small conference room, and Marvin began by thanking them for giving up their lunch hour. He was outwardly congenial, although he had a sinking feeling that the long-standing parking problem was bound to stir up some strong feelings and resentment.

Marvin soon found out that his fears were justified, as Wally criticized the company management for letting the parking situation get out of hand.

"Dammit, Marvin, you and the rest of management *knew* the State was going to build that highway over the parking lot. Now *we've* got to figure out new ways to get to work. What a lot of bull! That's management's job, not ours!"

Wally was an old-timer who had been passed over several times for promotions. He was bitter about this, and consequently he took advantage of every opportunity to condemn the company mangement. But Sylvia was tired of his negative attitude.

"Come on, Wally!" she said, "nobody knew *for sure* until yesterday that we would actually lose part of our parking area. I figure there must've been at least a fifty-fifty chance that the road would be rerouted; otherwise we'd have been told before now. And besides, if management *had* planned what to do about it, you would have complained that we never have a chance to get involved in making decisions!"

"Why don't you try to be objective about the situation?" Wally demanded, sneering at Sylvia. "Just once. That's all I ask. You're such a good company girl, you'd stick up for management no matter how badly they screwed up!"

Marvin was about to come to Sylvia's rescue, since Wally was now "playing dirty"—attacking Sylvia, rather than dealing with the point she was trying to make—when Neil intervened.

"Look, Wally, this is my lunch hour, and I've got better things to do than listen to your comments. You're not helping us solve the parking lot problem. Either try to be more constructive, or give the rest of us a chance to figure out what we're going to do."

Several others in the group nodded in agreement, and Wally sat back and folded his arms.

Marvin was glad Neil had taken the lead in using group pressure to handle a troublemaker like Wally. Otherwise, Marvin knew he would

have had to do it himself, and risk losing his "neutral" role in the meeting.

Jane broke the short, but embarrassing silence by offering the first constructive suggestion. "Maybe the Personnel Department could figure out which people live close together and come to work at the same time," she said, looking at Marvin. "Then it would be easy for people to get together and form car pools."

"Hey, that's a good idea," Marvin said. "I'll bet there's people working in other parts of the plant who live real close to me, and I don't even know it."

"Oh, that's just *great,*" Wally said sarcastically. "*Now* the company's gonna tell me who's going to ride in my car. . . . ."

"I'm in a carpool and it wasn't easy at first," Jane bravely continued, glancing around the table from one face to another, ignoring Wally's grumbling. "I guess we all like our independence."

Encouraged by Jane's boldness, another clerk, Kim, who was normally very shy, leaned forward and started to say something. But Wally cut her off with some loud remark about the young "punks" in Production he wasn't going to ride with.

"Hold on, Wally," Marvin said, raising his hand, but still looking at Kim. "Go ahead, Kim. You were going to say something?"

Kim spoke up, and turned out to have more factual information than anyone else, much of it obtained from a friend who worked in Personnel. The company had considered car pools, and had come up with some statistics. Kim explained that the 400 present parking spaces were used by 300 cars with a single driver; the other 100 were in car pool arrangements and carried about 300 employees.

Kim further added that the new road would result in losing one-half of the present lot, or 200 parking spaces. If all single-driver cars were replaced by car pools averaging three people each, there would be no parking problem.

Then, before anyone could break in, she quickly added, "I know that's not entirely realistic, but I agree with Jane that at least some of the shortage could be overcome by setting up more carpools."

"That's probably going to be our only way out of this mess in the short run," Neil said, nodding in agreement and looking at Jane and Kim. "But in the longer run," he continued, turning towards Marvin, "the company might be better off buying that old vacant building across the street and tearing it down."

"There's no way," Wally said, shaking his head, "that management would spend that much money to build a parking lot for its employees."

"Hey, not so fast, Wally!" Sylvia chided him. "We're supposed to be coming up with ideas. Let's let Marvin pass along Neil's idea to top management and let *them* decide if it costs too much money. We can't make that decision."

Marvin agreed to do so. "I've got it written down. You're right. We shouldn't be trying to second-guess top management when it comes to corporate finance!" Wally got the message about killing off suggestions, and returned to sitting back in his chair with his arms folded.

"Maybe you can add a footnote to the suggestion." Kim ventured. "Maybe the company could build a multilevel parking garage and rent out spaces to the general public. That would offset the costs."

Wally slumped down into his chair and rolled his eyes, but he didn't dare say anything else negative.

As Marvin was writing down Kim's latest contribution, Brian made a joke about knocking the vacant building down for free with a gigantic office party. The laughter broke the tension that had been growing.

After the laughter, Neil suggested that they use the next few minutes to move on to figuring out some other alternatives for traveling to work.

Neil was a "bulldog" for sticking to some kind of agenda. Marvin found this role helpful in keeping the meeting moving along and agreed that more alternatives should be discussed.

After twenty minutes of discussion (during which several alternatives were discussed, including such diverse ideas as using a "commuter bus" to transport workers from the big downtown public parking lot, and putting all the office workers on the day shift and all the production workers on the night shift), it was generally agreed that car pools held the most promise for an immediate solution for the crisis.

Wally had been quietly listening to the discussion, and was still very skeptical. Living up to his reputation for "throwing cold water" on any idea that would take some extra effort, he figured that now was the time to shoot down Jane's suggestion.

"Jane," he began, in an almost insulting tone of voice, "your idea of organizing more car pools will never work. I've talked to people in Sales and around the plant, and I know that you just can't force them into using car pools. They've paid for their cars and their gasoline, and will damn well use them any way they choose. They all feel *the company* is responsible for providing them with parking spaces."

Neil turned to Wally. "How many people did you actually talk to before arriving at your conclusion about car pools? We only found out there was a problem yesterday. Have you been interviewing around the clock?"

"Well," Wally sputtered, "I don't know *exactly* how many people

I talked to. At least ten. I guess I found out mostly when I used to work in the plant—but I've talked to people since."

Marvin picked up on Neil's comment.

"Let's see, Wally," he began, "if there are 300 persons not in car-pools and you've only talked to ten of them, that's about 3 percent of the total. Do you think that's really a big enough sample? Especially since much of your information may be out of date?"

Wally became flustered. "I don't know why you're getting so picky about exact numbers," he retorted.

"Five years ago," Neil added, "people had different attitudes toward car pools. There weren't as many workers in the plant back then, and besides, people used to be less conscious about wasting gas and making the oil companies richer."

Everyone was silent, looking down. Kim was concealing a smile. Neil had helped Marvin make his point.

It was getting close to one o'clock. Kim quickly added that the company where her husband worked had done some successful experi-menting with carpools and she would be willing to find out more about what they did, if anyone was interested. Jane then suggested they should all think about the problem some more and meet again early the following week.

Marvin took a quick poll, and set the time for the next meeting. He looked at the notes he'd made and told them that the agenda would be to look at the advantages and disadvantages of suggestions already proposed, as well as any new ideas, and then decide which ones their department would recommend for adoption by the company. Then he closed his notebook.

After they had all left the conference room to go back to their desks, Marvin sighed deeply and leaned back in his chair. He suddenly felt tired. Running a meeting, especially with so many different personalities, was hard work. It was especially difficult to separate how he felt as a car owner from how he should behave as a supervisor, setting a good example.

CHECK YOUR PROGRESS

1. If Marvin had proposed a specific agenda and then used tight control to see that it was followed, could a satisfactory decision have been reached at the end of the *first* meeting?

2. What should a supervisor do with a difficult or disruptive person at a meeting? With a creative person?

3. What can a supervisor do to be sure that a meeting sticks to the agenda?

4. How can a supervisor guard against scheduling a group meeting that is a waste of time and effort?

1. Marvin was wise in keeping the agenda open, as this permitted group members to "let off steam." Had he used tight control, there was little chance that a group with such varied opinions would have reached an agreement in only one hour's time.
2. The supervisor should try to remain "neutral" and permit other group members to handle a disruptive person. The creative thinker should be encouraged to contribute, even in the face of heckling.
3. Involve other group members, particularly those who are supportive or who are viewed as informal group leaders, to take some of the responsibility for sticking to the agenda.
4. Schedule a meeting *only* if there is good reason to believe that it can help sort out a controversial issue, or if it is necessary to get opinions and reactions before making a decision.

Further Thoughts

Meetings are not always held for the purpose of solving a specific problem. They can be designed to provide information, generate ideas, let people "blow off steam," arrive at a group decision, etc.—or any combination of these. What was the primary purpose of the meeting to discuss parking? To what extent did the meeting achieve its purpose?

The meeting appears to have had several objectives, although the primary goal was to reach group agreement on a short-run solution to the parking problem. A secondary goal was to generate ideas for a long-run solution to the parking problem. One of Marvin's goals was undoubtedly to give vent to some of the pent-up feelings about how an already bad parking problem was getting worse.

It is interesting to note that different people seemed to have different goals for the meeting. Top management was most concerned with the short-run problem of people's getting to work. It was probably hoped that the outcome of the meeting would be for workers to commit themselves to forming car pools.

The group defined the meeting primarily as a forum for generating ideas for a long-run solution to the parking problem. Marvin defined the meeting largely in terms of its usefulness in "taking the heat off."

The meeting was only partly successful in meeting its goal—as defined by top management—of coming up with a short-range solution to the immediate problem. However, feelings had been vented (partly against Wally!) that might have interfered with productive discussion, and the group had made a commitment to review further information on carpooling at the next meeting. The long-range ideas were useful, and didn't actually detract from the immediate objective. All in all, Marvin had reason to be optimistic, despite his uneasy feelings.

During meetings, what people say through nonverbal communication ("body language") can be as important as what they say in words. Re-read the "critical incident" and pick out *nonverbal cues* that (1) tell what people are thinking and feeling, and (2) are used to control the progress of the meeting.

1. Nonverbal cues that can be used as an indicator of peoples' thoughts and feelings include (in order of their appearance):

a. Workers' nodding in agreement when Neil first objected to Wally's lack of constructive criticism.

b. Wally's sitting back in his chair and folding his arms as a sign that he was "rejecting" his co-workers.

c. Wally's slumping down in his chair and rolling his eyes to convey disagreement and ridicule.

d. The group's looking downward (avoiding eye contact) as an expression of discomfort when Wally got his final "putdown" from Marvin.

e. Marvin's leaning back in his chair after the meeting, as an expression of his "withdrawal" from the meeting, and his feeling of closure.

2. Nonverbal gestures that can be used to control the progress of a meeting include:

a. An open-armed stance when Marvin wanted to receive suggestions.

b. Jane's use of eye contact, first looking directly at Marvin, when giving *him* an idea to write down, then looking around the table at her co-workers in explaining the suggestion to *them*.

c. Kim's leaning forward to indicate that she "wanted to be recognized," that is, given a chance to speak.

d. Marvin's raising his hand and looking directly at Kim, to shut off all other conversation.

e. Neil's swiveling his body towards Marvin when he wanted to indicate that he was making an important recommendation.

f. Marvin's closing his notebook to signal the end of the meeting.

It often happens that people have their own pet issues that they like to bring up at meetings. No matter what the topic of the meeting, somehow they are able to twist it around so that they can work in the points *they* want to discuss.

1. To what extent was Wally doing this?

2. How can a meeting be run so that important points do not become battlegrounds for irrelevant issues?

1. *Wally's pet issue was the incompetence and irresponsibility of management. He tried to focus the discussion on this issue, even though doing so would contribute nothing towards generating ideas to solve the parking problem.*

Wally probably needed to constantly condemn management as a defense mechanism to protect his ego. We know that Wally had been passed over several times for promotion. This generates a situation where Wally's self-concept (that he is competent, and worthy of promotion) is in conflict with management's decision in not promoting him.

To change his self-concept would be psychologically painful, so Wally needs to protect his self-concept by rationalizing, "Management must be incompetent if they can't recognize my talents." Thus, meetings represent an opportunity for Wally to try to convince his co-workers that management is incompetent, so that their social support will reinforce his defense mechanism.

2. Wally's case is somewhat atypical, because his pet issue is psychologically *motivated.* It more often happens that pet issues are politically *motivated; that is, people want to protect their interests, not their egos.* This has been observed so frequently in meetings that organizational theorists have studied what they call the "garbage can strategy."

The basic idea is that whenever there's a meeting, people will want to raise their pet issues, and won't really pay much attention to the real problem that the meeting is trying to solve until they have "made their pitch." The wise strategy, therefore, is to provide a "garbage can" into which these pet issues can be "dumped."

This can be done by putting two problems on the agenda for the meeting. The first problem is "invented"; it is specifically chosen to serve as the "garbage can." A typical garbage can question, for instance, is a general discussion of the mission of the department, or planning for the future. Anything vague enough to accommodate everyone's pet issues is a good garbage can "problem."

Once everyone has gotten his (or her) pet issue "off his chest," they all feel better, and thus are in a better position to give unbiased consideration to the second problem—the problem that the meeting was really designed to solve.

It should be kept in mind that a major problem in using the "garbage can strategy" is the additional time required when a garbage can problem is added to the agenda. Some people may see this as a waste of time, and thus may become antagonistic. This can be a problem if the feeling continues after the real agenda is confronted.

POSTTEST QUESTIONS

Now that you've read the five chapters in Section III, you might want to try to answer the same questions that you answered in the Pretest. The correct answers are given on page 172.

By comparing your score on the Posttest with your score on the Pretest, you will be able to get an idea of how much your knowledge of supervision has improved.

21. Choose the ending that describes the *best* long-run strategy for the supervisor, and then circle the corresponding letter.

Conflicts between loyalty to the boss and loyalty to subordinates should be resolved:

a. By explaining to the workers the dilemma being faced.
b. On the basis of what will keep the most people happy.
c. On the basis of what the boss desires.
d. On the basis of what is the fairest thing to do.
e. As quickly as possible.

22. Choose the *least* appropriate ending to the following statement by circling *one* of the five choices.

A supervisor's role in running a meeting is to:

a. Encourage group discussion.
b. Remain neutral as much as possible.
c. Help sort out controversial issues.
d. Stick to the agenda.
e. Take sole responsibility for handling disruptive persons.

23. Choose the answer that *best* completes the sentence, and then circle the corresponding letter.

A union contract usually _____ what supervisors are allowed to do in their departments.

a. Restricts
b. Avoids any mention of
c. Broadens
d. Is unclear about
e. None of the above

Questions 24 through 30 are to be answered by circling T if the statement is **true,** and F if the statement is **false.**

24. Workers vote for a union *primarily* to improve wages and fringe benefits.

T   F

25. Supervisors can avoid conflicts between loyalty to their bosses and loyalty to their workers. **T   F**

26. In order to be as fair as possible, a supervisor cannot afford to permit any exceptions to established rules. **T   F**

27. Nearly all worker grievances can be resolved at the supervisory level. **T   F**

28. A supervisor should always try to remain "neutral" when running a meeting, even if others have difficulty in pinpointing to what position the supervisor is committed. **T   F**

29. Fairness basically requires that a supervisor must not be too strict with his or her fellow workers. **T   F**

30. There are really no important differences between the effectiveness of a grievance procedure in a nonunion company, compared with a unionized shop. **T   F**

PRE- AND POSTTEST QUESTIONNAIRE—ANSWER SHEET

21. d
22. e
23. a
24. false
25. false
26. false
27. true
28. true
29. false
30. false

Here are ten questions. Try to answer them before you read the five chapters in Section IV. You'll have another chance to try to answer the same ten questions in the Posttest (pages 220–21).

An answer sheet is provided after the Posttest (page 221). You will be able to use this to score your Pretest and Posttest. By comparing the two scores, you will be able to get an idea of how much your knowledge of supervision has improved.

Select the *best* response to Questions 31 and 32, and circle the appropriate letter.

31. If you suspect that someone is playing "political games," you should:

   a. Retaliate by playing political games of your own.
   b. Avoid making any hasty accusations.
   c. Let your boss know what you suspect and get support.
   d. Confront face to face and have a showdown.
   e. Try to rally your workers to help you put it to a stop.

32. Every hiring requirement set by a supervisor must be

   a. Consistent with past hiring practices.
   b. Acceptable to members of the work group.
   c. First approved by the Personnel Department.

PROBLEMS
ON THE JOB

d. Able to attract the best-qualified candidates.

e. Related to actual job performance.

33. In dealing with a problem alcoholic worker, supervisors should NOT do which *one* of the following? (Circle one.)

a. Be supportive by assuring the worker that there is no danger of losing his or her job.

b. Find out what company or community programs are available to help.

c. Enlist the help of fellow workers.

d. Look for patterns of behavior that will show if the problem is getting worse.

e. Tell the worker that he or she *must* seek help, or else.

Questions 34 through 40 are to be answered by circling T if the statement is **true** and F if the statement is **false**.

34. If a person is really good at "politics" in the work place, there's no way to tell that his (or her) actions have hidden purposes.   T   F

35. Firing is strictly a private matter between the worker involved and the supervisor; other workers should be told that the entire matter is none of their business.   T   F

36. A supervisor should not tolerate any conflict, whenever it is possible to squelch it.   T   F

37. Trembling fingers, bloodshot eyes, and accidents are sufficient evidence to determine that a worker has a drinking problem.   T   F

38. It is usually wise for supervisors to let their bosses know about conflicts in their departments.   T   F

39. A supervisor with successful past experience in interviewing job applicants is unlikely to get into trouble with the law on discrimination.   T   F

40. A supervisor should try to avoid firing an unsatisfactory worker during his (or her) probation period after hiring, since it is at this time that the worker needs maximum help and support.   T   F

A PREVIEW

The five chapters in this fourth section cover some of the most difficult problems that a supervisor will encounter on the job. Each situation requires careful judgment because people's jobs and well-being may be "on the line," along with the supervisor's reputation.

One area that is usually a "mystery" to supervisors is *politics in the work place* (the subject of Chapter 16). This is largely because supervisors receive no training in developing political skills as a basis for power. In fact, the subject is often regarded as immoral, devious, or at least, "not nice to talk about," rather than as a crucial reality of what goes on in the work place. The chapter examines those "political intrigues" in which someone takes some action that appears to be straightforward, but in fact has some hidden purpose. It usually involves some unfair benefit to the "politician."

The political activity may backfire, however, and lead to intense *conflict* in the work place. In Chapter 17, the skills a supervisor needs for handling conflict are explored. It is important to note that some conflict is unavoidable, and even healthy. However, careful judgment is called for so that the conflict is not allowed to reach a potentially destructive level.

A less destructive, but perhaps more delicate problem for the supervisor is dealing with an *alcoholic worker.* Here a supervisor usually agonizes over the problem and procrastinates, thinking that it's none of his business. Chapter 18 points out that the supervisor who becomes sentimental does not do the alcoholic worker any favors. Once convinced that the drinking has become a problem *on* the job, the supervisor needs to face up to the need to tell the alcoholic worker the hard truth—that he must either seek help or risk losing his (or her) job.

Another area of anguish for supervisors is the legal restrictions against discrimination in hiring decisions. One problem is to be sure that job requirements are written so that they directly relate to actual job performance. Even more difficult is the interviewing of job applicants. Chapter 19 deals with a supervisor who unintentionally discriminates first in writing a hiring notice, and second by asking unlawful questions in an interview.

The last chapter in this section—Chapter 20—covers what most experienced supervisors will agree is the most difficult problem that they have to face—firing a worker. It's a hard thing to do even when such drastic action is logically justified. After all, the supervisor is using his or her power to perhaps make a major change in someone else's life. The responsibility is awesome, when you think about it.

With all these problems on the job, many people think twice about wanting to be a supervisor. There's more to the job than just prestige and high pay; there are a lot of headaches, too. The last section of the book will deal with these kinds of questions.

1. Become aware of the "politics" in the work place—
   the things people do and the decisions they make that
   have **hidden purposes.**

2. Notice that most "politicians" make a special point of
   **surrounding themselves with friends and loyal support-
   ers.** If they did this openly, they would be criticized for
   showing favoritism. So they usually do it indirectly, by
   carefully **arranging the right opportunities** for their
   pals.

3. Recognize that if a person is really good at "politics,"
   there's **no way to tell** whether decisions are designed
   to accomplish hidden purposes.

4. If you suspect that someone is playing political games,
   avoid making any hasty accusations, even when you
   think you know for sure. If you're right, you probably won't be able to prove it, and you'll come out
   looking bad. If you're wrong, you'll have done someone a great injustice. Either way, the person you accuse will become a permanent enemy.

"Politics"
in the Work Place

16

A CRITICAL INCIDENT: Some People Get All the Breaks

When the buzzer sounded for the morning coffee break, Zeke quickly shut down his stamping press. He offered to buy Sam, his supervisor, a cup of coffee, and the two of them took a stroll through the plant.

	Packaging Machine Operator Candidates for Position	
Employees Name	Zeke	Smitty
Present Position	Stamping Machine Operator	Stamping Machine Operator
Work Record	Good	Good
Years of Seniority	Over 15	14
Accepted for Position	No	Yes

Zeke was one of the older men in the Stamping Department at Globe Housewares. He was a huge man who, despite his formidable appearance, was (fortunately!) usually gentle and good-natured. But today, something was bothering him.

"Hey, Sam," he said as they sauntered by the paint shop, "I think I got screwed."

"What do you mean?" asked Sam, surprised.

"Well, I've been thinking it over and over about Smitty getting the job on the packaging machine. I figure Norman Reilley had that whole business planned that way, right from the start."

Zeke was referring to the recent transfer of his friend Smitty to the Shipping Department. Smitty had been working in the Stamping

Department for fourteen years, while Zeke had worked there for over fifteen.

The new job was much better than working on a stamping press. The packaging machine was cleaner and quieter; it involved a greater variety of things to do, and it paid slightly more. Norman Reilley was the supervisor in the Shipping Department, where the packaging machine was located.

"First of all," Zeke went on, "Norman Reilley and Smitty are pals—they bowl together every week. But Norman and I just don't get along somehow. Everybody knows that."

"Well, OK," Sam conceded. Over the years it had become obvious that these two rubbed each other the wrong way.

"So the idea of me being next in line for the packaging machine job must've galled the hell out of him, once he found out Grebstein was going to quit. I don't give a damn what Norman Reilley thinks of me personally, but I had a right to get that job, and I don't think Norman Reilley's likes and dislikes are a good enough reason to screw me out of it."

"But I don't see how he *could* have done that even if he wanted to," Sam interrupted. "Grebstein left suddenly, without telling anyone beforehand. Norman Reilley didn't have any choice in what he did; even the union didn't question it."

"You know what I figure?" growled Zeke. "I figure Norman Reilley knew *exactly* when Grebstein was going to quit, same as he knew beforehand when Grebstein was going to take his vacation last summer. In fact, I'll bet you Norman Reilley *told* Grebstein to take his vacation the same time as me, but to keep his mouth shut about it."

Sam frowned. Now that he thought about it, there *had* been something strange about Norman Reilley's dealings with Grebstein.

Sam remembered that during the past summer, two days before Zeke was to begin his three-week vacation, Norman Reilley had come over and told Sam that Grebstein had made a special request to take the same three weeks off. Norman Reilley had granted the request, which had something to do with an illness in the family.

Zeke had been "officially" offered the temporary position, which he would have liked, but obviously couldn't take; Zeke couldn't reschedule his vacation at the last moment. Neither could his wife, who also worked. So Smitty, who was next in line in seniority, took the temporary transfer.

At the end of his three-week vacation, Grebstein was back on the packaging machine and Smitty returned to his stamping press.

Sam had forgotten about the incident until the previous week, when Grebstein suddenly left. Norman Reilley immediately offered

Smitty the packaging machine job on a permanent basis. The experience Smitty had gained the previous summer put him first in line for the position. Although Zeke had more seniority, the union contract provided that only when two people had equal ability did the senior person have first chance at a transfer to a new job. Norman Reilley had claimed that because of Smitty's recent training, he had "superior ability" to run the packaging machine, and because of the urgency and disruption caused by Grebstein's sudden leaving, there "wasn't time to fool around breaking in a new man."

Sam was beginning to understand what Zeke was driving at.

"You mean you figure that Norman Reilley knew a long time in advance that Grebstein was going to quit in the fall, and he made some sort of deal with him?" asked Sam.

"Yeah," replied Zeke, getting visibly angry. "I figure he asked Grebstein to take his vacation the same time I did, but to say nothing about it 'til the last minute. That would be easy for Grebstein to do. He keeps to himself anyway. Then Norman Reilley must've worked out the business with Grebstein about giving the required two weeks' notice and then using up his accumulated sick leave those last two weeks, so that Norman Reilley would be forced to 'act fast' and the union couldn't raise hell. That's what I figure."

"Well, hell, I dunno," replied Sam, shrugging his shoulders. "What you're saying certainly makes a lot of sense. It *could've* happened that way, but then again, it *could've* all been coincidence. One thing's for sure: You'd better be damn certain you've got some solid evidence before you start making accusations."

"Yeah, I know," admitted Zeke, "and I don't want to put Smitty in the middle. He's still a good friend, and I'm sure he had nothing to do with all this."

"Come on," said Sam, relieved that Zeke seemed to feel better after getting it off his chest. "We'd better get back to work. Let's both keep our ears open for a couple of days, and then talk some more."

CHECK YOUR PROGRESS

1. What is meant by "politics" in the work place?

2. "Politicians" tend to avoid straightforward actions to accomplish their purposes, because this leaves them open to criticism from the union and from higher management. How does this strategy of "arranging opportunities" help to avoid such criticism?

3. How can a supervisor detect if a "politician" is trying to accomplish some hidden purpose?

4. Why should a supervisor *avoid* a hasty accusation of someone who is strongly suspected of a political game?

1. "Politics in the work place" involves the things people do and the decisions they make that have hidden purposes.

2. People are criticized for the choices they make. A smart "politician" will realize this, and escape criticism by making it *appear* that he has *little choice* in his decisions. He accomplishes this by thinking ahead and asking himself, "How can I make this look as though I didn't have much choice?" Then he does those things that will change the situation so that later on, people will think, "He did the right thing. It was his only reasonable choice."

3. If a person is really good at "politics," there may be no sure way to tell.

4. A supervisor can't win in this situation! If right, the accusation is hard to prove; if wrong, the accused person has been done a great injustice. Either way, the person accused will become a permanent enemy.

Further Thoughts

Given the facts before them, Sam and Zeke could not be sure whether or not Norman Reilley had pulled a "political move." How *could* they be sure?

> *A "politician" cannot be recognized on the basis of a single incident, which is all the information that Sam and Zeke have. To be certain, they need to observe the overall pattern of Norman Reilley's behavior. If there are many situations that look like they may have been "sneaky deals," then their suspicion becomes more justified. A really smart politician, however, will cover his tracks so well that it's almost impossible to discover a pattern.*

The political strategy that Norman Reilley was suspected of using was the *manipulation of opportunities* to serve his private interests. An equally common political strategy is to manipulate information. How does this work?

> *The politician wants decisions to "go his way"—that is, to be made in such a way that he (or she) will benefit. People in organizations make decisions on the basis of the information that comes to their attention, not on the basis of all the facts. Thus the politician tries to manipulate the information that comes to other peoples' attention. This may take a variety of forms:*

1. The politician may *withhold* key information so that the other person (who needs the information) will appear to be less competent. This helps the politician, for instance, when he's competing with the other person for a promotion and wants to discredit his competitor.

2. The politician may deliberately give *wrong* information, so that the

person using it will look bad. This is riskier than withholding information, since the victim will be more aware of the trick that was pulled on him, and will look for revenge, or the victim may succeed in getting off the hook by passing the blame to the politician.

3. The politician may give *incomplete* information or give it *too late* to help the other person. These are usually less risky strategies, since the politician can give the impression he was "doing his best to help."

There are many other forms of information manipulation, the strategies available being limited only by the politician's imagination. For instance,

4. The politician may *trade* information for favors. He may tap into the grapevine (by rewarding people who bring him valuable information) and thereby put himself into a position to "tip off" influential people in exchange for later favors.

5. He may *start rumors* (true or false) that will make competitors look bad.

6. He may *upstage* competitors by stealing their thunder—by providing valuable information, before his competitors do, to the people they seek to impress.

7. He, may, as a supervisor, *limit* the information that reaches his workers, so that he can keep tight control over the decisions they make.

8. The politician may *manipulate* the boss's *perception* of his performance. He does this by suppressing unfavorable information.

9. When the ambitious politician feels that the time is ripe to move up into his boss's job, he may bypass his boss and start dealing with the person two levels above him. This creates the image that the politician's immediate boss is incompetent, and that the politician needs to go around the boss in order to do his job properly. If this strategy works, the boss is seen as an obstacle to progress, while the politician is seen as being conscientious and showing a lot of initiative.

The "political" supervisor usually adopts the strategy of surrounding himself (or herself) with loyal supporters who will tend to look the other way when he bends the rules. How does he (or she) get away with doing this? How would he respond if someone accused him of bringing his pals (his "lieutenants") into the department and putting them in key positions?

The crux of the political supervisor's argument would be that he (or she) was building a team in order to accomplish the department's goals most effectively and efficiently. Such a team, he would argue, requires cooperative workers, and the supervisor himself is the best judge of whom he can work with. Higher management is not likely to quarrel with this argument, provided the supervisor has not openly violated any explicit rules (and good politicians seldom do!)

Virtually all employee performance rating forms (and recommendations of all sorts) include a rating of the cooperativeness of the worker. Sometimes a different phrase is used (e.g., "displays good work attitude," or "contributes willingly to departmental mission," etc.) but the general meaning remains the same. This item on a rating form is most useful to the political supervisor because it is not easily and not often challenged.

It is not easily challenged, because it is a matter of the supervisor's subjective judgment. For a worker to challenge a "cooperativeness" rating requires objective contradictory evidence, which is hard to produce. Even if the worker did succeed in making his case, the supervisor is not likely to be criticized, since he could claim that he was just stating his honest opinion.

It is not often challenged, because cooperativeness carries a lot of weight. Cooperativeness is accepted by American businessmen as a worker characteristic of great importance. In many cases, it is valued over technical skills. The reasoning is common sense. If most employees are generally cooperative, control is possible (see "Further Thoughts" in Chapter 3), and employees will work harmoniously towards the company goals.

The words "most" and "generally" are carefully chosen; there are dangers in extremes. If few employees were cooperative, there would be anarchy and chaos. If all employees were totally cooperative, the work force would consist of robots, and would lack the characteristics needed to adapt to a changing environment. There would be little innovation, since innovation is usually the work of the mavericks in the organization. More importantly, there would be no one to question assumptions—to force the supervisor to think through why he does things—and the lack of this vitalizing force (which some supervisors short-sightedly try to remove from their organizations) brings stagnation.

1. **Keep conflict to a healthy minimum.** A small amount is unavoidable, given human nature. But large amounts can be very destructive.

2. **Deal with conflict openly.** Allow workers to express their gripes, but encourage them to be **constructive** in doing so. (That is, make sure they focus on how to **correct** the problem.)

3. **Avoid inviting hidden conflict.** If your regular dealings with workers are full of hidden strategies, you're inviting them to resort to similar strategies as a defense.

4. **Don't underestimate the power of a work group.** Close-knit groups can "make or break" a supervisor, depending on what they feel he (or she) deserves.

Conflict in the Work Place

17

A CRITICAL INCIDENT: He Who Lives by the Sword. . . .

Norman Reilley, supervisor of the Shipping Department at Globe House-wares, was more than ready for his upcoming vacation. He really felt drained. It seemed his job had become one big nightmare—an endless stream of salesmen's complaints about shipping errors. The only thing worse than the complaints was the half-hearted, don't-give-a-damn excuses from his workers as to why the mistakes had happened.

The situation had been getting worse, over the past year, and Norman had no idea what to do about it. He'd worked hard to keep the sales force happy! He had accepted all their special orders, their rush orders, and all their last-minute changes. Norman figured that treating the salesmen right really paid off. The word was regularly passed along to Norman's boss that the sales force viewed him as a cooperative and very responsive supervisor.

However, the word was also reaching his boss that there was an increasing number of errors in "normal" shipments, and his boss had been leaning on him to straighten the problem out.

Norman refused to listen to his workers when they tried to ex-plain that there was a basic conflict between taking on rush orders, and the smooth, efficient handling of regular orders. He would just give them the command, "Drop everything, and get this special order out fast!" and not realize that all the "loose ends" he was thus creating increased the chances of mistakes.

Norman never talked over the problems in his department with his boss. Instead, he covered them up. A smooth talker, Norman had his boss convinced that there was no conflict in his department, that he was "running a tight ship" with everything under control. The shipping errors were blamed on the workers and the union. "You can't get good help any more," he would say. "You can't even shape up the zombies you've got! The union won't let you."

What was so upsetting to Norman was that no increase in effort on his part seemed to fix the problem. He practically hovered over his workers, spot-checking their work. He even read them the list of the previous week's errors at the weekly department meeting. Nothing seemed to help, because nobody cared. He was sick of the blank faces.

In a sense, Norman was right. Most of the workers in his depart-ment really *didn't* care any more. They had gotten sick of Norman's angry face long before he got sick of their blank faces.

They figured, why should they go out of their way only to make

Norman look good? He never did anything for them. All he cared about was good reports getting to his boss from the salesmen. He was helping himself at their expense.

Norman didn't even listen when they tried to talk to him about problems they were having doing the work. He just wanted RESULTS!

What bothered them most of all, though, was the slick way Norman would pull off deals to take care of his pals and the few workers who would "kiss his feet." It was obvious that the only thing you could get rewarded for was loyalty to Norman.

No one dared grumble in front of Norman; it was sure to bring on a humiliating "chewing out" in front of the other workers. He had an ugly temper, and was vicious when it was aroused. So people grumbled behind his back. It was their unhappiness which eventually brought about Norman's downfall.

The grumbling really increased when Norman Reilley had Smitty transferred from the Stamping Department to replace Grebstein on the packaging machine. The workers were sure that Norman had manipulated the situation so that his bowling pal, Smitty, got the job. The whole arrangement looked so much like other shady deals that Norman had pulled. It fell into a neat pattern.

After this particular incident, many workers who hadn't previously talked about their distrust of Norman began discussing his "political" tactics quite openly. As a result of these gripe sessions, it was generally agreed among the workers that if everyone put in only the minimum amount of work, Norman couldn't single out any one worker and fire him or her. The union wouldn't allow it! Consequently, over the past year, the number of salesmen's complaints had gradually increased from a previous average of ten per week to an average of nearly twenty-five.

The atmosphere of general hostility and fear in the department was just right when Grant, one of the shipping clerks, had a brainstorm on the eve of Norman's department for vacation.

On the Friday night that Norman Reilley had breathed a sigh of relief and left in his mobile home to start three weeks of vacation, Grant met with Maury, another shipping clerk. Over a beer, Grant explained his idea.

"Look, Maury, this is our big chance!" Grant said to a worried-looking Maury.

"But what if it backfires? Norman will have our heads!" replied Maury.

"He can't get *all* of us," Grant assured him, "and we know exactly who we can trust in the department not to talk about it."

Maury soon agreed to help Grant in getting support for his plan.

Over the weekend, they visited or telephoned all the other "trustworthy" workers—those who hadn't "sold out" to Norman. Very little persuasion was necessary!

The plan was for everyone to work very hard and very carefully for the next three weeks, while Norman Reilley was on vacation. The idea was to make it plain that the department was better off without Norman.

The following Monday morning, with Norman Reilley miles away, the Shipping Department really came alive. Gone were the long faces and the dragging feet. Workers were actually cheerful as they bustled about!

Inconspicuously, the workers made some changes in procedures. After an order was assembled for shipment, another worker would check it for accuracy. Workers consulted with each other on potential problems. No one, of course, tipped off Norman's cronies about what was happening.

The workers also began contacting salesmen to recheck orders that were not clear. Previously, the workers had said "to hell with it" and packed the shipments any old way, later using the unclear order as an excuse to get Norman off their backs. None of Norman's henchmen knew what was really going on, but the salesmen certainly noticed the changes, and rejoiced!

With all the extra care that was given to each shipment, the work took longer, but the workers were having so much fun getting back at Norman that they took shorter coffee breaks and occasionally worked part of the lunch hour.

As a result, not only could they keep pace, but the backlog of orders was cleaned out by the end of the first week. By the end of the second week, salesmen were no longer requesting rush orders, since *everything* was going out as if it were a rush order! By the end of the third week, the department was neat as a pin, and humming along like a well-oiled machine. And there were no salesmen's complaints.

Of course, when Norman Reilley's boss stopped by the department each morning to see how everything was going, he received glowing reports.

When Norman returned from his vacation, the department returned to normal. Back came the long faces and lifeless shuffling about, and back came the sloppy work habits. By the end of Norman's first week back on the job, there were twenty-two complaints and a backlog of unfilled orders.

This time, however, Norman's boss had little patience with Norman's excuses about the quality of the workers and the union. It was obvious that the department ran better without Norman, and there was a lot of heat from the sales manager, now that chaos had returned to the shipping operations. Norman Reilley was called in and told that his services were no longer needed.

CHECK YOUR PROGRESS

1. Should a supervisor try to eliminate *all* conflict in the department?

2. What strategy should a supervisor use in dealing with conflict when it occurs in the work place?

3. How does the supervisor *invite* hidden conflict?

4. How is it that workers, who have no authority at all, sometimes can muster enough power to make or break a supervisor?

ANSWERS TO PROGRESS QUESTIONS

1. No, since a small amount of conflict is unavoidable. A supervisor should try to keep conflict to a minimum, though, since large amounts can be very destructive.
2. Deal with conflict *openly*, by letting workers *express* what is bothering them. The supervisor, however, should insist that the worker is constructive in his (or her) complaint, focusing on how to *correct* the problem.
3. If a supervisor chooses "political" strategies as his way of operating, he (or she) will be setting a dangerous example for workers to follow.
4. Individually, workers are powerless. But a close-knit work *group* may have enough power to dominate what goes on in a department. This can work for or against a supervisor.

Further Thoughts

Was Norman Reilley's boss justified in firing Norman?

> *Yes. Norman's willingness to work hard and support the sales effort was not sufficient to offset his shortcomings, namely, mounting complaints, a boss unhappy with his performance, and the inability to resolve routine conflicts within his work group. He was barely hanging on to his job; the dramatic difference in results while he was away on vacation brought about his firing sooner, but it would likely have eventually happened anyway.*

Suppose that upon his return from vacation, Norman had somehow found *out* that Grant and Maury had planned this conspiracy against him. What alternatives did he then have, and what are the advantages and disadvantages of each one?

1. Talk with Maury and Grant to try and find out why they did it, and thereby learn from the experience.

2. Severely discipline Grant and Maury, such as by trying to get them fired.

3. Appeal to his boss that he was the victim of a conspiracy, and to be fired under such circumstances would be morally wrong.

4. Admit to his boss that he could have handled his department better. Then try to convince his boss he has learned something from the experience, and should be retained at least in some other position within the company.

> *Norman had four main alternatives available to him:*
>
> *1. He could have talked with the two conspirators, tried to find out why they did it, and hoped to learn from the experience.*

190

This alternative is probably a poor choice. Considering Norman's past behavior, it is unlikely he would have anything to gain from this course of action. After all, Grant and Maury would not have been able to achieve their goal without the long build-up of dissatisfaction. Thus Norman probably could not hope to become an effective supervisor of that department even if he was able to learn from his experience. Time had run out on Norman. There could be no going back.

2. *Norman could have severely disciplined Grant and Maury or even fired them.*

This would have also been a poor choice for Norman. At that point, he would have had no support from his work group or his boss for such an action. After all, the two conspirators had not broken any rules (they had only done their jobs!), thus Norman had no grounds for taking disciplinary action. The union would never permit it.

3. *Norman could have appealed to his boss that he had been the victim of a conspiracy, pointing out that to be fired under such circumstances would be morally wrong.*

This alternative may be worth a try, although it would have been unlikely to work. The difference in performance while Norman was away had been quite dramatic, so that it must have been fairly obvious to the boss that the workers must have been trying hard during Norman's absence. However, the boss would have felt justified in firing Norman merely because the workers were better motivated and the department functioned better without Norman. Thus Norman could expect little sympathy in contending that he was the victim of a conspiracy.

4. *He could have admitted to his boss that he could have handled his department better. Then he could have tried to convince his boss that he had learned something from the experience, and thus he should be retained at least in some other position within the company.*

This may also have been worth a try, although it would have been a long shot. Norman did not have the union to protect him, and at that point, he could expect little support from his boss.

Transfer to another position within the company could have solved the immediate conflict with the Shipping Department employees, but it wouldn't have given Norman a truly "fresh start," since his reputation by then had spread throughout the plant.

Why do you think Norman was more concerned with looking good to the sales force than in keeping pace in his own department? Could you advise a better strategy?

Norman faced a dilemma: If he responded to every special request from the sales force, it would disrupt the processing of routine orders. If, on the other hand, he devoted himself entirely to the smooth flow of routine work, it would disrupt the sales effort, because special situations do arise from time to time, and these require flexible performance in the shipping department.

In solving this dilemma, Norman thought only of his own selfish interests. He wanted to get ahead in the company—he wanted a promotion to a job with more pay, higher status, and greater power. He figured that this would require his being noticed by his boss and other people in higher management.

With "being noticed" foremost in his mind, Norman chose one extreme solution to his dilemma—he responded to every special request from the sales force. This made his performance as a supervisor highly visible. He realized that if he had followed the other strategy, and made his department run 100 percent smoothly, the department would tend to become "invisible"—no one would notice it; higher management would tend to take the department's performance for granted, and there would thus be no brownie points for Norman.

Of course, the side effects of Norman's taking the extreme position became quite visible! The resulting disruption of routines caused a landslide of customer and sales complaints. A better strategy for Norman would have been to handle some of the special orders, but to make a point of educating the sales force as to the probable repercussions of his workers' having to handle too many special orders. Salesmen might thus be able to see that too many exceptions would hinder, rather than help, the overall sales program. Unfortunately, Norman was too shortsighted to seek "cooperation through understanding."

1. Become aware of **patterns in workers' behavior** that give **early warning of an alcohol problem.**
2. Focus on the problem drinker's desire to keep from losing his (or her) job. Otherwise, there is usually little you can do to **motivate him to help himself.**
3. Find out what company or community programs are available to help the alcoholic worker. Then **be firm** in telling the worker that he must either **seek help, or risk losing his job.**
4. **Enlist help from the alcoholic's fellow workers** in supporting his efforts to help himself.

The Alcoholic Worker

18

A CRITICAL INCIDENT: Where Do You Draw the Line?

Alan glanced anxiously out the window. It was after 2 PM and one of his mechanics, Kirk, was more than an hour late in coming back from lunch.

Kirk's long lunches were not unusual. For quite some time, they had been a source of irritation for Alan. Kirk had never expressed the least objection when Alan had docked his pay for the time lost, so the matter never came to a head. But lately, it seemed to be happening more often, and the time away appeared to be getting longer and longer.

Alan was particularly upset this time, however. A customer had come in at 1:30 to pick up his car, which Kirk had used to go out for lunch. Alan had explained to the customer that the work *had* been completed, and that the mechanic was out road-testing the car.

Alan had, in fact, told a partial truth: Kirk had worked on the car right up until lunchtime. Then he had left, telling Alan he would grab a sandwich while he was out road-testing the car. This was a common practice among the mechanics at Foreign Auto Repair, Inc.

At 2 PM, the customer asked why his car needed such a long road test after just a regular tune-up. Alan had weakly replied that he didn't know; that perhaps a more serious problem had developed on the road.

At 2:30, the customer asked Alan why his mechanic wouldn't call in for help if the car was stuck somewhere.

"Maybe he couldn't get to a phone," Alan offered as an alibi.

By 2:45, the customer had taken to pacing back and forth across Alan's office, saying nothing, but occasionally glaring at Alan. The air was very tense in the shop.

At 3:10, Kirk drove up, a silly grin on his face. As he walked into the office, he seemed a bit unsteady. Alan asked him, in front of the customer, what the delay had been, pointing out that the customer had been waiting for more than an hour and a half.

"Mechanical troubles," Kirk replied, unconcerned, his words somewhat slurred. "The car quit on me—an electrical problem—It was damn hard to fix without my shop tools. But it's running OK now."

He tossed the keys on Alan's desk and headed into the shop, as if nothing had happened.

Kirk had smelled like a brewery, but neither Alan nor the customer mentioned the fact. Alan apologized to the customer for the delay, shrugging his shoulders helplessly.

The customer obviously wasn't satisfied with Kirk's excuse, or Alan's apology. But he was anxious to get out of there, and almost too angry to speak.

Alan was also fuming over the incident, but didn't know what his next step should be.

The following week, however, something happened that reminded Alan that Kirk's drinking at lunchtime was not a dead issue. Kirk got into an accident on the way back from another late lunch.

It was only a minor accident, and fortunately Kirk had been driving his own car. But it was obvious to Alan that he could no longer avoid facing his responsibilities as a supervisor. He had an obligation to do something about what was becoming a serious problem.

Alan sensed that his first move should be to clamp down on Kirk's drinking at lunchtime, but he also felt that what his mechanics did on their own time was *their* business. He figured the only justification for interfering in the private lives of his mechanics was that work schedules and the reputation of the shop were being affected.

As a further complication, he didn't know how he could tell Kirk not to drink at lunchtime, and not make the rule apply to all the mechanics. Most of them liked an occasional beer, and there had been no problems with anyone except Kirk.

Despite his being convinced that he ought to do something, it took a chance meeting with a long-time customer—a man who regularly dealt with these problems—to get things moving.

At 5 PM, Mr. Lentz, the personnel manager of the largest company in town, dropped his car off for servicing the next day. He arrived just as the mechanics were leaving for the day. His wife was to pick him up at 5:30, and Alan had to stay late anyway to catch up on some paper-work.

Alan knew that he could talk confidentially to Mr. Lentz, so he explained his problem with Kirk. Mr. Lentz listened sympathetically while Alan gave a brief account of Kirk's drinking history.

"You know, Alan," he said, when Alan had finished, "alcohol is one of *our* biggest personnel headaches. We have more problem drinkers in the plant than you'd ever believe! And it's really difficult for any-one—including a personnel expert—who has never been an alcoholic to understand what it means to be one."

"Well, how do *you* usually handle the problem?" Alan asked.

"Not very well, I'm afraid," Mr. Lentz admitted. "Some people we can help, but many we can't. It depends on how much the worker wants to help himself and if he is honest in admitting he *is* an alcoholic."

"I don't even know how to approach the problem, much less help the guy," Alan confessed. "All I know is that Kirk is one of my most loyal workers and he likes working here. I'd really like to be able to do something to help him."

Mr. Lentz suggested that the place to start was to look for various clues to decide whether the worker had an overall pattern to his be-havior that pointed to alcohol addiction.

As Mr. Lentz began to describe the key symptoms, Alan became increasingly dismayed. He realized that he'd been overlooking many clues that applied to Kirk. Three clues in particular stood out.

First, Kirk's work was inconsistent. Much of the time, he worked quickly and to high-quality standards. But occasionally—and more so in recent weeks—he seemed to take too long to complete a job, and some of his work was of poor quality, which led to customers' coming back for corrections.

Second, Kirk seemed to be getting more clumsy. Mid-morning was usually the worst time; he was particularly prone to dropping things from his trembling fingers.

In addition, Kirk was always bumping into things. The other mechanics kidded him about this, and at one point they even made him wear Herbie's motorcycle helmet—"to prevent brain damage"—when he was working under a car raised up on the lift.

Third, Alan recalled that Kirk had more "mysterious" absences than anyone else, particularly on Mondays. Kirk usually came in on the following Tuesday with a good excuse.

Alan recalled being skeptical on several occasions—he had won-dered how so many calamities could happen to one individual! But since these absences had never cost Alan anything in wages, and he could usually pinch-hit himself on jobs that couldn't wait another day, he had always let the matter slide.

All of these clues—which fit Kirk so well—were indirect evidence that a worker might be having a problem with alcohol, Mr. Lentz was explaining. When he went on to explain the more direct evidence, Alan's fears were confirmed; Kirk showed all the signs of being a problem alcoholic.

To start with, there was no escaping the constant smell of alcohol on Kirk's breath. In addition, his eyes were often bloodshot, and his face was usually flushed.

Finally, Kirk often looked drawn—almost haggard—and tended to be sluggish, particularly after one of his Monday absences. In retrospect, Alan suspected that these symptoms might have resulted from Kirk's "drinking his lunch," instead of eating solid foods.

Mr. Lentz then emphasized that individually, any of these symptoms didn't necessarily mean a thing, but that if there was a *pattern,* then something should be done.

Sensing Alan's despair, Mr. Lentz went on to suggest some positive steps that Alan might take with Kirk. In effect, he was recommending the procedures developed in his plant—after much experience and professional consultation—for supervisors who faced the same problems with a worker.

He suggested that Alan should first focus on Kirk's liking his job and wanting to keep it. Alan should be as supportive as possible in leveling with Kirk, explaining that while he liked Kirk personally, and wanted to keep him on the payroll, the drinking would have to stop. Otherwise, Kirk would lose his job.

Alan should next suggest, as diplomatically as possible, that Kirk seek help at the local chapter of Alcoholics Anonymous or the local clinic, which also had an alcohol and drug abuse program.

Mr. Lentz also advised that the other mechanics should be encouraged to support Kirk in his effort to overcome the drinking problem. They could be very influential, especially if Kirk liked and respected them. Alan resolved to talk to each one of the mechanics privately about the importance of their encouragement.

Last, Mr. Lentz convinced Alan to take a firm stand, even at the risk of losing a well-intentioned mechanic. It was important for Kirk to fully understand that he was being given an ultimatum: He must either control the drinking by himself, or accept professional help. There was no third alternative.

Alan knew that he hadn't been facing up to his responsibility as a supervisor. He also realized that he'd reached the point where he couldn't put it off any longer. It was time to draw the line. He owed that much to his customers—and to his loyal employee, Kirk.

Alan was not looking forward to the face-to-face session. Neither was he overly optimistic that Kirk would recognize he had a drinking problem, and agree to do something about it. . . .

CHECK YOUR PROGRESS

1. When you suspect that a worker is having a drinking problem, what *clues* do you look for, and how do you use these clues in making a decision to take action?

2. How does the supervisor *motivate* a problem alcoholic to help himself (or herself)?

3. Where can the supervisor find *programs* to help the worker who is addicted to alcohol?

4. Why is the support of fellow workers so crucial for an alcoholic trying to help himself?

1. The clues are inconsistent performance, accidents, trembling fingers, unexcused absences, liquor on the breath, bloodshot eyes, flushing, sluggishness, and malnutrition. Single clues may mean nothing; however, an established *pattern* is usually sufficient evidence to require taking action.

2. The supervisor must focus on the worker's desire to keep his (or her) job, and make it perfectly clear that unless the problem alcoholic does something to help himself, he risks losing his job.

3. Large companies, which recognize alcoholics as persons who are sick, often have their own medical treatment programs. Otherwise, there are usually Alcoholics Anonymous and other community programs available to the addict seeking help.

4. It is very difficult for the problem drinker to reform. If co-workers continue to provide *social support* for his drinking, the alcoholic finds reform even more difficult.

Further Thoughts

What is the relationship of accidents to alcoholism?

Studies show that although alcoholics lose more work time than nonalcoholics, they, surprisingly, do not have a higher rate of occupational accidents. This is apparently because many alcoholics, while on the job, tend to be overcautious in a deliberate attempt to avoid accidents so that they won't be discovered. Further, if in an alcoholic or hangover state, they tend to be absent rather than risk being confronted about their drinking problem. An exception is for jobs away from direct supervision, which require geographic mobility and thereby offer easier access to alcohol without the risk of discovery.

As for experiences away from work, the alcoholic clearly has a higher accident rate. For example:

1. Problem drinkers have about twice as many accidents per mile of driving as does the nondrinking population. Also, about 50 percent of auto-related fatalities involved significant blood alcohol levels in either or both drivers and pedestrians, if the latter were involved.

2. The total fatal accident rate in alcoholic workers is twice that of nondrinkers. Other than auto accidents, this is attributed to a much higher incidence of home accidents caused by excessive drinking.

What are the characteristics of the work group that could help Alan in dealing with Kirk's drinking problem?

The group of auto mechanics, of which Kirk is a long-term mem-

ber, is basically close-knit (cohesive); therefore, its members will tend to stick together, to help and protect one another. Individuals in groups such as this can be seen doing such things as loaning one another their cars or "ten bucks" 'til payday," going on picnics with each others' families, sharing both happy and sad personal happenings, remembering and celebrating birthdays, and paying visits to hospitals, etc. Since Kirk is an established and well-liked member of such a group, Alan can probably count on their willingness to help with Kirk's problem.

Also, there is no evidence to indicate that other members of the group are problem drinkers, nor that the group norm endorses heavy drinking. If Kirk could accept the group's moderate drinking pattern as his standard and adhere to it, the problem would be a lot easier for him.

One can also assume that the group has good rapport with Alan and trusts him. It is not likely that skilled mechanics would stay with a small independent owner-operator for many years if they mistrusted him, since they usually can easily find jobs elsewhere. Alan can take advantage of this bond of trust by leveling with the group about the severity of Kirk's problem and the strong possibility that Kirk will have to be fired. In return, Alan will likely get their assurance of help and understanding.

Note that Alan would have little or no hope of getting help from the work group if:

1. Kirk were an "outcast" or disliked by the informal leader(s) of the group.
2. Group members were competitive and chose not to help one another for fear it would hurt their position, status, or earnings.
3. The group were not close-knit, but rather unconcerned about dealing with matters affecting its members.
4. The technology were such that there was little chance to build up bonds of friendship and trust (such as a farm operation employing migrant workers, or isolated jobs in a factory).
5. The group did not want to deal with the issue of alcoholism—perhaps because it was complex and "scary," and therefore they felt it should only be handled by professionals.
6. The group sensed that Alan wasn't really serious about going so far as to fire Kirk, because of his willingness to overlook Kirk's drinking problems in the past.

What is the difference between alcohol, heroin, and marijuana?

Medically speaking, all three are drugs. There are two significant differences, however.

1. There is a social difference between these drugs in that two are illegal in our culture, while the third, alcohol, happens to be legal.

Two receive social disapproval; the third receives considerable social approval.

The legality and the social approval are closely connected. During the prohibition era, the legal status of alcohol was changed so that it became, in effect, a controlled drug. Prohibition didn't work, however, because the social approval continued. The recent softening of the laws relating to marijuana can also be attributed to growing social approval by younger people. Heroin, however, continues to be tightly controlled, since its legal status is congruent with its social disapproval.

2. The medical difference between the three drugs is actually quite shocking. Alcohol is considered by some medical experts to be the worst of the three. It takes longer to get addicted to alcohol than to heroin, but the effects of addiction are much more severe with alcohol.

A heroin addict can be cured "cold turkey" (i.e., simply deprived of the drug and confined until the withdrawal symptoms subside). The same cure can literally kill an alcoholic, since his whole metabolism becomes adapted to his overdoses. Furthermore, alcohol overdoses often cause brain damage, a chronic condition which is seldom curable, and may even be fatal.

Since marijuana is nonaddictive and there is controversy over whether it has any medically proven physiological consequences, it is a curious quirk of history that it has been outlawed while alcohol remains, as strongly as ever, the basis of the social institution of drinking!

1. Avoid being charged with **discrimination** when writing up the requirements that job applicants have to meet. **Get expert advice** if you aren't sure of the law.
2. Make sure that every requirement you set is **significantly related to actual job performance.**
3. **Watch carefully how you ask questions** when interviewing job applicants. Many kinds of inquiries that **were acceptable** in the past are **now unlawful.**
4. **Don't waste your energy fighting "affirmative action"** policies. What may seem "unfair" to nonminority workers is really for the good of all **in the long run.**

Discrimination
and the Law

19

A CRITICAL INCIDENT: Learning about the Law—The Hard Way!

Albert was about to retire from his job. He had run the tool crib in the Machining Department at Precision Electronics for more than twenty years.

Vince needed to find a replacement, so he had to write up a hiring notice for the Personnel Department. What made Vince's task difficult was that there was no job description to refer to. No one had ever taken the trouble to write one up.

Vince asked Albert what was involved in the job, and what skills were necessary. Then he wrote up what he thought was a good hiring notice (see Exhibit 19-1), which he sent to Personnel.

POSITION OPENING IN MACHINING DEPARTMENT
PRECISION ELECTRONICS CO.

Title: _____ Tool Crib Man _____

Major Responsibilities: Care and inventory of micrometers,
testing equipment, machine tools,
drill bits, special machine attachments,
and related equipment.

Qualifications
Required for the Job: Machine shop experience, in good health,
under age 55, ability to work accurately
with numbers.

Starting Date: Soon as possible

EXHIBIT 19-1

Within two hours, the Personnel Manager dropped by Vince's office to tell him that the notice was discriminatory and would have to be rewritten.

Vince was surprised to learn that the hiring notice actually could have led to at least four charges of discrimination, due to violations of the Equal Employment Opportunity Act.

First, by using the title, "Tool Crib *Man*" instead of "Tool Crib *Attendant*," Vince was discriminating on the basis of sex.

Second, the "machine shop experience" requirement implied that job applicants should be able to operate machines in the shop. This was obviously not a truly job-related requirement. The Personnel Manager suggested that Vince change the wording to read, "Knowledge of machine shop equipment and parts is desirable."

As Vince sat stunned, it was further pointed out to him that the "good health" requirement could be interpreted as discrimination against the handicapped.

"Look, I don't care if the person's handicapped!" Vince protested. "I just want someone who'll show up at work regularly. Whenever Albert was out sick, *I* had to jump in and cover the tool crib."

"Yeah, I know, Vince," The Personnel Manager replied, sympathetically. "But you really ought to change it to something more in line with the law."

They rewrote it to read, "able to meet climbing and lifting job requirements." This didn't get at the "good health" requirement, but at least it was job-related, and nondiscriminatory.

The fourth objectionable standard in the hiring notice was the "under age 55" requirement. The Personnel Manager explained that it was illegal to discriminate on the basis of age between forty and sixty-five.

Vince threw up his hands. He explained that he had only specified "under age fifty-five" because of the company's retirement program. Ten years' service was necessary in order to be eligible for benefits upon mandatory retirement at age sixty-five.

The Personnel Manager advised Vince to make no reference at all to age in the hiring notice. The retirement issue could be handled informally. Qualified applicants from outside the company over fifty-five years old would be warned of their ineligibility for retirement benefits. Then it would be *their* decision to turn down the job.

With these changes made, the revised hiring notice was posted around the plant and appeared in local newspapers (see Exhibit 19–2). Within the next week, Vince interviewed five candidates. Each one would have been competent to do the job, but Vince picked out a forty-year-old man who had the advantage of prior machine shop experience.

Two weeks later, however, Vince had another visit from the Personnel Manager. One of the female applicants had filed a discrimination complaint against Vince and the company.

"You got yourself in trouble," the personnel manager explained, "when you ask her whether she had someone to take care of her kids."

"Aw, come on!" Vince groaned, in disbelief. "That just came up in a general conversation we were having. I was explaining to her that the tool crib absolutely *had* to be open at 8 AM. Otherwise my machinists would be standing around waiting for their machine tools. I've

```
┌─────────────────────────────────────────────────────────────┐
│        POSITION OPENING IN MACHINING DEPARTMENT              │
│               PRECISION ELECTRONICS CO.                      │
│                                                              │
│   Title:              Tool Crib Attendant                    │
│   ─────────────────────────────────────────────────────     │
│                                                              │
│   Major Responsibilities:  Care and inventory of micrometers,│
│                            testing equipment, machine tools, │
│                            drill bits, special machine       │
│                            attachments,                      │
│                            and related equipment.            │
│                                                              │
│   Qualifications                                             │
│    Required for the Job:   Knowledge of machine shop         │
│                            equipment and                     │
│                            parts is desirable; able to meet  │
│                            climbing                          │
│                            and lifting job requirements;     │
│                            ability                           │
│                            to work accurately with numbers.  │
│                                                              │
│   Starting Date:           Soon as possible                  │
│                                                              │
└─────────────────────────────────────────────────────────────┘
```

EXHIBIT 19-2

always asked questions about peoples' reliability. It's good business sense."

"Your intentions were good, Vince," the Personnel Manager assured him, "but your question was unlawful. It discriminates against women and wasn't *specifically* related to her ability to do the job. I'm afraid she has a strong case against us."

"I don't believe it!" Vince exclaimed. "How the hell was I supposed to ask her if she could show up on time every day? My wife can't drop off our kids before 8:30. I needed to know if the applicant had the same problem."

"Well, it's always easier to figure out what a guy should have done after the fact," the Personnel Manager began, trying to be supportive. "But times have changed. Questions have to be asked differently. In the eyes of the law, all you can say is, 'It's very important that the tool crib be open no later than 8 AM, and stay open until 5 PM. Is that going to be a problem for you?'"

Vince just sat in his chair looking dejected, so the personnel manager went on to explain.

"You see, Vince, in this way, she knows the company requirements for working hours *without* bringing up the subject of children. It's really none of the company's business *who* takes care of the children, so long as she does her job properly."

"OK," Vince conceded. "I get the point. But what do I do now?"

"I don't know," he replied. "Sit tight for now. The woman has an application pending for another job in the plant, which pays more, anyway. If she gets that job, she'll probably drop the complaint."

Vince just shook his head.

"In the meantime, I'd like to bring up the fact that you turned down a minority male in your final choice. I'll be honest with you. The subject came up in a management meeting we had on Affirmative Action. The Plant Manager *had* considered overruling your decision, but decided not to."

Vince was shocked. "I made my final decision on the basis of who was best qualified," he explained. "From a *personal* standpoint, I thought the black guy could have done the job almost as well, and he had a much better sense of humor. I would have rather hired *him*, except his qualifications were weaker."

"You probably *should* have hired him," the Personnel Manager said seriously. "There aren't enough blacks working in the plant. Top management keeps pointing this out to me, since we've got to be careful about compliance procedures with our federal government contracts."

"How do you know when you've got enough?" Vince asked, irritably. "We seem to have quite a few."

"Thirty percent of the people in this city are black," was the reply. "Company policy is that we should have at least thirty percent of our labor force black."

"But if I *had* hired the black guy, I would have been discriminating against the better-qualified white guy!" Vince pointed out.

"Look, Vince. I don't disagree with what you're saying, but there's another way of looking at the situation. You picked the white guy because he had previous experience in a machine shop.

Well, it's likely the black guy never got the *chance* to work in a machine shop. That's because not so long ago, blacks were excluded from the crafts. That means the white guy started out by getting a break! And without Affirmative Action, the white guy's gonna get *more* breaks, just because he got the first one.

"The cycle has to be broken somewhere, and this company is going along with Affirmative Action guidelines. It may *seem* unfair in the short run, and maybe it is. But in the long run, its going to be best for everyone."

"Well, I dunno," Vince grunted. "I gotta think about it."

CHECK YOUR PROGRESS

1. How can you be sure that job requirements are in line with the law?

2. How can a supervisor avoid being charged with discrimination when setting up job requirements for new applicants?

3. A supervisor with many years of experience in interviewing job applicants is unlikely to get into trouble with the law. True or false?

4. Affirmative Action programs are designed to eliminate unfairness to minorities. But in some cases, they operate in a way that is unfair to *non*minorities. Why, then, are these programs tolerated?

ANSWERS TO PROGRESS QUESTIONS

1. Read and try to understand the laws applicable in your state. If in doubt, seek expert advice.
2. Job requirements must be significantly related to actual job performance. Thus decisions based on such irrelevant characteristics regarding ability to perform as race, sex, and national origin are discriminatory and unlawful.
3. False. Many kinds of inquiries that were acceptable in the past are now unlawful. Supervisors with lots of pre-Affirmative Action interviewing experience need to change their approach, to conform to the latest laws.
4. In the short run, there may be some "discrimination" against nonminorities. But in the long run, Affirmative Action should create more equal opportunities for everyone.

Further Thoughts

Management policy regarding employment of minorities can reflect a wide range of alternatives. At one extreme, a company may continue to discriminate, in violation of the law, even though it risks penalties if detected. At the other extreme, a company may go to the extra expense of trying to adjust or create jobs so that they are within the capabilities of minority workers who are socially disadvantaged. Experience has shown that most companies choose to operate somewhere in between these extremes. What are four workable approaches that reflect various "middle-ground" positions?

Four "moderate" policy alternatives regarding the employment of minorities are:

1. *Be neutral and "color blind,"* not changing hiring policies, but insisting that decisions be made *strictly on ability* without regard to color. (This was essentially what Vince tried to do.)
2. Maintain current job standards, but make *greater efforts to recruit minorities* who meet the standards. (Employment agencies and extensive advertising can help here.)
3. Hire minority members even though they are not the *best* qualified, as long as they meet *minimum standards*. (This was the position supported by the personnel manager at Precision Electronics.)
4. Hire and then *provide special training* for minorities who do not meet minimum standards but eventually might be qualified. [This was done under the National Alliance of Businessmen (NAB) programs (between 1967 and 1971).]

In order to enforce affirmative action laws, the federal government uses a *contract compliance* procedure to help eliminate discrimination. How does this procedure work?

The contract compliance procedure takes advantage of the federal government's role as a large purchaser from private industry. Any company with a substantial government contract must have effective Affirmative Action programs. The company is required periodically to report the racial composition of its work force on a job-by-job basis. If there is an insufficient number of minority members in any job category, the company is required to specify steps that it will take to eliminate the imbalance. Failure to do so can result in loss of the government contract. Obviously, supervisors in such situations need to be particularly sensitive to quotas on all jobs within their departments.

Exceptions can be made to the *age* and *sex* provisions of fair employment laws, but only when such exceptions are based on bona fide (i.e., sincere) occupational qualifications. How can a legal exception be made for (1) hiring *only* a male or *only* a female; and (2) hiring based on age.

Exceptions regarding sex can be made where it is a bona fide occupational qualification, such as a female to model women's clothes; or where it is a bona fide factor in terms of community standards of morality or propriety, such as a male to work as an attendant in a men's washroom or a woman to work as a fitter in a women's foundation garment store.

Exceptions regarding age can be made where it is a bona fide factor in connection with job performance, such as airline pilots; where it is a bona fide factor in an apprentice training or on-the-job training program of long duration; and where it is a bona fide factor in fulfilling the provisions of other statutes, such as laws regulating employment of minors.

An employer or supervisor who is not sure if a particular job qualifies as an exception may file with the Division of Human Rights within his state for a supplemental interpretation of the bona fide occupational qualification provisions of the law.

1. **Fire only as a last resort.** Always do your best to **first try to "salvage" the worker.** Then you'll get more respect and support from other workers if firing later becomes necessary.

2. **Use probation periods** to protect your right to dismiss questionable workers. Remember, the longer a worker is on the payroll, the harder it is to fire that person.

3. If you decide that you **must** fire a worker, **be impersonal and businesslike.** Build a sound case to support your decision, using as many facts and witnesses as possible.

4. **Ease the pain of being fired** by suggesting or even helping with alternative employment for the worker. Take the approach that the worker would be "better off working somewhere else."

Firing a Worker

20

A CRITICAL INCIDENT: When All Else Fails. . . .

Marvin walked into his office in the Accounts Receivable Department at Allied Industries on Monday morning to find Sylvia already sitting there waiting for him. One look told Marvin she was furious.

"You wanna know why Jennifer quit?" she asked, before he could even say hello.

"Why did she?" Marvin asked her, somewhat startled.

"Because Wally wouldn't leave her alone," Sylvia replied, icily.

"You mean . . ." Marvin began.

"I mean sexually," she snapped.

Marvin sank down into his chair, his coat still on.

"How do you know?" he asked, weakly.

"I ran into Jennifer yesterday," Sylvia replied. "She told me the whole thing. Wally was after the poor girl from the moment she started working here. He threatened to see she got fired for incompetence if she opened her mouth."

"Well if that's true . . ."

"I *know* it's true," she interrupted him, slapping her hand on the armrest.

"Just *hold on,* Sylvia!" Marvin said, emphatically. "If it's true, Jennifer's going to have to file a complaint before I can do anything about it."

"She won't," Sylvia said, sullenly. "She's too scared. I tried to talk her into it, but she doesn't want a scene."

Marvin took his coat off and began pacing.

"All I can do is *talk* to Wally," Marvin finally said. "If Jennifer won't come forward, I can't make any accusations. I can't fire someone just on the basis of hearsay. Especially someone with a lot of seniority with the company."

"Well, Wally isn't any prize as a worker!" Sylvia reminded him. "He only puts in the bare minimum of effort. And he's so negative about everything! You should fire him just for constantly disrupting the teamwork around here."

"I know it's no secret that Wally's bitter about never having been promoted," Marvin admitted. "And frankly, you're not the first to suggest to me that the department would run better if Wally was replaced. But to fire him on the basis of a sexual intimidation charge I can't prove—that's just asking for a grievance."

"Well if you do *nothing,* what does that tell the rest of us?"

Sylvia demanded to know. "That as long as we do a minimum job and don't actually get caught doing anything bad, then everything's OK?"

"Sylvia, please try to see the position I'm in," Marvin pleaded. "I've got to treat Wally fairly even if he's a bad worker. If he'd been caught stealing or beating somebody up, we'd have a different situation. But as it is, he's never given me sufficient grounds to fire him."

"Yeah, I guess you're right," Sylvia said, more sympathetically. "But please don't give up trying!"

When Sylvia had left his office, Marvin thought back to Jennifer's sudden disappearance from the office two weeks previously. She had worked as a clerk for only a month, then had suddenly quit. She had given no explanation, other than "personal reasons."

Wally had been coaching Jennifer's work. (Actually, he had volunteered to do so.) When she left, Wally had *seemed* as surprised as everyone else. When Marvin asked for an explanation for her sudden quitting, Wally had told him that Jennifer seemed "unstable" and that her work quality had been inconsistent.

Marvin had accepted Wally's explanation at the time. Somehow, though, Marvin's intuition now told him that something had happend between Wally and Jennifer.

Marvin called Wally into the office.

He began by telling Wally that his performance seemed to have been declining recently. Marvin cited several examples of mistakes that Wally had made, and instances where other workers had to do part of his work in order to meet deadlines.

Wally shrugged it off, however, He said that nobody is perfect, and that everyone makes a few mistakes.

Marvin went on to remark that Wally had seemed more nervous and moody recently, and asked if everything was going well in his home life.

Hoping to get Marvin off his back for the poor performance, Wally admitted his marriage was on the rocks. He said that adjusting to being a bachelor was rough. He was frequently depressed, and though he tried not to let it affect his work, may be it sometimes did.

"Perhaps that explains a rumor that's been going around about you," Marvin said.

Wally didn't show any reaction, so Marvin decided to be blunt.

"Do you know that some people are saying that Jennifer quit because you were after her for sex?"

Wally scoffed at the rumor. "She was a mixed-up kid," he told Marvin. "Did you talk to her personally?"

"No, I didn't," Marvin admitted.

"Then let's not waste your time and mine with vicious rumors," Wally replied, getting up to leave.

"No. Let's talk about it some more," Marvin said, unemotionally, beckoning Wally to sit down again. "I'm surprised that with all the coaching you gave her she suddenly turned out so 'mixed up.'"

Wally just shrugged his shoulders.

"Look, Wally. This is too serious a matter for me to overlook."

"Well, since you don't have any evidence, . . ." Wally began.

"I'm not going to take any disciplinary action against you concerning Jennifer," Marvin interrupted him. "What I *am* going to do is put you on general probation, until you can straighten out these irregularities in your performance.

"If there's no truth to the rumor, then you've got nothing to worry about," Marvin pointed out. "And I'm also going to *assume* that your poor performance and your bad attitude is only a temporary problem—due to your marriage breaking up. In time, things will get better, and you'll be off probation."

"*Thanks*, Marvin," Wally replied, sarcastically.

"Meanwhile," Marvin added, ignoring Wally's sarcasm, "if I can help you get some professional help to sort out your personal problems, . . ."

"Don't bother," Wally retorted.

"I hope you understand that if you cause any further problems in this department, you'll leave me no choice but to dismiss you," Marvin added, as Wally was leaving.

"Yeah, I understand," Wally replied icily, not even looking at Marvin as he went out.

Marvin confirmed in writing the terms of the "general probation," and had Wally sign that he'd read the copy, which would be going into his personnel file. Finally, Marvin told his own boss, in confidence, everything that had happened.

The department seemed to run a little more smoothly during the next few weeks. Wally said nothing at the weekly department meetings, which was a great improvement, compared with his usual negativism! And he was making fewer mistakes. Furthermore, the new clerk was working out well.

Marvin had tried to forget the incident with Jennifer, since there was nothing he could do about it.

Three months later, however, the issue came alive again, when Marvin's dinner was interrupted by a telephone call. It was from the Industrial Sales Manager. He had just caught Wally molesting the new clerk. She and Wally had been working overtime on an end-of-year report.

The Industrial Sales Manager, also working late, had been walking down the hall to the coffee machine when he happened to see Wally cornering the protesting young woman. Welcoming the Indus-

trial Sales Manager's sudden presence, she had quickly grabbed her coat and purse, and left, in tears. Wally had awkwardly stuttered that it was "only fooling around—a game," and then gone back to his desk.

After hearing the whole story from the Industrial Sales Manager, Marvin thanked him and called the clerk at her home that same evening to console her. She agreed to file a formal complaint, although she had been afraid of Wally's threats to "make sure she got a bad recommendation if she didn't cooperate."

Marvin spent that whole evening mulling over what he should do. Certainly he had ground for firing Wally the next morning, but it wasn't so easy to make that decision now that he was confronted with it.

The responsibility was awesome. After all, who was he, Marvin Green, to make such an important decision about someone else's life? He weighed the evidence for and against firing Wally a hundred times in his mind, as he paced back and forth across his study at home.

After hardly sleeping all night, the next morning, complaint in hand, Marvin confronted Wally. Wally, of course, whined that "the girl" had been "leading him on."

Marvin was in no mood to listen to any excuses, however. This was the second sexual intimidation complaint he'd had about Wally, and this time, there was a reliable witness. He made it clear that if Wally was willing to "level with him," he'd try to help Wally. Otherwise, there was going to be big trouble—perhaps including criminal assault charges.

Wally decided he'd better not make a bad situation even worse. Unhappily, he told Marvin that he had been feeling very lonely since his wife left. He admitted that he'd used very bad judgment in "replacing" her affection. He also confessed that there was some truth both to the rumor about Jennifer and the complaint filed by the new clerk.

Marvin was relieved, and became more sympathetic, now that he no longer had a battle on his hands.

"Look, Wally," Marvin began, "you and I both know you're going to have to work someplace else."

"Yeah. I guess I'm not going to be too popular around here," Wally replied, looking down.

"You can't say you weren't warned," Marvin continued. "I even tried to help you get sorted out, but you wouldn't let me."

"Yeah. I know," Wally said mournfully, "but what can I do now to make a living?"

"If you'll cooperate, I'll try to help you," Marvin told him. "Here's what I'm willing to do, if my boss will approve it.

"You've still got six weeks of unused vacation. I want you to see a counselor during that period, to help you with your personal problems. The expenses will be covered under the company medical plan.

"If you go through with it, I'll let you resign when your vacation's all used up. That way, your personnel record won't show you were fired. In addition, I'm willing to write a general letter of recommendation for you. It will cover *only* your technical skills."

Wally looked a little relieved.

"But you've *got* to go through with it. You've got to see a counselor and try to get straightened out," Marvin reminded him. "If you don't, . . ."

"I'll do it, I promise," Wally replied, sadly but gratefully.

As Wally left his office, Marvin noticed that the other workers were looking at both of them for "facial clues" as to Wally's fate.

Marvin was certain that he wouldn't get any complaints about not being fair with Wally. The problem was, what could he tell the workers without giving away information that was still confidential among himself, his boss, and Wally?

CHECK YOUR PROGRESS

1. When should firing be used to solve disciplinary or performance problems?
2. What conditions make it hard for a supervisor to fire a worker?
3. How can the supervisor be impersonal and businesslike in firing a worker?
4. How can the supervisor ease the pain of a worker who must be fired?

ANSWERS TO PROGRESS QUESTIONS

1. Firing should be a *last resort*. The supervisor should always try hard to "salvage" the worker, unless there are grounds for immediate dismissal, such as stealing, assault and battery, etc.
2. If a worker has long seniority, if there is no prior probation, or if there are no grounds for immediate firing, higher management will be hesitant to back a supervisor's decision to fire a worker.
3. The supervisor should build a sound case, using as many facts and witnesses as possible.
4. The supervisor can suggest alternative employment, and perhaps even help the fired worker to get it.

Further Thoughts

The workers in Marvin's department were curious and concerned about what action Marvin took concerning Wally. What could Marvin tell them, without giving away information that was still confidential among himself, his boss, and Wally?

> *The whole incident with Wally had both "public" and "private" aspects. Wally's poor performance was "public," as was his constant opposition to anything that Marvin was trying to accomplish in the department. The two incidents involving sexual intimidation were fairly public, too. Sylvia probably told Jennifer's story to people in the department other than Marvin, and the new clerk probably told her story to her co-workers. Consequently, the "evidence" that formed the basis for Marvin's firing decision was probably "public knowledge" in the department, and perhaps even beyond the department.*
>
> *Because the situation that Marvin faced was common knowledge, he had to be particularly careful in how he handled it. His decision would set a precedent—that is, other workers who cause equally serious problems would expect to be treated the same way. Unequal treatment might be grounds for a grievance.*
>
> *To add to other workers' curiosity, Wally had proven himself to be somewhat of a "sexual menace," so that the other workers, particularly the women, probably began to feel they had a right to know whether Marvin would take actions to make the department safe from any further harassment.*
>
> *On the other hand, firing is also generally thought to be a private matter between the worker and the supervisor. After all, it is really just another transaction in the worker's personnel file, which is confidential. In Wally's case, where the agreement to seek professional help was a condition of "honorable discharge," medical confidentiality increased Wally's right to privacy.*

217

> *Marvin's best strategy is probably to issue a memo to each member of the department. The memo would say that Wally had resigned, effective immediately, and that his work would henceforth be covered by so-and-so. In this way, Marvin would not be disclosing the exact "deal" he made with Wally, nor would he be distorting the truth. (It is no one else's concern what happens to Wally's unused vacation time.)*

How fair is it to put a worker on "*general* probation"? If no single offense deserves probation, can a group of offenses justify it?

> *This is a deceptively difficult question, which can be argued either way. It makes a difference whether one applies rules of evidence or rules of judgment.*
>
> *Let's first consider rules of evidence. Suppose a man is thought to be speeding, but turns off the highway before the police can "clock" him. They stop him anyway, and notice that he almost fits the description of someone who held up a bank two weeks previously. They also smell beer on his breath, but don't see any symptoms that he is at all incapacitated by alcohol. Finally, they notice his inspection sticker will expire at midnight that night. Can they arrest him for "general lawlessness?"*
>
> *Of course they can't. The rules of evidence say that offenders must be "booked" on specific charges, on the basis of specific evidence that supports each charge.*
>
> *Picture, however, a clerk who is regularly late for work, and is frequently sick or absent on Mondays—always with a "good" excuse, of course; whose difficult tasks "somehow get lost in the mail" quite often; and who suffers "lapses in memory" when it is discovered that direct orders have been ignored.*
>
> *Any supervisor concerned with smooth workflow will sooner or later have to come to the judgment that no matter whether every single event is justified, the worker's overall performance is disrupting departmental efficiency. Higher management would probably back the supervisor's putting such a worker on general probation, based on the pattern or "group" of offenses.*

Marvin has agreed to write a *general* letter of recommendation that discusses only Wally's technical skills. It will say nothing about his character or his ability to get along with other workers. What are the ethical considerations?

> *There could be some very serious ethical problems here. If Wally's problem is more than a matter of "poor judgment in replacing his wife's affection"—for instance, if there is some sexual psychopathology—Marvin may be ethically obliged to warn other employers*

(over the phone, not in writing) so that other young women are not exposed to the same risks in an unsupervised situation.

On the other hand, Marvin has no business "playing psychiatrist," since his training is not in psychiatry but in accounting. Thus if he tells other prospective employers, in effect, "Watch out for Wally—he's a pervert," Marvin could end up with a slander or a libel suit.

Whatever decision Marvin makes, the law would judge it on the basis of what a "reasonably prudent man" would have done in the same circumstances. If Marvin is conscientious in resolving his dilemma, he probably doesn't need to fear any legal consequences.

POSTTEST QUESTIONS

Now that you've read the five chapters in Section IV, you might want to try to answer the same questions that you answered in the Pretest. The correct answers are given on page 221.

By comparing your score on the Posttest with your score on the Pretest, you will be able to get an idea of how much your knowledge of supervision has improved.

Select the *best* response to Questions 31 and 32, and circle the appropriate letter.

31. If you suspect that someone is playing "political games," you should:
   a. Retaliate by playing political games of your own.
   b. Avoid making any hasty accusations.
   c. Let your boss know what you suspect and get support.
   d. Confront face to face and have a showdown.
   e. Try to rally your workers to help you put it to a stop.

32. Every hiring requirement set by a supervisor must be
   a. Consistent with past hiring practices.
   b. Acceptable to members of the work group.
   c. First approved by the Personnel Department.
   d. Able to attract the best-qualified candidates.
   e. Related to actual job performance.

33. In dealing with a problem alcoholic worker, supervisors should NOT do which *one* of the following? (Circle one.)
   a. Be supportive by assuring the worker that there is no danger of losing his or her job.
   b. Find out what company or community programs are available to help.
   c. Enlist the help of fellow workers.
   d. Look for patterns of behavior that will show if the problem is getting worse.
   e. Tell the worker that he or she *must* seek help, or else.

Questions 34 through 40 are to be answered by circling T if the statement is **true** and F if the statement is **false.**

34. If a person is really good at "politics" in the work place, there's no way to tell that his (or her) actions have hidden purposes.   T   F

35. Firing is strictly a private matter between the worker involved and the supervisor; other workers should be told that the entire matter is none of their business.   T   F

36. A supervisor should not tolerate any conflict, whenever it is possible to squelch it.   **T   F**

37. Trembling fingers, bloodshot eyes, and accidents are sufficient evidence to determine that a worker has a drinking problem.   **T   F**

38. It is usually wise for supervisors to let their bosses know about conflicts in their departments.   **T   F**

39. A supervisor with successful past experience in interviewing job applicants is unlikely to get into trouble with the law on discrimination.   **T   F**

40. A supervisor should try to avoid firing an unsatisfactory worker during his (or her) probation period after hiring, since it is at this time that the worker needs maximum help and support.   **T   F**

PRE- AND POSTTEST QUESTIONNAIRE—ANSWER SHEET

31. b
32. e
33. a
34. true
35. false
36. false
37. false
38. true
39. false
40. false

Here are ten questions. Try to answer them before you read the five chapters in Section V. You'll have another chance to try to answer the same ten questions in the Posttest (pages 265–66).

An answer sheet is provided after the Posttest (page 266). You will be able to use this to score your Pretest and Posttest. By comparing the two scores, you will be able to get an idea of how much your knowledge of supervision has improved.

41. The important difference between line positions and staff positions is that line managers pass down _____, while staff people pass along _____ . (Choose from the alternatives below and write the corresponding letters in the two blanks.)

 a. Recommendations
 b. Communications
 c. Information
 d. Orders
 e. Accountability

42. Resistance to change is primarily caused by (circle the *best* response):

 a. The change itself.
 b. The meaning of the change to the persons affected.
 c. Workers' having a chance to discuss the change beforehand.

DEVELOPING YOURSELF AS A SUPERVISOR

d. People who would be inflexible about altering the status quo, no
      matter what.
   e. An increase in communications from top management.

43. The type of skill that is usually *least* important to a supervisor moving
further up the career ladder is (circle one)

   a. Administrative
   b. Political
   c. Interpersonal
   d. Bargaining
   e. Technical

Questions 44 through 50 are to be answered by circling T if the
statement is **true**, and F if the statement is **false**.

44. If staff people get involved in what goes on in a supervisor's department,
they should be held responsible if something goes wrong.   T   F

45. While actually on the job, the worker loses his (or her) right to "do his
own thing."   T   F

46. A promotion from worker to supervisor always means more take-home
pay.   T   F

47. A supervisor wishing to advance up the organizational ladder can't go
wrong by having a capable replacement.   T   F

48. The best way to minimize resistance to a change in the workplace is to
make the change as *slowly* as possible.   T   F

49. After a promotion, supervisors should expect to have a different relationship with their former co-workers.   T   F

50. In many cases, a supervisor has the power to deny a worker's constitutional rights.   T   F

A PREVIEW

The first three chapters in this section cover some *higher-level* supervisory skills. You will need to develop these in order to advance yourself in the organization.

First, you need to be able to take advantage of the special knowledge of *staff* experts in the organization. Supervisors are not expected to know everything, but they *are* expected to know how to tap the resources of staff specialists. Chapter 21 illustrates this, using quality control as an example.

After getting staff advice, however, the supervisor still has to make the actual operating decisions. The supervisor has the *right* to make such decisions, and also the *responsibility* to make them wisely. Workers also have rights and responsibilities, for which the supervisor sometimes becomes a "referee," as we see in Chapter 22. This is a delicate process, since it involves *ethical judgments,* but it is one of the most important areas of judgment that the supervisor must develop.

Another crucial area of judgment is in handling worker resistance to change. Chapter 23 provides some guidelines for the most common situation involving change—when technological improvements disrupt the established work patterns and work environment.

When you have mastered these higher-level skills, you may feel that you're ready to take another step up the organizational ladder. The last two chapters are written to help you in thinking about your career.

Chapter 24 looks at promotions from a different perspective than you're probably expecting: It looks at the *drawbacks.* Promotion is not "a step ahead" for everyone; for some people it's a step into a life of frustration. We want *you* to be sure that promotion is right for you before you get locked into anything.

The final chapter of the book, Chapter 25, will be an even more personal experience for you. It encourages you to do some planning for your own future, and explores how you can make the best of your career possibilities.

At the end of this last section, we have written an epilogue. The Epilogue summarizes where the four organizations and the supervisors you have met are headed as we leave them. In taking a "final look" at each setting, we encourage the reader to try to get a feel for what

has happened over time. This will provide a final supervisory skill—
the ability to put events into the perspective of where the organization has been, and what the future seems to hold for persons in supervisory positions.

1. Understand the important difference between line positions and staff positions: **Line managers pass down orders,** while **staff people pass along recommendations.**

2. **Take a positive approach:** Use your initiative to benefit from a staff person's special knowledge and experience. Don't wait until you're in trouble and the staff person is sent to you!

3. **Insist on constructive recommendations.** Make sure they focus on how to **correct problems,** rather than on **who is to blame.**

4. **Avoid trying to pass the buck** to staff people on matters that are really **your responsibility** as a supervisor.

Line
and Staff Relationships

21

A CRITICAL INCIDENT: Friend or Foe?

It had been a busy day in the Machining Department of Precision Electronics, so Vince, the supervisor, had let the paperwork pile up in his in-basket. After all his workers had punched out for the weekend, Vince slumped down in his chair and casually thumbed through the day's mail.

He didn't stay there for long, however. As soon as he read the memorandum from Quality Control, he angrily leapt to his feet. Memo in hand, he hurried over to try to catch Wilbur Wilson, the Quality Control Supervisor, before he, too, left for the weekend.

Vince was in luck. Wilbur was still in his office, digging through piles of reports. Vince walked right in and leaned over Wilbur's desk.

"What are you trying to do to me?" Vince demanded, shaking the memo in the face of a very surprised Wilbur.

"What the hell are you talking about?" asked Wilbur, annoyed. "What's that?"

Vince didn't reply. He just threw the memo down in front of Wilbur (see Exhibit 21–1). Wilbur read it carefully.

After he had finished reading it, he looked Vince in the eye and said, "I don't know what this is all about. I've been out of state for the past week. I got back into town this afternoon and I just came in to the office to catch up on some paperwork so it wouldn't all hit me Monday morning. So you tell *me* what's going on!"

"I don't *know* what's going on," Vince replied. "I just got this memo in the mail this afternoon. That's the first I heard from you guys all week!"

"Well, let me pull out the inspection reports," said Wilbur, walking over to the filing cabinets. Vince waited, his hands on his hips.

"Well," said Wilbur, after scanning the reports, "the memo is accurate. There *are* a lot of defective pieces. All too large on the O.D.* Floyd was in charge of the inspections. Didn't you talk to him?"

"I haven't heard a word from Floyd. You'd better straighten that jerk out before he screws up anything else!" retorted Vince.

"Now hold on a minute, Vince," Wilbur said firmly. "Floyd has done his job properly. He didn't mess up. It was *your* department that messed up!"

*The outside diameter.

228

MEMORANDUM

To: Machining Department
From: Quality Control Department
Subject: Problems on new Defense Dept. Contract

Random samples of parts produced by your
department over the past week contain too many
defective pieces. You need to pay more attention
to making sure the pieces stay within the tolerances
allowed in the Government Specification.

By copy of this memo, I am advising the
Production Manager to hold up assembly operations
until 100% inspection and removal of defective
pieces is complete.

Quality control will be more intensive in its
inspection of machined parts for this important
contract until these production problems are cleared
up.

cc: Production Manager
     Vice President, Marketing   FH/as

EXHIBIT 21-1

"You call *this* 'doing his job properly?'" demanded Vince, holding up the memo. "That meathead went over my head and sent a copy directly to the Production Manager! What did he have to do *that* for?"

"He's *supposed* to do that, Vince." Wilbur replied. "Quality Control reports directly to the Production Manager. Floyd reports directly to me. So when I'm not here, he has to send the memo upstairs. It's standard operating procedure. . . ."

"Come on, Wilbur!" Vince interjected. "Don't give me that 'official procedure' stuff: Your procedure has always been to give me a call if you think there's a problem. Then we talk about it, and I fix whatever's going wrong. If Floyd had any common sense at all, he'd realize that *I'm* the guy that's turning out the parts, not the production manager! There's no *need* to get them involved upstairs."

"Well, let me explain," Wilbur replied. "Floyd is pretty new on the job here, but he's had a lot of experience in quality control. The standard operating procedures are pretty much the same in every company—Quality Control is a staff function reporting directly to the top. Our job is to make independent checks on production operations. We couldn't be independent without reporting directly to the Production Manager, could we?"

Vince didn't disagree, so Wilbur went on.

"So it looks like Floyd did what he was supposed to do. There *was* a problem, and Floyd simply made his recommendations. You want me to get on his back for that?"

"But why the hell couldn't he call me as soon as he found the faulty pieces in the first batch?" Vince asked.

"I'm not sure, Vince," Wilbur replied honestly. "I would have. He *should* have. I know he's been very busy trying to get the low-temperature test rig working properly. Maybe he didn't have time to see you during the day and dictated the memo after hours to be sure that the problem was reported."

"Well, then; you mean you actually agree that Floyd messed up by not calling me before sending the memo?" asked Vince, his tone a little sarcastic.

"Sure. I said he should have called you," Wilbur admitted.

"And if you read the memo carefully, you'll see that it makes no mention of what I'm supposed to do to *correct* the problem. It just says we messed up," Vince pointed out.

"You're right," Wilbur conceded, after rereading the memo. "I'll have to talk to him about that."

"So if he's making mistakes left and right," Vince continued, hopefully, "it could be that he measured the O.D.'s wrong!"

"Come on, Vince," Wilbur said good-naturedly, "Floyd may need a lesson in diplomacy, but he sure as hell knows how to measure diameters. I'm sure the inspection reports are accurate. So don't get your hopes up! You and I both know the parts must be defective."

"Well, if a whole week's parts are defective, Floyd is partly responsible anyway!" Vince replied, in a final, weak attempt to get off the hook. "Why didn't he catch the problem right away?"

"Come on!" Wilbur said, smiling. "Don't try to pass the buck to us! We inspected the first batch as soon as we got them. If you want to work out a different inspection schedule. . ."

"Yeah, I guess you're right," Vince interrupted, the hostility gone from his voice, "but I wish you'd get Floyd to use the telephone instead of sending me memos."

"Look, Vince," Wilbur said sincerely, "why don't you help me out? How about spending some time talking to Floyd so he's comfortable dealing with you over the phone? Floyd is a smart and very experienced guy. He can help you head off production problems long before they get you in hot water. Pick his brains!"

By the end of the following week, Vince and Floyd had gotten together and traced the production problem to an overheating bearing in one of the lathes. They also had installed "process controls": At

each work station, there was a "go/no-go" gauge in which the machinists could test every tenth piece, so that they would get *early* warning if their lathes were creeping out of adjustment.

The quality problem was solved. And Vince was left wondering how he could have ever concluded that Floyd was "an enemy."

CHECK YOUR PROGRESS

1. When a *staff* person decides that something needs to be done, he takes action that is different from what a *line* person would do. What is the difference?

2. Contact between line supervisors and staff experts takes place under a variety of circumstances. What are the ideal circumstances?

3. How does the line supervisor avoid a relationship in which the staff person becomes a "policeman" rather than an advisor?

4. Since staff people are supposed to get involved in what goes on in the supervisor's department, they should also be held responsible when something goes wrong. Isn't this correct?

ANSWERS TO PROGRESS QUESTIONS

1. Staff people "give advice," whereas line people—such as supervisors—give orders.
2. It is always better for the line supervisor to use his (or her) initiative and *seek out* the help of staff experts, rather than waiting until there's a problem and the staff person is required to get involved.
3. The supervisor should insist on *constructive* recommendations—advice that focuses on *how to correct the problem,* not on who is to blame.
4. No. Staff advisors have no *authority* to give orders to correct a problem; therefore, they cannot be held *responsible.*

Further Thoughts

Quality control is only one of the staff functions in a modern business organization. What are some other typical staff functions?

> *Other staff functions include:*

1. Personnel/Industrial Relations
2. Safety
3. Industrial engineering (e.g., time and motion study)
4. Legal staff
5. Research and Development

Even though staff people are only supposed to give advice, quite often they, in effect, give orders. How does such a situation come about, and how does it affect the supervisor?

> *1. If the line supervisor* always *follows the staff recommendations, as a matter of expediency his workers will tend to follow the staff recommendations without double-checking with the supervisor. Thus, over time, workers will come to view staff people in a chain-of-command ("line") role, and the staff people will respond to workers' expectations by tending to give orders rather than recommendations. This can have the unfortunate effect of the workers' having two bosses, which gives rise to confusion and the opportunity to "play one boss off against the other" (just as children do with their two parents!).*
>
> *2. Sometimes, the line supervisor* wants *more than recommendations. This happened in Chapter 3, where Marvin tried to persuade Catherine, the Personnel Supervisor, to make a selection decision for him. For many staff people, this temptation is often too strong to resist.*
>
> *In the long run, giving up authority in this manner is a poor policy for the line supervisor. He relies on the advice of staff people because they have specialized knowledge he lacks. Ideally, he should*

learn *from the process of incorporating their advice into his decisions to increase his own expertise. If the supervisor chooses to give up completely the decision making, he learns nothing, loses some control over his workers, and yet still is responsible for the decisions.*

3. The third factor is the supervisor's extra risk if he doesn't accept staff advice as "gospel."

Staff people give one kind of "advice" to line supervisors, and another kind to the higher-level managers. Using Floyd as an example, explain what is different about the two kinds of "advice."

Staff people give expert advice to supervisors. No supervisor is expected to possess all the technical knowledge that is useful in running a department in a modern company. The organization makes staff people available to help supervisors solve problems where highly specialized knowledge is required.

Staff people also provide some expert advice to higher-level managers, but their primary usefulness to higher management is in the control advice they give. Quality Control is a good example.

Quality Control, as we saw in the Precision Electronics critical incident in this chapter, would provide expert advice to the supervisor, if he asked for it. However, as Wilbur pointed out, Quality Control reports directly to the Production Manager, and advises him when the actual production output has drifted "out of control"—in other words, when the output no longer meets the control standards. (Recall Chapter 2.)

These dual roles of staff positions can cause some role conflict. To get good expert advice, the supervisor may have to confide in the staff person that (1) something is going wrong in his department, and (2) he doesn't know how to "fix it." This poses no problem insofar as the staff person is giving expert advice. But "wearing his other hat" as a control agent of higher management, the staff person is under some obligation to report "upstairs" that something is going wrong and recommend that steps be taken to correct the problem. The supervisor may (wisely, sometimes) fear that one of the recommended steps might be to replace him with a more competent supervisor! Fearing this, the supervisor may hesitate to ask for help in the first place.

1. Recognize that the people you deal with have **rights.**
    One of your **responsibilities** is to make an effort not to
    interfere with those rights, even if you're uncomfort-
    able when they "do their own thing."
2. Know the difference between people's responsibilities
    when they are **acting as individuals,** and their responsi-
    bilities when they are acting as **representatives of the
    organization.**
3. When one person's rights **interfere** with another person's
    rights, favor the person who is likely to come to **the
    most harm** if his rights are denied.
4. Remember that one of the most important of the
    workers' rights is their right to "tell their half of the
    story," **before** any disciplinary action is taken.

Rights
and Responsibilities

22

A CRITICAL INCIDENT: The Limits to "Freedom of Speech"

Alan had made a special point of telling the customer to bring his Datsun pickup truck in early to Foreign Auto Repair, Inc., if he wanted it back the same day. When the appointment was made, the customer had explained to Alan that the pickup had been plagued for quite some time with a misfiring problem. The dealer hadn't been able to fix it. Neither had the two other foreign auto repair shops in town.

At 10:30, Alan decided he couldn't wait any longer for the customer to show up. He had to go to the bank to deposit the cash and checks that had been accumulating in his desk for the past week or so. Before he left, he explained the whole thing to Herbie, who was to write up the service order and start working on the pickup right away.

It was natural to have Herbie working on that particular project, rather than on the more-routine service jobs. Actually, Herbie was given nearly all the difficult troubleshooting jobs. He was a real wizard at diagnosing engine problems; time after time he amazed the other mechanics!

What was so amazing was that Herbie never used the sophisticated diagnostic equipment Alan had bought. Instead, he would test-drive whatever vehicle he was working on, to "get a feel" for the problem. Then he would bring it into the shop and carefully listen to the engine, while disconnecting wires and making a series of trial adjustments. In a very short time, he would isolate the problem. And he was never wrong!

Herbie amazed the rest of the mechanics in other ways too—especially in his appearance and his ideas.

He was fairly short and skinny, and had a huge mop of curly hair, which was kept out of his eyes by a badly frayed headband. He always seemed to be wearing exactly the same tattered sweatshirt and jeans. Although they were always clean, they were so torn and ragged that they appeared to be in danger of actually falling off his body at any moment. His appearance provided a regular topic for jokes in the shop, but Herbie didn't seem to mind at all.

Herbie's ideas amazed the others because he had a different way of interpreting everything that happened. For instance, when the news came on the radio, which was playing constantly in the shop, Herbie would retell the news stories, using his own terminology: Government and business officials were always "the ruling class"; all private prop-

erty really belonged to "the people"; and so on. The other mechanics were amused with what they called his "heavy raps," and would often ask Herbie for a reinterpretation of the news or the radio commercials if he didn't provide it right away.

Although they didn't agree with his views, except on environmental issues, the others respected Herbie for being very well-read on the topics he would "rap" about, and also for being very good at explaining things in simple, down-to-earth terms. Besides that, he was a natural comic, and they liked him.

On this particular day, Herbie was off in the corner assembling the front forks of a motorcycle when in marched the customer with the misfiring pickup truck. Herbie put down his tools and sauntered over to greet him. He soon found himself confronted with a very irritable, square-jawed, heavy-set man, who insisted on talking to "the boss."

Herbie patiently explained that they had expected to get the truck before 9, and that Alan had waited around until 10:30, at which point he just *had* to go to the bank. Furthermore, it would be he, Herbie, not Alan, who would actually be working on the truck.

The customer grunted something, then reluctantly gave Herbie all the necessary information. He also made a point of telling Herbie how he was sick of getting "jerked around" by auto repair shops who "never fix things right but rip you off anyway." He further complained about what an inconvenience it was for his wife to follow him down. Herbie didn't comment; he just continued writing up the service order.

Next, the customer refused to sign his name on the bottom of the service order. Though Herbie's patience was exhausted by this time, he politely but firmly convinced the abrasive customer that no work could be done on the pickup until the order was signed, and that the man was welcome to wait around until Alan came back, and discuss it with *him.* Grumbling, the customer agreed to sign.

As the customer was scrawling his signature on the service order, Herbie glanced out the window. What he saw made his aggravation level go from uncomfortably hot to the boiling point!

First, Herbie noticed that the pickup had a gun rack in the back window. Herbie loathed hunters; he called them "bloodthirsty barbarians." Second, the customer's wife was sitting in a Cadillac with the engine running. Herbie noticed her because she had blown the horn and was making impatient gestures to her husband. Herbie despised Cadillacs. They were "the tasteless symbol of the ruling class." To make matters worse, the impatient woman was wearing a fur coat, and Herbie considered trapping to be the ultimate cruelty to animals.

This combination of irritants would have been hard for Herbie to handle under ideal conditions. With his patience already strained to the breaking point at the outset, Herbie had no mercy. He figured what this "dude" needed was some "shaking up" so he'd come to his senses.

"Hey, I see you've got a gun rack. You hunt, huh?" asked Herbie, amiably.

"Yeah," replied the customer in a more friendly tone of voice.

"No kidding!" said Herbie, appearing to be very interested. "What do you hunt?"

"Deer, mostly," the customer replied, becoming interested himself in the conversation. "I use a 30–06 with a special scope. You hunt, too?" he asked.

"No. Actually, I don't have any goddam troubles at all with my masculinity." replied Herbie, still smiling. "I don't need to go out and prove what a big hero I am by standing behind a great big cannon and blowing the guts out of a poor defenseless deer."

The customer frowned deeply, not yet understanding what was going on. Herbie still had a friendly smile, and continued to talk.

"I'll bet you're one of those guys," he went on enthusiastically, "who just *wounds* a deer and lets it go off and bleed to death somewhere. It's more of a *sport* that way, right?"

The customer was getting red in the face, and his anger was rising. "What the hell's going on?" he demanded. "I didn't come here to listen to a lot of crap from you."

"Well, part of the problem is that you came to the wrong place," retorted Herbie. "You should have gone to see a psychiatrist. Your head needs a lot more attention than your truck!"

The customer was speechless. He crumpled up the service order and threw it at the wastebasket in the corner (he missed). Then he headed for the door.

Herbie escorted him to his truck, and before the man was able to escape, Herbie delivered a fast lecture, covering (1) how Cadillacs waste "the people's fuel," especially when the motor is left running; (2) how buying furs subsidizes and encourages the torture of animals; and (3) why he shouldn't have bought a Japanese pickup in the first place, since "most conscientious citizens" were boycotting that country's products "in protest of their extermination of whales." As the man was roaring out of the driveway, Herbie added his prediction of how the man would likely fare "when the revolution comes."

As the man was roaring out of the driveway, he almost hit Alan, who was driving in. The man leaped out of the pickup and angrily told a very surprised Alan what had happened. The wife, at that point, jumped out of the Cadillac and started yelling at her husband. Herbie went back inside the shop to resume working on the motorcycle.

Five minutes later, a very hassled-looking Alan came into the shop.

"Look, Herbie," he said wearily, "I don't mind what you look like around here, and I don't care what your ideas are. But when you start jumping all over customers, . . ."

Alan was interrupted by Hans, one of the older mechanics: "Hey, Alan, hold on a minute. You've only heard one side of the story so far. Be fair to the kid."

"Yeah, you're right," Alan conceded. "OK, Herbie, what happened?"

As Herbie recounted what had happened, the others stopped working and listened. Someone turned the radio off. Every once in a while, someone would interject "That's right," or "That's *exactly* what happened" to support Herbie's story.

When Herbie had finished, Alan said, "OK, so you had a good reason to be uptight. But you had no right to lay that 'rap' on him."

"Don't I have the right to freedom of speech?" asked Herbie.

"Yeah," replied Alan, "sure you do. But what's more important is that guy had the right to be treated like a customer. If you want to convert someone to whatever the hell it is you believe in, take some time off and do it as a private citizen. Don't do it as my mechanic—as a representative of this place. You've got no right to do that."

"Come on, Alan. If the guy wasn't so offensive, I wouldn't have told him about the rest of the things that were wrong with him. You know that," Herbie protested. "Just what did you expect me to do? Take all that crap he feels like dishing out? Lie there like a doormat and let him wipe his feet on me?"

"No," Alan replied firmly. "As a representative of this place, you can refuse his business. That's *all*. And I'll back you up. You can't hassle him, though. *No lectures*! And you can't refuse his business just because he's a 'capitalist pig' or whatever name you use. You can't discriminate against a customer just because you don't agree with where he's at. *We've* got responsibilities as a business, and *you've* got responsibilities as a mechanic."

"I gotta think about that," said Herbie seriously, as he went back to working on the bike.

"OK. You think about it," Alan replied; then he went back to the office to put the bank statements in his desk.

The others went back to work, too. Moments later, the radio began playing again.

CHECK YOUR PROGRESS

1. What is a supervisor's basic responsibility towards the rights of his (or her) workers?

2. What is the difference between a worker's responsibility when acting as an individual as opposed to acting as a representative of the organization?

3. If one person's rights conflict with another person's rights, how do you, as a supervisor, choose which person's rights to uphold?

4. What is one of the most important rights of a worker who is about to be disciplined?

ANSWERS TO PROGRESS QUESTIONS

1. The supervisor has a responsibility to not interfere with a worker's rights, even if his "doing his own thing" makes the supervisor uncomfortable.
2. Workers' responsibilities are less restricted when they are acting as individuals; when representing the organization, workers are responsible for respecting the right of customers to be treated as customers.
3. You should figure out which person is likely to be harmed more if his (or her) rights are denied, and then favor that person in your decision.
4. A worker who is about to be disciplined has the right of due process—that is, the right to tell his (or her) version of what happened.

Further Thoughts

What are the differences between the following three rights which Herbie claimed?

1. The right to tell his half of the story.
2. The right to dress as sloppily as he wanted.
3. The right to freedom of speech.

> *There are important differences between each of the three rights. Specifically:*
>
> 1. Herbie's right to tell his half of the story is fairly straightforward and has its basis in the Constitution and in common law.
> 2. Whether Herbie had the right to dress as sloppily as he wanted is less clearcut. Since he is exposed to customers, the shop's image could be affected (i.e., customers might associate sloppy dress with sloppy workmanship).
> 3. What is really controversial, however, is whether people can reasonably be expected to leave their values outside of the work place—that is, to function purely in their work role when they have conflicting personal values. In Herbie's specific situation, however, this has to be decided in the context of the customer's right to be treated as a customer, without harassment from Herbie because of his different values.

If you reread the critical incidents in Chapter 7 (rules) and Chapter 8 (safety), you will notice that the two supervisors—Maria and Sam—have similar rights and responsibilities. What are they?

> *As supervisors, Maria and Sam have the right to give orders. They also have the right to refuse to give an order, such as when they exercise discretion in enforcing rules.*
>
> *Along with these rights goes the responsibility to supervise and to enforce rules in such a way as to protect their workers from accidents. When they permit a rule to be relaxed, there is an added responsibil-*

ity to be reasonably sure that more harm (e.g., intolerably restrictive working conditions) would result from rigidly enforcing the rule than from being more lax (e.g., the probability and severity of an accident).

In these two particular cases, Sam (in Chapter 8) was somewhat irresponsible in his loose enforcement of the safety rule. By contrast, Maria's laxity (in Chapter 7) was less serious, given the relatively mild danger involved with the toy mouse, as compared with the hazard of spilled oil.

Alan is a businessman (an "entrepreneur"), as well as a supervisor. What are his rights and responsibilities as a businessman?

Alan has the same rights as any businessman. These are so taken for granted that we normally don't even notice them, much less recognize them as rights.

For instance, Alan has a right to use some land for business purposes, land which in some respects, really "belongs to society" rather than to Alan. He also has the right to decide what services he will provide to citizens, and even which citizens he will serve. (He can refuse to fix a car if he so chooses.) It is also Alan's right to choose which citizens he will hire, how much he pays them, how much energy and water will be used in his business, and so on. In addition, he has the right to expect police and firefighter protection, and also the right to have courts of law protect all these rights!

In exchange for all these rights *granted to him by society, the businessman has* responsibilities *to society. First, he has the responsibility not to abuse any of these rights. These responsibilities are outlined by society in zoning and environmental laws, consumer protection and fraud laws, wage and hour laws, anti-discrimination laws, and so on.*

Beyond not abusing his rights, the businessman has a responsibility to serve the needs of the public, and to do it efficiently, conscientiously, and fairly. If he carries out these responsibilities, he has the right to "make a living" from his business. The businessman who serves society more responsibly should make a better living than one who does not.

Thus profit is a reward for serving society well—it is not merely the difference between what it costs the businessman to provide the goods or services and what the businessman can charge for them. The businessman has no right to take the second approach; this only leads to cheating the consumer. Capitalism is founded on fair, ethical principles, not on greed.

1. Recognize that **change in itself doesn't cause resistance.** What does cause resistance is the **meaning of the change** as seen by the workers affected.

2. Be prepared to receive and deal with **considerable worker resistance** if changes are made that affect **job security, status,** or **friendship** patterns.

3. Wherever possible, **let your workers participate** in decisions involving changes that affect them.

4. **Increase communications** during times of change. Otherwise, the rumor mill may supply wrong information that could increase resistance.

Resistance to Change

23

A CRITICAL INCIDENT: An Unwelcome Surprise

"Well, it looks like we're in for another rough week!" Vince commented, as he joined Maria in the cafeteria. "I figured that things would have calmed down a bit over the weekend, but they seem to be getting worse!"

Vince was referring to the poor morale in the Machining Department at Precision Electronics, which he supervised.

"My department's getting worse, too," replied Maria, Supervisor of the Assembly Department. "I've had nothing but complaints and long faces all morning."

The problem had begun three weeks earlier, on the day before the plant's two-week summer shutdown. A memo had been circulated to all supervisors announcing a meeting of the entire work force at the end of the workday.

No one had known what it was all about—not even the supervisors. As a result, the plant had been alive with rumors. By the time the meeting had started, the workers were so nervous that Vince and Maria could feel the tension in the air.

The Production Manager gave a short speech about the high quality of the work effort over the past year. Next he expressed his hopes that everyone would have an enjoyable, relaxing vacation. Then he casually told everyone they could expect to find a few improvements in the layout of the plant's ground floor when they got back to work.

Using an overhead projector, he carefully explained the inefficiencies of the present ground floor layout. (See Exhibit 23-1.) Too much manpower and money was being wasted in moving materials in and out of storage, and across halls (see arrows in Exhibit 23-1). Changes were necessary to maintain the company's competitive position.

The new layout (see Exhibit 23-2) would be more efficient, since materials would flow in a straight line on conveyors.

The Production Manager then pointed out that worker productivity was expected to rise in each of the departments affected, but he promised that piece rates would not be revised. This, he said, was "like giving workers a raise!"

The Production Manager then asked for questions, as he stood there, smiling benevolently. He didn't get any questions. Nor did he get any smiles. All he got was puzzled frowns and confused, angry stares.

There were even fewer smiles when the workers returned from

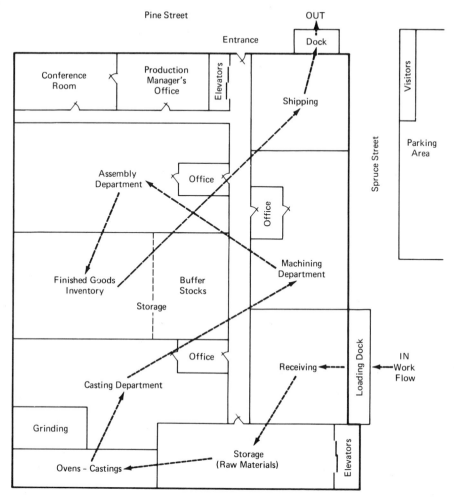

EXHIBIT 23-1 *First-floor Plan Precision Electronics Company*

vacation. In explaining the diagrams, the Production Manager had tried to convince them that the changes would be insignificant, and would involve only "moving a few machines around, plus a little interior decorating." However, the actual change in the appearance of the work area took the workers quite by surprise.

Whereas previously they had worked in cozy little departments separated by walls from the rest of the factory, workers now found themselves in one large production area. Gone also was the clutter; the shop was neat and antiseptic-looking, with fresh paint everywhere.

Furthermore, the conveyors didn't affect only materials-handling

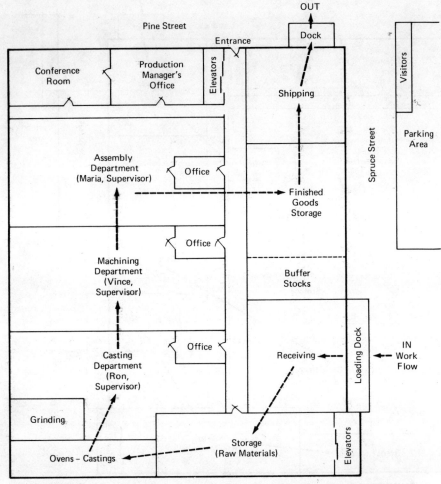

EXHIBIT 23-2 *New Layout First-floor Plan Precision Electronics Company*

procedures. They also affected work stations. For instance, assemblers had worked for years in groups of eight around large assembly benches, in a fairly quiet room. They now found themselves in a noisy room, sitting alone at small work stations spaced along a whirring conveyor.

Vince's machinists didn't mind the physical separation so much, because they were used to it. But they complained more about the noise, since they were closer to the whining air tools and roaring exhaust fans in the grinding booths of the Casting Department.

Reading between the lines, however, Vince had come to the con-

246

clusion that what bothered his machinists the most was being thrown in with lower-status workers. They had come to regard their old room as the "private territory" of skilled machinists. They didn't like working practically alongside unskilled grinders and semi-skilled assemblers.

"You know, we could have easily avoided most of the bitterness we're getting right now," Vince told Maria. "We shouldn't have surprised the workers with a decision already made."

"Yeah. I agree," Maria replied.

"The Production Manager could have explained the problem of materials-handling costs making us uncompetitive, and asked for suggestions," Vince continued. "He should have done this in the early planning. Probably a lot of workers would have come to these same conclusions about changing the layout. Then they probably wouldn't be fighting the changes so hard."

"Yeah," she replied, "and probably the worst thing he could have done was to keep people on edge all day waiting for an official announcement. All those rumors poisoned any chances of having the workers accept the changes as a good idea."

Vince nodded in agreement.

"By the way, Vince, did you know that the union organizer contacted several workers over the weekend?" she asked him. "The union only lost by a narrow margin last year. This time it looks like they'll be in for sure!"

1. From the Production Manager's point of view, the changes in layout seemed insignificant. Yet the workers got very upset and resisted the changes. Why?
2. What kind of changes usually cause the greatest worker resistance?
3. What can supervisors do to minimize worker resistance to change?
4. How can the "rumor mill" be held in check during times of change?

ANSWERS TO PROGRESS QUESTIONS

1. It was the meaning of the change, as seen by the workers affected, not the change itself, which caused worker resistance.
2. The greatest worker resistance can be expected when changes affect job security, status, or friendship patterns.
3. Workers should be given some voice in change decisions that affect them, *before* such decisions are finalized.
4. Workers are hungry for information during times of change. Thus management must increase the flow of communications. Otherwise, information will be supplied in the form of rumors, which may be false and harmful.

Further Thoughts

The machinists responded to the changes differently than the assemblers. This might be expected, given the differences between skilled "craft" work and semi-skilled assembly work. What are some of these differences?

Craft workers generally see a number of advantages to their jobs as compared with assembly operations. These include:

1. Greater interest, variety, and opportunity to move around, change pace, or take breaks.
2. More opportunity to develop their own work methods (autonomy), to use initiative, and for self-expression.
3. Greater sense of completion of a "whole" product.
4. Closer sense of identity as a member of a prestigious occupational group (peer status).
5. Greater sense of accomplishment (ego satisfaction) and job security (since skilled workers are not easily replaced).
6. Common bond for communicating readily with others in the work group, due to special skills and technical language.

Why did Maria believe that the union now had a very good chance to win the election?

Maria knows that union support was relatively strong in the plant before the new layout was made, because the vote had been very close the previous year. She apparently feels that management's mishandling of the layout change will sway enough pro-management workers to change their minds so that the union will gain majority support. Her reasoning assumes that:

1. The union's new organizing attempt will move quickly and make the most of the workers' anxiety over the layout change.
2. A number of workers will continue to resist the change and openly

talk about how badly it was handled, no matter what management does to try to appease them.

3. Not all workers believe the Production Manager's claim that the change is "like getting a raise," since productivity would rise with no change in the piece rates. Doubters believe that (a) it will lead to a speedup in order to make the company more competitive; or (b) unless there are more orders, the increased productivity will mean that the company can get by with fewer workers and can make some layoffs to lower costs still further.

4. The new layout will be perceived as giving management increased control (work will now be machine-paced) over workers and the work process; a union will be necessary to collectively counter this greater control.

The management at Precision Electronics made the layout changes quickly, and they backfired. Would making the changes slowly have avoided worker resistance?

Fast changes, if forced on workers (as was done at Precision Electronics), can lead to intense resistance and poor morale. Although there may have been some resistance to slow change, the resistance probably would have been less intense (and change might possibly have been accepted as a "natural process") if the change had been introduced slowly enough.

Slow change is not without problems, however. Economic circumstances supposedly required moving ahead rather quickly. Also, under a slow rate of change, workers may have sensed that something was continually happening, but they wouldn't have known where the change was leading, or what the full impact would be. The key to change seems to be communicating with workers in such a way that they understand the nature and reasons for the proposed change before it happens.

Usually, if employees fully understand and accept a change, there is little reason not to make the change rapidly. Fast change avoids the constant series of adjustments that are required when it happens slowly, and which leave everyone guessing as to what will happen next.

1. Recognize that **supervising a job requires different skills than doing the job.** Learn in advance what these differences are, so you'll be able to avoid promotions that are beyond your ability and will make you feel incompetent.

2. Be prepared for the **different sense of accomplishment** and a **different basis of evaluation** by superiors, when you become a supervisor. Quite often, it won't be obvious to you (or anyone else) when you're doing a good job.

3. After a promotion, **expect to have a different relationship with your former co-workers.** They'll think of you as **"one of them"** (part of management) rather than "one of us" (part of the work group).

4. **Build yourself an out**—negotiate in advance with your boss so that you can step down without embarrassment if the promotion doesn't work out for you.

Promotion
from the Ranks

24

A CRITICAL INCIDENT: "Congratulations and Condolences!"

Alan decided that he needed help in supervising his mechanics. Foreign Auto Repair, Inc., had been growing steadily, and as it grew, he found he needed to spend more time on planning and control. Lately, he'd been spending most of his time in the office, and not enough on the shop floor.

In addition, he was working on a deal with a taxi service in town, which would involve adding two more bays to the south end of the shop. This was taking a lot of his time, and he didn't want to be bothered with a lot of day-to-day headaches supervising the regular service work.

Gil, the oldest mechanic, heard what Alan had in mind, and came right out and asked Alan if he could take over as supervisor. Gil felt he deserved the job, since he was the oldest, and had put in the longest service with Alan, now that Kirk had left. Furthermore, being the most highly skilled, he was well respected by the other mechanics.

Two days later, Alan gave Gil the promotion. They closed the shop an hour early that afternoon, and had a small party to celebrate.

Gil was very happy about his promotion. So was his family. He was now a first-line supervisor, instead of "just a mechanic." And he now had a grandiose title—"Service Manager"—which impressed friends and neighbors.

It took only a week, however, for Gil to start having second thoughts about his promotion. When he had first considered asking Alan for the position, Gil had visualized it as being "sort of the same job as before, but with a nicer title.

He soon found out, however, that being a supervisor was totally different from being a mechanic. Gil figured that there were several major drawbacks to the promotion.

First, he disliked dealing with customers face to face. Most of them knew very little about the mechanical side of cars, and didn't appreciate the beauty of precision engineering and craftsmanship.

To make matters worse, Gil had great difficulty in "translating" explanations from the technical terms the mechanics used, to everyday terms that the customers could understand. And he hated complainers —he soon got to the point where he would become irritated and defensive even if someone asked an innocent question about a service bill.

Also, Gil felt awkward dealing with the other mechanics. He had always been "one of the boys"; he minded his own business and worked alone on the high-precision jobs. Now he had to supervise less-skilled mechanics doing some of the same jobs. The others gave him a ribbing every time he gave an order, and Gil wasn't handling their gibes very well.

Finally, Gil was still doing a small amount of mechanical work on the side, just as Alan had done, as the supervisor. But it was driving Gil crazy to continually have to drop what he was doing to deal with a customer or coordinate the work of the other mechanics. This was a particular problem in that Gil would reserve the highest-precision jobs for himself, the jobs that were least suited to on-again, off-again attention.

Because actual mechanical work represented only a small fraction of his daily tasks, Gil found that he missed the sense of satisfaction he got from completing such jobs and doing them well. Also, as the supervisor, it seemed that the only time Gil got any feedback at all was when something went wrong! *He* heard all the complaints from customers, for example, even though someone else had made the mistakes! Gil figured he didn't need that kind of aggravation.

Noticing that Gil had been looking increasingly unhappy, at the end of the second week, Alan took him out to lunch to talk things over. Gil was quite frank in expressing his disillusionment, but was hesitant to step down, knowing all the fuss that had been made over his promotion. What would he tell his family and the neighbors?

Alan was sympathetic and supportive. He told Gil he'd try to figure something out.

That afternoon, Alan took Hans (the second oldest mechanic)

aside and explained the situation to him. Alan asked him if he would like to take over as Service Manager if Gil stepped down.

Hans said he *would* like to try the job, but on certain conditions. Hans wanted to know exactly what was expected of him, and how much time he would have to learn the job. He also wanted to take the job only on a trial basis, so that he could decide later whether it was a good idea.

With Gil's agreement, Alan changed Gil's title to "Service Manager —specialty cars." This allowed Gil to return to his old job at his previous pay, with no explanations necessary for the neighbors.

Alan gave Hans the title "General Manager" and instructed the mechanics that Hans would have full supervisory responsibility for the shop. Alan also explained to them that he'd found Gil's talents for doing the high-precision jobs were much too valuable to remain idle while Gil did supervisory work. Then Alan made a joke about Hans "messing up so many jobs that he'd been made supervisor to keep him away from cars."

Alan hoped everyone would feel better about this arrangement. Looking back, he wondered how well he had handled the promotion of a new supervisor.

CHECK YOUR PROGRESS

1. How do you avoid promotions that are beyond your ability and will make you feel incompetent?

2. As a new supervisor, how will you (and your superiors) know when you're doing a good job?

3. How will your relationship with your co-workers change after your promotion?

4. How can you step down gracefully from a promotion that doesn't work out for you?

ANSWERS TO PROGRESS QUESTIONS

1. You should recognize that *supervising* a job requires different skills than *doing* the job. Learn in advance what these differences are, and make sure that you can measure up to what will be expected of you.
2. What a supervisor does is not very obvious, compared to most workers. Thus it's hard to get a sense of having accomplished something, and often you only hear about how you're doing when something goes wrong!
3. Instead of seeing you as "one of *us,*" you'll probably be seen as "one of *them.*"
4. Negotiate in advance with your boss. Make it understood to everyone that you want to take the promotion *on a trial basis.* Then if it doesn't work out, *you* can reject the job, rather than losing face when it seems that "the job has rejected you."

Further Thoughts

Does a promotion always mean receiving more take-home pay?

> *Promotions are usually thought to mean more money, but it doesn't always work out that way. For example, if a fast and efficient mechanic like Gil received a bonus or incentive for beating the flat-rate (see Chapter 2 on control), he could earn more by rate-busting than by receiving a nominal increase in his base pay at the time of promotion to supervisor. In the supervisory position, Gil was now exempt from receiving overtime or incentive pay. Thus, unless the promotion carried a substantial increase in base salary, Gil could have less annual take-home pay than he would have had as a mechanic on incentive.*
>
> *Another example would be the case of a supervisor who prefers the nonmonetary rewards of a new job (such as the prestige of wearing a suit, mingling with the bosses, greater future opportunity to advance, etc.) as the "real" rewards rather than more take-home pay.*

What did Alan do well in opening up a promotion opportunity for one of his mechanics? What did he do poorly?

Steps Alan handled well include:

1. He decided to *promote from within,* thus providing a motivator to mechanics who want to advance.
2. He made a change *quickly,* when he recognized that promoting Gil had been a mistake.
3. Gil was permitted to *save face* and return to a job where he could make contributions more in line with his abilities.
4. A *ceremony* (or "rite of passage") regarding promotion was held that played up the importance of Gil's change of status.

Steps Alan handled poorly *include:*

1. The promotion was based initially entirely on *seniority and age.* It should also have included recognition of *ability* to do a supervisory job.

2. The new job was *not spelled out* as to skill, knowledge, responsibility, relationships with customers, and other such requirements from which the best potential supervisor could be selected and trained.

3. *Career ladders* for future promotions were not spelled out; the decision was based on the expediency of the moment, and left doubts in all mechanics' minds of what other promotion opportunities, if any, were available.

4. The new supervisor was *left entirely on his own*—the first follow-up was done only after Gil was completely discouraged.

Merit, ability, and seniority can be factors in a promotion decision, and each can be weighted more or less heavily. What are the consequences of different weightings of these factors?

There are a number of options available in trying to balance ability, merit, and seniority when one is making promotion decisions. At one extreme, length of service may be the only factor considered (such as Alan's initial decision to select Gil). At the other extreme, only merit (i.e., past service record) and ability (i.e., future potential) may be considered. In between, are the more realistic options of:

1. After excluding the truly incompetent, select the *most senior* person.

2. Require a *minimum length of service* before individuals can be considered for promotion.

3. Select the most able, but only if *clearly superior* to the longest-service (most senior) worker.

4. *From the most able,* select the most senior person.

Almost all companies give some weight to seniority, although unionized firms tend to give it greater weight than those that are not.

1. If you wish to advance to a better job, **start working on the move** as soon as you are **running out of fresh challenges,** or you have stopped learning in your present position.

2. **Develop a capable replacement** for yourself. This will improve your chances of getting management's approval of a move.

3. **Stay flexible** if you seek a fast advancement. **Avoid traps** that make it difficult for you to relocate, such as large debts.

4. Realize that as you move up the organizational ladder, **interpersonal and managerial skills become more important** than technical skills. Take advantage of training opportunities to develop these skills.

Your Future

25

A CRITICAL INCIDENT: What Price Success?

Sam felt good as he sat in an easy chair in his boss's office. His boss, Mr. Armstrong, was reading out loud from Sam's annual performance review. Sam had done a good job in his third year as supervisor of the Stamping Department at Globe Housewares.

"You have a good future with this company," Mr. Armstrong assured him, in conclusion. "Have you done any thinking about the next step in your career?"

"Yeah. Actually, I have," Sam replied. "I've got a growing family, and a bigger job would sure help pay the bills. I'm ready to move ahead now."

"What makes you think you're ready now?" Mr. Armstrong asked, seriously.

"I dunno." Sam replied, a little puzzled at the question. "I guess I'm ready now because, as you've told me, I've been doing a good job. And besides, I need more money now."

"I didn't mean in terms of money," Mr. Armstrong pointed out. "We can all use more money! What I meant was in terms of your career. For instance, I figure I'm ready to move up once I get to the point where I'm not learning anything new on my present job. Are you at that point yet?"

"Well, maybe not quite," Sam admitted. "I'm still learning some, and every day brings a few new challenges. But I still feel I'm ready to move up. The only thing is, I don't know what the next step is after the Stamping Department."

"Well, over the next few years, several positions are going to open up." Mr. Armstrong told him. "There's going to be a couple of retirements next year, for instance. And maybe *I'll* be moving to a different position. But even if I don't, I may need an assistant. . ."

"I was hoping to be moving sooner than next year," Sam interjected, looking concerned.

"Let's be realistic about this, Sam," Mr. Armstrong said, in a fatherly tone of voice. "You're going to need new skills to do a decent job at a higher management level."

"Like what?" Sam asked, a trace of impatience in his voice.

"Well, we promoted you from press operator to supervisor because you had a good technical knowledge of how the presses worked, and you were well liked and respected by the other press operators.

"Look at my job, though," he continued. "I spend most of my

258

time on the phone, sorting out problems, or trying to convince people to actually do what I think needs to be done. I also have to go to meetings every day. And the time that's left I spend traveling, doing the same kinds of things at our other plants.

"So you see, I don't need a technical knowledge of how a stamping press works. And it doesn't matter that much whether your press operators respect me or not! It's a different ball game."

"So where do I learn those kinds of skills?" Sam asked him.

"I don't know exactly," Mr. Armstrong admitted. "The Community College offers some communications courses—you know, things like public speaking, debating, and group dynamics. You could probably learn a lot from those kinds of courses. Some general business courses would be very helpful, too.

"Of course, you're not going to learn everything you need to know that way," Mr. Armstrong added, "but you'll sure be in a better position than others who haven't made any effort to get special training."

"The summer sessions start next week," Sam pointed out, looking a little more hopeful. "In three months, I can have picked up the special training."

"There's more to it than that," Mr. Armstrong warned him. "Let me ask you something. Have you been grooming someone to step into your shoes when you move up?"

"Well, not exactly," Sam replied, somewhat taken aback. "I've got a lead man who covers for me sometimes. But he isn't ready to do all my job yet."

"Look at the situation from the company's point of view," Mr. Armstrong advised him. "Chances are, if moving you up to a bigger job is going to mean that the Stamping Department won't have adequate supervision, then top management is going to be hesitant about moving you. Isn't that reasonable?"

"Yeah," Sam admitted. "I guess I couldn't blame them for that. I guess I've got to do a little more training and delegating."

"There's something else you ought to think about, too," Mr. Armstrong went on. "You may have to relocate, if you want to get ahead as fast as you've told me. We have two subsidiaries that are growing fast. We'll need to send some good middle management people in there soon. Are you and your family prepared to move out of state, if it's necessary?"

"I honestly don't know," Sam admitted, after a few moments' thought. "Actually, I guess we somehow avoid the subject at home. We've got a lot invested in the house, and we owe quite a bit of money. Besides, we have relatives and friends nearby. Moving to another community would be especially hard for my wife and kids."

"I appreciate your concerns, Sam, but if you want to move up fast, you will have to stay flexible so you can take whatever opportunities come along."

"Then I've got to do more thinking about whether I should be in such a hurry," Sam said, resignedly.

As Sam was leaving the office, he thought to himself, "If getting ahead fast here is going to come at the expense of my family's happiness, maybe my future's not with this company. . . ."

CHECK YOUR PROGRESS

1. If you want to advance to a better job, when should you start working on the move?

2. Higher management will be hesitant to promote you if your department can't afford to lose you. How do you get around this?

3. How do supervisors become inflexible, so that it's difficult to move rapidly into a new position?

4. What skills become more important as you move up the career ladder? How can these skills be developed?

ANSWERS TO PROGRESS QUESTIONS

1. Start working on the move as soon as you find that you're running out of fresh challenges, or you have stopped learning in your present job.
2. Develop a capable replacement who is ready to step into your shoes when you move.
3. Supervisors who are anxious to move up can be made inflexible by such things as strong family ties or large debts.
4. Interpersonal and managerial skills become more important than technical skills. Thus you should take advantage of training opportunities to develop these skills.

Further Thoughts

Sometimes a supervisor is offered a promotion that he (or she) doesn't want to take, for one reason or another. What are the consequences of *turning down* a promotion, and how can these be minimized or avoided?

The supervisor may have a good reason for not wanting to take a specific promotion that is offered to him (or her). For instance,

1. The promotion may be to a position at which the supervisor cannot succeed. (It could, for instance, involve a department that has been left in chaos by the previous supervisor, with workers who are alienated and antagonistic.)
2. The new position may be in danger of being eliminated. (Past contribution to profits or future plans may result in a department's being earmarked to be phased out.)
3. The new position may be a dead end. (For instance, it may require the development of special skills that are of no use elsewhere in the company.)

Actually turning down the promotion, however, may be a very delicate matter. In offering the promotion, higher management is expressing its judgment that there is a good match between the person and the job. In turning down the promotion, the supervisor is, in effect, contradicting that judgment; he (or she) is saying, "That job doesn't suit me." This may result in a reassessment of the supervisor, which may turn out to be unfavorable. Thus the supervisor needs to give reasons that will not hurt management's reappraisal of him; otherwise, he may be passed over when other positions are being offered. Some reasons that might be acceptable to higher management include:

1. The supervisor could convince higher management that the (unwanted) promotion would be a poor use of his present skills or future

261

potential, so that it would be *in the company's interest* to offer him a promotion more suited to his ability to contribute.

2. The supervisor could point out *extenuating circumstances* of which higher management was unaware. For instance, the supervisor's "replacement" may have changed his mind about taking over the position that would be left vacant; or perhaps a serious crisis has arisen that requires the supervisor to stay in the department and work it out.

3. The supervisor could pass up the offer for *personal reasons,* implying that a crisis in his private life has limited his ability to cope with the additional, new responsibilities that would arise in his work life if he accepted the promotion offer. This, of course, is only a temporary stalling measure, and can probably be used effectively only once.

4. Where the promotion involves relocation, a variety of *local ties* can be invoked, such as special responsibilities in the community, although the only really unquestionable reason involves religious affiliation (such as Mormons not wishing to leave the Salt Lake City area, or Amish people not wishing to leave Amish country).

There are some clear advantages to a supervisor's having a trained and capable back-up person ready to step into his (or her) shoes. What *disadvantages* are there?

Some of the disadvantages are:

1. An understudy may get restless and "push" the supervisor, or leave, if his (her) timetable isn't met.

2. A capable understudy can "outshine" the supervisor and create insecurity for him.

3. Split loyalties may develop among the workers as to who the "real" leader is.

4. A capable assistant may demand more salary, thereby disrupting the department budget (or equity among department members).

5. The successor may be acceptable to the supervisor and not to the company, especially if selected by the supervisor without prior approval of higher management (or if not known to management in terms of loyalty, ability under pressure, etc.)

"Success" is often viewed in terms of more money, or the prestige of a higher management position. Yet these are often thought to be associated with insecurity, ulcers, heart attacks, and divorce. What would *you* consider to be better things to shoot for in a successful career?

This is a highly personal question aimed at helping you explore your own values. In the process, you will have to critically evaluate the cultural norm which says that "bigger," "higher," or "more" is always "better." For many people it is not, even though they receive a steady brainwashing that indicates it is.

There can be unfortunate consequences for people who allow themselves to get caught up in striving to advance their careers when further advancement is not really right for them. *Here are a few examples:*

1. People come to feel *alienated* when the opportunities available do not match the aspirations they are led to hold.
2. A feeling of *isolation* can afflict people who find that in their striving to "get to the top," their friends become enemies competing for the same few positions at the higher levels of the organizational pyramid.
3. *Insecurity* can be more of a problem the farther up one goes. Higher management positions frequently have low job security, especially in times of profit decline. If there is unsatisfactory performance at higher levels, seldom is there the retraining that is often given to lower-level workers (particularly if they are unionized). The higher-level manager is often quickly replaced. This may even be unrelated to that person's performance; in "big business," there are many cases where whole management teams are summarily replaced—in effect, the manager can get fired purely because his boss got fired, and the new boss wanted to bring in his own team.
4. The *greater responsibilities* of higher management positions can produce increased pressure, anxiety, and tension. These are "occupational hazards" of higher management, and can lead to ulcers, high blood pressure, chronic digestive problems, excessive smoking, alcoholism and other types of drug dependence, and an unhappy home life.
5. Higher managers tend to work *longer hours.* This can add to the home-life problems caused by constant tension.
6. The *increase in pay may be illusory.* First, the higher manager usually works longer hours for his greater salary, and he (or she) is always "on call," when not actually working. Second, the higher manager has greater expenses. There is a certain image that must be maintained (and usually substantial social pressure to do so). The higher manager usually is expected to wear more expensive clothing, eat in more expensive restaurants, entertain more lavishly, live in a home that is appropriate for his position, drive an expensive car, and so on. The result may be that he isn't really that far ahead, financially.
7. There may be a *loss in self-respect.* This can happen as a result of the political moves necessary to get ahead in some organizations; the loss of self-confidence and the feeling of incompetence that comes with advancing too far or too fast (i.e., the "Peter Principle"); or the discomfort of assuming an unnatural role—in other words, "trying to be something you're not."

Lest this listing sound too pessimistic, it should be cautioned that these kinds of problems don't necessarily afflict all higher managers, although they are quite common. Even when they do arise, many people feel that the benefits are worth the costs anyway.

However, there are alternative ways of looking at success:

1. For some people, the delight in doing one's present job well is more important than the middle-class norm of "getting ahead."
2. Some people don't want a more challenging job; they want to do

work that requires minimum involvement, so that they can be "alone with their fantasies" or so that they can socialize freely without worrying much about the task.

3. There is an increasing number of people who consciously reject the middle-class "progress" ethic. For them, "bigger" and "higher" are not necessarily better. Perhaps aesthetic and humanistic values are more important to them than what they call "blind" progress.

4. For many people, good health and a good home life are more important than the prestige, status, and power of a higher management position.

There are no "right" answers to this question, of course. If you explore your own values, rather than blindly accepting the values embodied in the traditional organizational success notion, then you will probably be the wisest—and only—judge of what's best for your future.

POSTTEST QUESTIONS

Now that you've read the five chapters in Section V, you might want to try to answer the same questions that you answered in the Pretest. The correct answers are given on page 266.

By comparing your score on the Posttest with your score on the Pretest, you will be able to get an idea of how much your knowledge of supervision has improved.

41. The important difference between line positions and staff positions is that line managers pass down _____ , while staff people pass along _____ . (Choose from the alternatives below and write the corresponding letters in the two blanks.)

    a. Recommendations
    b. Communications
    c. Information
    d. Orders
    e. Accountability

42. Resistance to change is primarily caused by (circle the *best* response):

    a. The change itself.
    b. The meaning of the change to the persons affected.
    c. Workers' having a chance to discuss the change beforehand.
    d. People who would be inflexible about altering the status quo, no matter what.
    e. An increase in communications from top management.

43. The type of skill that is usually least important to a supervisor moving further up the career ladder is (circle one)

    a. Administrative
    b. Political
    c. Interpersonal
    d. Bargaining
    e. Technical

Questions 44 through 50 are to be answered by circling T if the statement is **true**, and F if the statement is **false**.

44. If staff people get involved in what goes on in a supervisor's department, they should be held responsible if something goes wrong.　**T　F**

45. While actually on the job, the worker loses his (or her) right to "do his own thing."　**T　F**

46. A promotion from worker to supervisor always means more take-home pay. **T   F**

47. A supervisor wishing to advance up the organizational ladder can't go wrong by having a capable replacement. **T   F**

48. The best way to minimize resistance to a change in the workplace is to make the change as *slowly* as possible. **T   F**

49. After a promotion, supervisors should expect to have a different relationship with their former co-workers. **T   F**

50. In many cases, a supervisor has the power to deny a worker's constitutional rights. **T   F**

PRE- AND POSTTEST QUESTIONNAIRE – ANSWER SHEET

41. d, a
42. b
43. e
44. false
45. false
46. false
47. false
48. false
49. true
50. true

As we leave Precision Electronics, there is a lot of doubt as to what the company's fate will be. Tensions have increased to the point where production workers distrust higher management, seeing them as "the enemy." The first-line supervisors are caught in the middle. Unfortunately, they may in the near future become victims of the cross-fire when the union comes in to oppose the power that higher management has been abusing.

This "cold war" evolved over time; it wasn't always that way. The senior workers still have fond memories of when Precision Electronics used to be a "fun" place to work. In the early years, the thirty or forty people on the work force got to know each other on a first-name basis. The atmosphere was very informal, with lots of good-natured kidding. No one seemed to worry about status or special recognition. Everyone just "pitched in" and got a lot of quality work done each day.

With high quality, competitive prices, and a work force that was willing to adapt to the constantly changing needs of the electronics market, Precision Electronics grew fast. As it grew, the atmosphere became more impersonal. The old-timers couldn't keep up with the constant influx of new hires, and after a while, didn't even try. Soon, friendship networks tended to become restricted to within single departments, and the "company spirit" was replaced with petty conflicts and jealousies between departments.

The company had other growing pains, besides its becoming impersonal. There were many more rules to follow—in fact, these eventually filled a fairly thick book! Also, there was less chance for chatting and enjoying the companionship of fellow workers.

But perhaps worst of all, higher management didn't seem to be listening to workers as they used to. Oh, sure, there was still talk that

Epilogue:
A Final Look
at Precision Electronics

everyone's ideas were welcome, but the lack of response from higher management led the workers to believe that such talk wasn't sincere.

This book visited Precision Electronics in its later years. During this period, higher management came under increasing pressure. This pressure came from other firms—both domestic and foreign—who were competing in the same product market. Higher management, in turn, put more pressure on the workers, but didn't go about it wisely.

Their worst mistake was to put all the pressure on the production workers. It was almost as if other costs didn't exist. Even during the worst layoffs, nothing was mentioned about reducing the size of the engineering staff or the sales force, or of cutting down on the executive office frills. Even the clerical workers seemed immune from any cutbacks.

The Production Manager was the focus of the production workers' increasing resentment. They felt that he should have been the one to go to the President and get a fair deal for them. But he turned out to be more their oppressor than their defender!

The desperate work force welcomed the union organizer when he first appeared in the plant. Here, at last, was a means of representing their interests to top management. In the election supervised by the National Labor Relations Board, the union was narrowly defeated. But while the company "won the first battle" with the union, it seems they will eventually "lose the war."

Higher management has responded to the union's organizing drive by hiring a Director of Industrial Relations (see Exhibit A-1), for the purpose of convincing enough "undecided" workers to vote against the union to insure its defeat. However, the union has not given up at Precision Electronics. Indeed, its position is now stronger than ever. A rallying point in the union's latest campaign is that the company is willing to pay the additional costs of a high salary to the Director of Industrial Relations, yet insists that workers must be laid off and worked harder to save money!

All of the first-line supervisors are caught in a squeeze: There is pressure from workers, and pressure from the Production Manager. Vince, Supervisor of Machining, and Maria, Supervisor of Assembly, are particularly sensitive to their predicament. They don't like being caught in the middle (see Exhibit A-2).

Vince, in this regard, has shown an interesting shift in attitude. When the union organizer first appeared on the scene, Vince and Maria stood far apart in their reactions. Maria was very close to her workers, and sympathized with what the union was trying to accomplish. Vince, on the other hand, staunchly opposed the union; he saw it as an invasion of management rights.

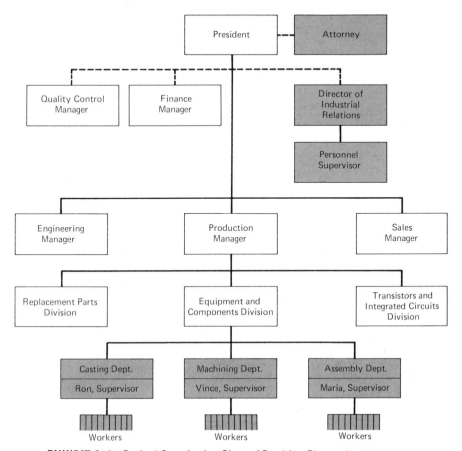

EXHIBIT A-1 *Revised Organization Chart of Precision Electronics*

Most recently, however, Vince has reexamined his attitude towards the union, and has started to suspect that the union may be the workers' only hope to protect themselves against top management, and particularly against the Production Manager. This shift in attitude bothered Vince, since it made him feel disloyal, somehow. So he thought back over the Production Manager's "history," to try to figure out what had happened.

As best Vince could recall, the Production Manager had started out on the right foot. He had talked about how important supervisors and workers are to the success of the company, and he had seemed sincere in trying to make meaningful improvements in various employee programs, such as the performance rating system. But for reasons Vince came to understand only gradually, the "honeymoon" didn't last long.

PRODUCTION MANAGER

Exerting pressure downward by asking for:

A speed-up work pace   More cost savings   More efficient layout

SUPERVISORS
(squeezed in the middle)

Vince   Maria

Requesting fairer treatment   Threatening unionization   Filing more grievances against higher management

Upward pressure from the WORKERS

WORKERS

First, it upset Vince that the Production Manager wouldn't go to bat for the production workers, in the President's office. Instead, he blindly accepted cuts in the production work force when other divisions of the company escaped completely. Vince was particularly sensitive on this issue, since he himself has made a stand supporting fair treatment for good workers. So had Maria, and she felt just as strongly about the Production Manager's letting them down in this matter.

Second, it had become apparent that the Production Manager was too "sneaky" to be trusted. Although he kept *saying* that he wanted everyone's ideas, since he never seemed to seriously consider them, Vince realized that this was manipulation, rather than a sincere invitation to participate in decision making. Vince figured he'd been "used" all along.

All in all, Vince had become as pessimistic as Maria about how things were going to work out in the future with this Production Manager. Their challenge was to hang on, and do their best to maintain a good relationship with their workers. They realized that they would need to have some "money in the bank" with their subordinates to maintain productivity and some semblance of order when (not "if") the union won the upcoming election.

Few changes have taken place at Allied Industries since you first met Marvin. None of them has been major. Certainly Marvin has learned a few things; he has become a little more effective as a supervisor; his department is running more smoothly. But on the whole, we leave the Accounts Receivable Department pretty much as we found it.

This stability may not continue into the future, however. The garment industry is highly competitive, and many firms fall victim to the intense competition, especially from abroad. Where a large company owns several plants (as in the case of Allied Industries), it "hurts" less to close down plants in expensive labor areas, and reopen them where lower wages can be paid. Thus while Marvin's situation *seems* very stable, because of the nature of the garment industry the stability could disappear quite suddenly.

As long as the plant remains open, Marvin's future seems fairly secure. Fortunately, Marvin isn't especially anxious to get ahead fast. There is low turnover among the office staff, especially at the middle-management level. Thus Marvin may have to wait for a retirement before a higher-level position opens up.

In any event, Marvin may have to go back to school if he wants to progress up the career ladder. His present boss (the Fiscal Manager) was formally trained as a C.P.A. (Certified Public Accountant), whereas Marvin has learned his job through experience, supplemented by a few accounting courses in night school. Neither man knows very much about production processes; they don't need to, in order to do their jobs well.

Marvin's contentedness was a great contrast to Wally's frustrations. Both Marvin and Wally had started as clerks in the Accounts Receivable Department the same year. Wally had been working in

Epilogue:
A Final Look
at Allied Industries

production, whereas Marvin had come to Allied Industries as soon as he got out of the Air Force.

Some years later, when the supervisor retired, Marvin was surprised to be offered the promotion, while Wally became extremely bitter that it wasn't offered to *him.* This bitterness continued, and contributed to his later being fired. Wally, by the way, was able to get another job, thanks to Marvin's assistance. He has settled down, and is doing quite well.

The teamwork improved substantially after Wally left. Wally had scorned any worker who seemed to be doing a good job. He would accuse the worker of "buttering up the boss for a raise," or worse. Workers who wanted to be cooperative were made to feel self-conscious.

With Wally gone, the supportive atmosphere created by a management that generally wanted workers to participate in decisions started to "pay dividends." Marvin continued trying to delegate more and more of his routine work, and workers began to willingly accept the challenge without fear of Wally's insults. And Sylvia's disposition improved considerably once Wally wasn't constantly getting on her nerves.

As we leave Allied Industries, however, we see a bright spot on Marvin's horizon. Marvin had done a good job on the task force that studied the feasibility of buying out a competitor's plant. The acquisition of this plant *is* going through, and the office work will be transferred to the "home office" at Allied.

One result of this change will be the opening of some new administrative positions at the new plant. Higher management is considering Marvin for one of the new positions. Neil is almost ready to take over Marvin's present responsibilities, since most of these have been delegated to Neil at one time or another. Marvin likes his present job, and can live comfortably on his salary, so he hasn't been pushing to make a move. Neil may just have to do some nudging. . . .

Alan had been running Foreign Auto Repair, Inc., for six years when we made our first visit to the shop.

The first thing we noticed was that although there had been steady growth in the business, Alan, the owner, was lagging behind in his growth as a supervisor.

The business began with Alan and Kirk operating a gas station and doing repair work as a sideline. In those early days, the business was so simple that Alan could keep fairly good track of it "in his head."

However, as the business moved from the gas station to the larger shop and more mechanics were hired, the whole operation became much more complicated. Alan discovered that he was losing money because of a lack of supervisory controls.

Alan was able to solve this problem with the help of an experienced bookkeeper, and from that point on, he introduced additional control systems wherever they became necessary.

The business continued to grow, and this forced other changes in Alan's supervisory style. Alan had originally chosen the auto repair business because he enjoyed working on cars. The more the business grew, however, the less time he could spend actually pitching in and doing mechanical work, since more time was taken up with paperwork and other administrative matters.

Alan didn't spend a whole lot of time in actually directing his mechanics' work. He planned their work schedules, and then got involved only if they needed technical advice. This style of leadership suited his easygoing personality, and besides, their own standards of craftsmanship guided the mechanics' work. So Alan didn't need to exercise close supervision.

Epilogue:
A Last Look at Foreign
Auto Repair, Inc.

Although Alan could be firm—perhaps even tough—in an emergency, his casual, easygoing manner got him in trouble occasionally. For instance, Alan was too lax—for too long—with Kirk's drinking problem.

(Kirk, by the way, never did solve his drinking problem. He left Foreign Auto Repair after a particularly bad drinking binge, and went to work for one of the big dealerships in town. He died in a single-car accident three months later.)

But Alan's fairness and openness served him well, since this earned his mechanics' continuing respect and trust. His decisions were always accepted, largely because he encouraged his workers to participate in making the decisions. Most importantly, his mechanics knew that Alan was sincere in asking their opinions—he wasn't just doing it as a manipulative strategy to minimize their opposition to decisions that had already been made.

The *personal* quality of Alan's style of supervision may pose some problems for further growth. As we leave Foreign Auto Repair, he has delegated his supervisory responsibilities to Hans, and now Alan is busy taking over a taxi service (see Exhibit A–3).

Just as the supervisor's job doesn't suit every personality (it drove Gil crazy within two weeks!), the mechanics will not accept just anyone

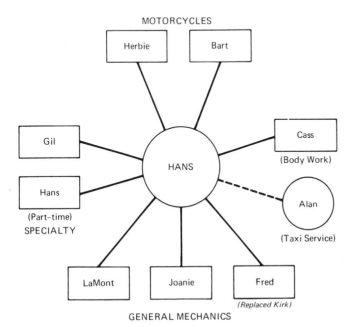

EXHIBIT A-3 *Revised Organizational Relationships*

as their supervisor. Hans is not as flexible and easy-going as Alan, and the mechanics may resent his tendency to be more rigid.

If this happens, Alan may be in trouble. He may spend as much time handling grievances as he saves by letting Hans take over the supervisory responsibilities. Worse, the mechanics may become alienated, and start doing just the bare minimum.

Obviously, Alan will be very wise to watch closely what happens in the shop for the next year or two. Otherwise, the business he started as a hobby may become a nightmare.

We leave Sam in good shape. His Stamping Department is running fairly smoothly, the company seems to have a good future, and the relationship between the union and management is healthy despite some layoffs and tighter work standards.

From a personal point of view, Sam has come a long way as a supervisor since we first met him. He started out with high technical skills, and has since been supplementing these with other kinds of necessary skills.

For instance, we learned that Sam's technical skill with the stamping presses was a large factor in his original promotion from press operator to pressroom supervisor. Furthermore, Sam's night school courses in workflow planning enabled him to skillfully analyze bottleneck problems in the company cafeteria.

But Sam learned what all supervisors must learn: That being effective as a supervisor calls for more than just technical skills. It involves knowing *when* to "pull rank" and let your former co-workers know that you're not fooling around on issues like safety. It also involves judgment—the sensitivity to look behind appearances and see what's really going on. Sam learned this in dealing with grievances.

Later, Sam learned that political skills are important, too. Otherwise, a supervisor can become the victim of a manipulator. In these circumstances, a supervisor can survive and prosper only through awareness and the careful use of ethical counter-moves. Sam was fortunate to have learned this almost instinctively. Many supervisors, such as Norman Reilley, who was fired from his Shipping Department job, learn from much more "expensive" lessons!

Even though Sam has come a long way, he still has quite a way to go. With regard to his own career, he still hasn't thought through

Epilogue:
A Final Look
at Globe Housewares

where he wants to go and how to plan to get there. Sam wants to get ahead fast, but he has no idea of the costs, in terms of his personal and family life.

To make matters worse, Sam isn't a good listener when his own future is involved. His boss, Mr. Armstrong, tried to give him some food for thought—some hints that would guide Sam's thinking about what he really wanted out of life, and what sacrifices he and his family were willing to make to obtain it. More concerned with what he saw as roadblocks to his progress, Sam did not follow up on the advice. If Sam is serious about a promotion, we can only hope that he is not headed for the "expensive" type of learning that he was able to avoid in acquiring political supervisory skills.

FINAL REVIEW TEST

Now that you've finished reading the book, you have the opportunity to test yourself on all twenty-five chapters.

The fifty questions listed below are taken from the Posttests in each of the sections. You can score your answers yourself, using the answer key given on pages 284–85. Each correct answer is worth two points, so you can "grade" yourself on a 100-point scale.

For any wrong answers, we encourage you to go back to the appropriate chapter and make sure that you understand the material.

Section I: Multiple Choice or Completion: In Questions 1–17, please CIRCLE the letter that corresponds to the *best* answer to each questtion.

1. Conflicts between loyalty to the boss and loyalty to subordinates should be resolved

    a. By explaining to the workers the dilemma being faced.
    b. On the basis of what will keep the most people happy.
    c. On the basis of what the boss desires.
    d. On the basis of what is the fairest thing to do.
    e. As quickly as possible.

2. Every hiring requirement set by a supervisor must be

    a. Consistent with past hiring practices.
    b. Acceptable to members of the work group.
    c. First approved by the Personnel Department.
    d. Able to attract the best-qualified candidates.
    e. Related to actual job performance.

3. The four steps involved in on-the-job training are listed below, but they are not in the proper sequence. Indicate the correct sequence by writing in the appropriate number (1, 2, 3, or 4) in the blanks provided.

    supervised work practice: This should be step ____ .
    job breakdown: This should be step ____ .
    follow-up: This should be step ____ .
    explanation and demonstration: This should be step ____ .

4. The type of skill that is usually *least* important to a supervisor moving further up the career ladder is (circle one)

    a. Administrative
    b. Political
    c. Interpersonal
    d. Bargaining
    e. Technical

5. In order for delegation to be effective, it is important that (circle one):

    a. Workers be capable of doing the work assigned.

    b. Workers who make some errors learn from them.

    c. Tasks delegated not need the supervisor's close attention.

    d. All of the above.

    e. None of the above.

6. Choose the answer that *best* completes the sentence, and then circle the corresponding letter.

A union contract usually ____ what supervisors are allowed to do in their departments.

    a. Restricts

    b. Avoids any mention of

    c. Broadens

    d. Is unclear about

    e. None of the above.

7. Resistance to change is primarily caused by (circle the *best* answer):

    a. The change itself.

    b. The meaning of the change to the persons affected.

    c. Workers' having a chance to discuss the change beforehand.

    d. People who would be inflexible about altering the status quo, no matter what.

    e. An increase in communications from top management.

8. One of the following statements about on-the-job training is *false*. Which one is it?

    a. Trainees should be watched most closely during training and immediately after it.

    b. A good worker is not necessarily a good trainer.

    c. The *rate* of training should be adjusted to what each individual trainee can handle.

    d. An overqualified trainee can cause as many training problems for a supervisor as one who is underqualified.

    e. Trainees who reach an acceptable level of performance rarely decline from that level.

9. If you suspect that someone is playing "political games," you should (select the *best* answer and circle the appropriate letter):

    a. Retaliate by playing political games of your own.

    b. Avoid making any hasty accusations.

    c. Let your boss know what you suspect and get support.

    d. Confront face to face and have a showdown.

    e. Try to rally your workers to help you put it to a stop.

10. A supervisor's department is free of bottlenecks when there is (circle the best answer)

    a. A source of technical help.
    b. A trained back-up staff.
    c. Smooth work flow.
    d. A preventive maintenance program.
    e. A number of workable standby machines of equipment.

11. Circle the letter corresponding to the one statement that is *least* true.

    a. Rules can sometimes create problems if they are followed to the letter.
    b. Rules reduce the need for a supervisor to constantly give orders.
    c. Rules protect workers from arbitrary actions by supervisors.
    d. Rules can be used to "pass the buck" for unpleasant decisions.
    e. Rules make it harder for a supervisor to exercise authority.

12. The important difference between line positions and staff positions is that line managers pass down ____ , while staff people pass along ____ . (Choose from the alternatives below and write the corresponding letters in the two blanks.)

    a. Recommendations
    b. Communications
    c. Information
    d. Orders
    e. Accountability

13. A supervisor can help avoid *people bottlenecks* by having (circle the best answer):

    a. A source of technical help.
    b. A trained back-up staff.
    c. A surplus of employees.
    d. A preventive maintenance program.
    e. A number of workable standby machines or equipment.

14. In dealing with a problem alcoholic worker, supervisors should NOT do which *one* of the following? (Circle one.)

    a. Be supportive by assuring the worker that there is no danger of losing his or her job.
    b. Find out what company or community programs are available to help.
    c. Enlist the help of fellow workers.
    d. Look for patterns of behavior that will show if the problem is getting worse.
    e. Tell the worker he or she *must* seek help, or else!

15. When a worker has a preventable accident, the blame rests *mainly* on (circle one):

    a. The worker.
    b. The supervisor.
    c. The worker and the supervisor.
    d. The maintenance department.
    e. The personnel department.

16. Circle the letter corresponding to the one statement that is LEAST true.

    a. Workers tend to "test" rules and stretch them to the limit.
    b. Rules create problems if they are applied too strictly.
    c. The biggest objection to rules is that they are impersonal.
    d. Rules tend to reflect experiences and problems of the past.

17. Choose the *least* appropriate "ending" to the following statement by circling *one* of the five choices.

A supervisor's role in running a meeting is to:

    a. Encourage group discussion.
    b. Remain neutral as much as possible.
    c. Help sort out controversial issues.
    d. Stick to the agenda.
    e. Take sole responsibility for handling disruptive persons.

Section II: True or False. In Questions 18–50, circle T if the statement is **true** and F if the statement is **false**.

18. As a leader it is particularly important to maintain one's normal leadership style *during emergencies.*　　**T**　　**F**

19. There are really no important differences between the effectiveness of a grievance procedure in a nonunion company, compared with a unionized shop. **T**　　**F**

20. A supervisor should try to avoid firing an unsatisfactory worker during his (or her) probation period after hiring, since it is at this time the worker needs maximum help and support.　　**T**　　**F**

21. A good performance rating plan will focus on "ability to get along with others" and basic personality traits.　　**T**　　**F**

22. To be a skillful communicator, a supervisor should not waste time by rephrasing or repeating what others say.　　**T**　　**F**

23. A supervisor wishing to advance up the organizational ladder can't go wrong by having a capable replacement.　　**T**　　**F**

24. A supervisor should always try to remain "neutral" when running a

meeting, even if others have difficulty in pinpointing what position the supervisor is committed to.   **T   F**

25. The final decision to hire a new worker should be made by the line supervisor.   **T   F**

26. Trembling fingers, bloodshot eyes, and accidents are sufficient evidence to determine that a worker has a drinking problem.   **T   F**

27. The best way to minimize resistance to change in the workplace is to make the change as slowly as possible.   **T   F**

28. The best time to get tough on safety rules is after an accident, when everyone will realize how bad the consequences can be.   **T   F**

29. Workers vote for a union primarily to improve wages and fringe benefits.   **T   F**

30. Controlling is a distinctive process that needs to be kept separate from the planning process.   **T   F**

31. If a person is really good at "politics" in the work place, there's no way to tell that his (or her) actions have hidden purposes.   **T   F**

32. Nearly all worker grievances can be resolved at the supervisory level.   **T   F**

33. While actually on the job, the worker loses his (or her) right to "do his own thing."   **T   F**

34. A supervisor should spend his (or her) time doing the things he knows best.   **T   F**

35. A supervisor should give preference in hiring to women and minorities even if they don't have perfect job qualifications.   **T   F**

36. It is usually wise for supervisors to let their bosses know about conflicts in their departments.   **T   F**

37. Supervisors can avoid conflicts between loyalty to their bosses and loyalty to their workers.   **T   F**

38. After a promotion, supervisors should expect to have a different relationship with their former co-workers.   **T   F**

39. A supervisor who copies the leadership style of someone he admires risks being seen as a phony.   **T   F**

40. Firing is strictly a private matter between the worker involved and the supervisor; other workers should be told that the entire matter is none of their business.   **T   F**

41. Tight controls should be used by a supervisor when there is the first sign of problems in meeting standards.   **T   F**

42. In order to be as fair as possible, a supervisor cannot afford to permit any exceptions to established rules.   **T**   **F**

43. If staff people get involved in what goes on in a supervisor's department, they should be held responsible if something goes wrong.   **T**   **F**

44. Spoken words usually tell more about what the communicator really thinks and feels than do nonverbal cues.   **T**   **F**

45. A supervisor should not tolerate any conflict, whenever it is possible to squelch it.   **T**   **F**

46. Supervisors can benefit from giving all of their workers "satisfactory" performance ratings, in order to demonstrate that they have a good work force. **T**   **F**

47. Fairness basically requires that a supervisor must not be too strict with his or her fellow workers.   **T**   **F**

48. In many cases, a supervisor has the power to deny a worker's constitutional rights.   **T**   **F**

49. A supervisor with successful past experience in interviewing job applicants is unlikely to get into trouble with the law on discrimination.   **T**   **F**

50. A promotion from worker to supervisor always means more take-home pay.   **T**   **F**

FINAL QUESTIONNAIRE—ANSWER SHEET

1. d
2. e
3. 3, 1, 4, 2
4. e
5. d
6. a
7. b
8. e
9. b
10. c
11. e
12. d, a
13. b
14. a
15. c
16. c
17. e

18. false
19. false
20. false
21. false
22. false
23. false
24. true
25. true
26. false
27. false
28. false
29. false
30. false
31. true
32. true
33. false
34. false
35. true
36. true
37. false
38. true
39. true
40. false
41. false
42. false
43. false
44. false
45. false
46. false
47. false
48. true
49. false
50. false

A

Absenteeism, 196, 204, 218
Accidents, 14, 46, 93, 98–103, 196, 275
Affirmative Action, 49, 122, 202–9
Alcohol problems, 193–201, 275
Alienation, 52, 96, 117, 120
Appraising performance, 54–65, 106, 159, 183–84, 186, 212, 251, 269
Arbitration, 159
Authoritarian leadership style, 116–17, 121
Authority, 53, 95, 96–97, 112, 114, 141, 150–52, 160, 206, 227, 233, 241, 277
Automation, 130, 157, 245–46

B

Backup workers, 25
Blind loyalty, 136
Body language, 88, 169,215
Bottlenecks, 25–34, 74
Buffers against disruptions, 32, 68
Bumping, 65

C

Challenges, 109, 257, 263–64
Closeness of supervision, 13, 66, 90, 96, 199, 274
Communications, 83–89, 244, 252, 259
Compromise, 88, 135
Confidentiality, 106, 196, 213, 216, 217–18
Conflict, 185–192

Control, 35–42, 93, 230, 234, 252, 274
Cooperation, 42, 64, 110, 120, 184, 192
Cost control, 36–40, 93, 130
Creativity of workers, 8, 93, 95, 111, 117, 168

D

Delegation, 104–10, 259, 273
Democratic leadership style, 116–17, 121
Developing a replacement, 257, 273
Dilemmas of managing, 55, 135, 140, 167, 192, 214, 218–19
Discipline, 92, 93, 118, 119–20, 210–19, 235
Discretion in decision making, 133
Discrimination, 52, 202–9
"Drawing the line," 90, 93, 100

E

Employment application, 47
Equal Employment Opportunity Act, 203
Equity theory, 62–64, 119
Ethics, 64, 135, 141, 191, 218–19, 242
Example-setting, 69, 137, 139

F

Face-saving, 73, 88, 122, 135, 215, 251–56
Fairness, 54, 59, 74, 129, 132, 137–41, 146, 207, 212, 216, 217, 271

Index